The Story of
the City Companies

Also from Westphalia Press

westphaliapress.org

The Story of
the City Companies

by P. H. Ditchfield

WESTPHALIA PRESS
An imprint of Policy Studies Organization

The Story of the City Compnaies
All Rights Reserved © 2014 by Policy Studies Organization

Westphalia Press
An imprint of Policy Studies Organization
1527 New Hampshire Ave., NW
Washington, D.C. 20036
dgutierrezs@ipsonet.org

ISBN-13: 978-1935907794
ISBN-10: 1935907794

Updated material and comments on this edition
can be found at the Westphalia Press website:
www.westphaliapress.org

THE STORY OF
THE CITY COMPANIES

THE STORY OF
THE GREAT WAR

DICK   WHITTINGTON'S   HOUSE

THE STORY
OF THE CITY
COMPANIES

BY

P. H. DITCHFIELD, M.A., F.S.A.

Author of "London Survivals," "The City of London,"
"London's West End," etc., etc., etc.

TO

COLONEL THE RIGHT HONOURABLE

SIR WILLIAM PRYKE
LORD MAYOR OF LONDON

CITIZEN AND FREEMAN OF THE WORSHIPFUL COMPANIES

OF PAINTER-STAINERS AND PLUMBERS

THIS ACCOUNT OF THE CITY GUILDS

ASSOCIATED FOR CENTURIES WITH THE GOVERNMENT OF

THE CITY

AND FROM THE RANKS OF WHICH

THE LORD MAYORS HAVE FROM TIME IMMEMORIAL BEEN

CHOSEN

IS DEDICATED WITH MUCH RESPECT

AND WITH HIS LORDSHIP'S KIND PERMISSION

BY THE AUTHOR

v

PREFACE

THE purpose of this volume is to present a succinct account of the origin, history, character and object of those ancient and interesting institutions denominated the City Companies of London. It is intended to inform the general public with regard to their usefulness and the debt the country owes to them for their services in ancient and modern times. Even their Freemen are not always perfectly acquainted with the fascinating story of their achievements, their triumphs, their struggles and vicissitudes, and may be interested to learn how gallantly their forefathers contended for the honour of their fraternity, supported it in all their trials, and won the victory. The spirit of brotherhood, of which much is said to-day, was never more perfectly exemplified than in the annals of the City Guilds. It is true that in former days there were frequently jealousies and rivalries and contentions between them, but each man strove to maintain the welfare and honour of his Company, to support it to the utmost of his power, and to make it the repository of his benefactions for future generations of its members.

In spite of much that has been written there still remains much ignorance in the mind of the public with regard to the past history of the City Gilds and the enormous benefits which they confer upon the Nation. Monographs have appeared upon several, written by some patriotic member thereof. There are excellent works on the wor-

THE CITY COMPANIES

shipful Companies of the Mercers, Grocers, Ironmongers, Haberdashers, Merchant Taylors, Skinners, Leather sellers, Vintners, Armourers and Braziers, Barber-Surgeons, Gold and Silver Wire Drawers, Carpenters, Founders, Masons, Horners, Stationers ; and other smaller histories in the form of pamphlets which need not be particularized. Many of them I am glad to possess, but most of these are large and comprehensive volumes usually published for private circulation amongst the members, and not generally accessible to the public. Herbert's great work on the *History of the Twelve Great Companies*, published in 1834, is valuable, but copies are scarce. Moreover many changes have taken place since Mr. Herbert lived and wrote ; not a few Halls have been rebuilt, and the book contains only scant references to the other Gilds of which there are sixty-three. A learned and lengthy work entitled *The Livery Companies of the City of London* was published by the late Mr. W. Carew Hazlitt in 1882, in which he enumerates not only the existing gilds but the voluntary associations which have disappeared or have merged into the Livery Companies Gilds.

The report of the Royal Commission on the City Companies of 1880 issued in the form of a Blue Book is an extremely valuable document, but Blue Books are not easy reading and somewhat formidable for the ordinary reader. It is of great importance as it vindicates most thor-

PREFACE

oughly the honour and integrity of the Companies, and exposes the fallacy of certain slanderous statements and misconceptions which were current some time ago. These were advanced by a Mr. Firth in his book *Municipal London*, and supported by a few men who in the language of the commissioner were " not competent by reason of their situation, knowledge and experience to afford correct information on the subject of the inquiry." The slanders were stifled and killed, and the Companies were able to continue their good works unhindered by the calumnies of the ignorant and unscrupulous.

In the following pages it will be seen how strongly the religious element was woven with the constitution of the Gilds. It remains so still. Most of the Companies have their Chaplain. They attend in state a service in one of the City Churches nigh their Hall on the occasion of the installation of the Master and hear a sermon. In former days Religion and Life were blended together more closely than in modern times. Each Company had its Patron saint, and sought Divine aid in all its undertakings, acting in the spirit of the motto of the Merchant Adventurers' Company " Dieu nous donne bonne adventure," or " God be our Friend," or of the East India Merchants " Deo ducente nil nocet."

The origin of the term livery, as applied to the Companies, signifies that it was the custom and reputation of the higher members of the Gild to

wear a distinctive dress called " the livery."
Examples will be given in the following pages of
their love for bright colours. Chaucer in his
description of " a merchant " in the Canterbury
Tales, pictures him :

> " In motley, and high on his horse he sat,
> Upon his head a Flandrish beaver hat."

This garb was a badge of brotherhood, each
Company having its own livery, the outward and
visible sign of membership and graduated dignity.
It is quite possible that the adoption of the Livery
had some religious signification and was analogous
to the monastic garb ; only members adopted
their multi-coloured robes to indicate that they
served God in carrying on their trades honestly
and in good faith, relying upon His protection
as well as " loving the brotherhood " and being
good citizens.

In spite of the vicissitudes of the Companies
they retain many treasures of art and vertu and
plate. The recent exhibition of these in the
Victoria and Albert Museum has called the
attention of the public to some of their priceless
objects. A special chapter in this book has been
devoted to a description of some of these.

I may add that my first acquaintance with the
Livery Companies began some thirty years ago
when I was invited by an old friend, Canon
Erskine Clarke, Vicar of Battersea, to contribute
a series of articles on the subject to one of his peri-

PREFACE

odicals.   It was my pleasure and privilege to visit all the Halls and examine their treasures.   A quarter of a century ago I published a large quarto volume bearing the title *The History of the City Companies of London and their Good Works*, which was published by Messrs. J. M. Dent & Sons, with abundant illustrations.   It was a costly volume and has been long out of print.   The present work is an entirely new book and is in no way a repetition of the former.   It is hoped that it may be useful in spreading information with regard to those municipal bodies which have so long formed a constituent part of the government of the City of London and conferred so many benefits on the nation.

My grateful thanks are due to the Clerks of the Companies and several members thereof for their courtesy and kindness in supplying information, and to my brother-in-law, Mr. Lionel Monk Smith, for bestowing so much care and pains in reading and correcting the proofs.

P. H. Ditchfield

Barkham Rectory,
October, 1926

13

CONTENTS

LIST OF ILLUSTRATIONS

I. INTRODUCTION

IN these days of change, which have obliterated most of the old landmarks of the City, when the County Council has almost transformed London, and high warehouses and glaring shops have replaced the old picturesque buildings of our forefathers, it is refreshing to find some institutions which have preserved through the ages their old customs and usages, and retain their ancient homes and treasures. Such are the Livery Companies of the City of London, the history of which teems with vivid pictures of bygone times and manners; and the accounts of their pageantries, their feasts, and customs furnish us with curious glimpses of early civic life. When we visit the ancient homes of these venerable societies, we are impressed by their magnificence and interesting associations. Portraits of old city worthies gaze at us from the walls and link our times with theirs when they, too, strove to uphold the honour of their gild and benefit their generations. Many a quaint old-time custom and curious ceremonial usage linger on within the old walls, and there, too, are enshrined cuirass and targe, helmet, sword and buckler, which tell the story of the past and of the part which the Companies played in national defence, or in the protection of civic rights. Turning down some little alley and entering the portals of one of these halls, we are transported at once from the busy streets and din of modern London into a region of old-world

19

THE CITY COMPANIES

memories, which has a fascination that is all its
own. We see the old city merchants resplendent
in their liveries of " red and white with the
cognizances of their mysteries embroidered on
their sleeves," or when fashions changed, then
dominating the sterner sex as it now does only
the fair, clad in " scarlet and green," or " scarlet
and black," or " murry and plunket," a " darkly
red," or a " kind of blue," preparing to attend
some great State function, or to march in procession through the streets to their gild services.
Again, the great hall is filled with a gallant
company. Nobles and princes are the guests of
the Company, and the mighty "baron" makes
the table groan, and " frumentie with venyson,"
brawn, fat swan, boar, conger, sea-hog, and other
delicacies crown the feast, while the merry music
of the minstrels or the performance of the players
delights the gay throng. Pictures of ancient
pageantry, their truimphs, their magnificent
shows and gorgeous ceremonies, flit before our
eyes when we visit the halls of the Companies.

There was a grand procession in 1686, when
Sir John Peake, Mercer, was Lord Mayor.
The Master, Wardens and Assistants, dressed
in their gowns faced with foins and their hoods,
marched first, followed by the livery in their
gowns faced with satin, and the Company's
almsmen, each one bearing a banner. Then
came the gentlemen ushers in velvet coats, each
wearing a chain of gold, followed by the bachelors

INTRODUCTION

invested in gowns and scarlet satin hoods,
banner bearers, trumpeters, drummers, the City
marshals, and many others, while the gentlemen
of the Artillery Company, led by Sir John Moore,
brought up the rear. From the Hall of the
Grocers' Company, which was the usual rendez-
vous on account of its convenient situation or its
size, they marched to the Guildhall, the Lord
Mayor, sheriffs and aldermen riding on horse-
back. Thence they went to Three-cranes wharf
and took barge to Westminster. On their return
the pageants met them at St. Paul's Churchyard.
These were most gorgeous. The first consisted
of a rock of coral, with Neptune at the summit,
mounted on a dolphin which bore a throne of
mother-of-pearl, with tritons, mermaids and
other marine creatures in attendance. But the
most magnificent of all was the " maiden chariot,"
a virgin's head being the arms of the Company.
Strype tells us that " . . . when any of this Company is chosen Mayor, or makes one of the
triumph of the day wherein he goes to Westminster to be sworn, a most beautiful virgin is
carried through the streets in a chariot, with all
the glory and majesty possible, with her hair all
dishevelled about her shoulders, to represent the
maidenhead which the Company give for their
arms. And this lady is plentifully gratified for
her pains besides the gift of all the rich attire
she wears."

The chariot in which she rode was " . . . an

21

imperial triumphal car of Roman form, elegantly adorned with variety of paintings, commixed with richest metals, beautified and embellished with several embellishments of gold and silver illustrated with divers inestimable and various coloured jewels of dazzling splendour, adorned and replenished with several lively figures bearing the banners of the kings, the lords mayor, and companies."

Upon a throne sits the virgin in great state, " hieroglyphically attired " in a robe of white satin, richly adorned with precious stones, fringed and embroidered with gold, signifying the graceful blushes of virginity ; on her head a long dishevelled hair of flaxen colour, decked with pearls and precious gems, on which is a coronet of gold beset with emeralds, diamonds, sapphires, and other precious jewels of inestimable value. Her buskins are of gold laced with scarlet ribbons, adorned with pearls and other costly jewels. In one hand she holds a sceptre ; in the other a shield with the arms of the right honourable the Company of Mercers.

Such is the gorgeous being who presides over the maiden's chariot. But she rides not in solitary state. Fame perched on a golden canopy blows her trumpet ; Vigilance, Wisdom, Charity, Prudence, Justice, Fortitude, Temperance, Faith, Hope, Charity, Loyalty and the Nine Muses, attend upon her. She has eight pages of honour dressed in cloth of silver to walk by her side, and

22

INTRODUCTION

Triumph acts as charioteer. The whole machine is drawn by nine white Flanders horses, each horse ridden by some emblematical personage—such as Victory, Fame, Loyalty, Europe attended by Peace and Plenty, Africa, Asia and America. The foot attendants are numerous—eight grooms, forty Roman lictors in crimson garb, twenty servants to clear the way, and twenty savages or green men throwing squibs and fireworks, to keep off the crowd, and a host of workmen ready to repair any part of the cumbersome chariot which might, as was not unlikely, get out of order during its progress through the city.

Beside such magnificent pageants, our present Lord Mayor's processions seem poor and insignificant. We might go back to an earlier day, and see Henry V returning from his victorious campaign in France, and being greeted by his loyal subjects at Blackheath, the mayor and brethren of the City Companies wearing red gowns with hoods of red and white, " well mounted and gorgeously horsed with rich collars and great chains, rejoicing in his victorious returns." The river, too, was often the scene of their splendour, as when Elizabeth, the Queen of King Henry VII, was crowned. At her coming forth from Greenwich by water, ". . . there was attending upon her then the major, shrifes, and aldermen of the citie, and divers and many worshipful commoners, chosen out of evry crafte, in their liveries, in barges freshly furnished

23

THE CITY COMPANIES

with banners and streamers of solke, rechly
beaton with the arms and bagges of their craftes ;
and in especiall a barge, called the bachelors'
barge, garnished and apparelled, passing all
other, wherein was ordeyned a great read dragon,
spowting flames of fyer into the Thames ; and
many other gentlemanlie pagiaunts, well and
curiously devised, to do her Highness sport and
pleasure with." With such pleasant devices did
our forefathers disport themselves.

CHURCH OF ST. LAWRENCE & OLD GUILDHALL

II. THE GUILDHALL

THE Guildhall, the home of the civic government of London, is one of the most important buildings in London. It has been the battle-ground of many a hard-won fight for civic and religious liberty. According to Professor Lethaby, " it is a fine fragment of a great civic palace which followed the same general type as the larger houses, having gate-tower, court, great hall, chambers, chapel and offices. It was a very splendid and romantic palace, worthy of the City and of the Lord Mayor and Barons of London." The Great Fire and the eccentricities of the 18th and early 19th century architects have done their best to mutilate it, but it still possesses features of great interest, and a study of its history forms a fitting introduction to the story of the gilds.

In Norman times, there was a Guildhall which stood upon the site of the present building.[1] This was removed and a fine new one erected between the years 1411 and 1435. The Great Fire in 1666 swept over it and destroyed much, including the roof, but the walls were strong, and were only partially damaged. A 15th century window, with cusped-leaded lights may be seen in the south-western side of the hall, and the porch which was damaged ; but through it have entered the worthy citizens of London, the Lord Mayors and Aldermen in all their glory followed by the

[1] Stow mentions this Hall, and states that it faced Alderman-bury, but this modern authorities consider to have been an error.

25

THE CITY COMPANIES

Livery Companies for nigh 500 years. Beneath
the hall are two large crypts, one of which is now
used for the Guildhall Museum in which are
stored the relics of Old London. The other crypt
is now used partly as a kitchen. After the Fire
had done its worst, Sir Christopher Wren
immediately set to work to restore the blackened
chambers and hall, and replaced the old open
roof by a flat ceiling. Since then various alterations have been made. The Gatehouse was
restored in 1789 by George Dance, Junior. The
east wing was removed under the auspices of
Sir Horace Jones in 1868, but it was rebuilt
in 1909 by Sir Sidney Parks, who restored the
façade after the manner set by Mr. Dance, which
Bayley satirically described as " the truly Gothic
façade."

In older days vast multitudes used to resort
here at the elections of the Mayor and Sheriffs,
and often riots and tumults ensued. Hence a
strict law was passed in 1419, ordering that no
one should be present on these occasions, except
the Aldermen and four discreet and best men of
each Ward who should select the Mayor for the
ensuing year. " This yere the Geldhalle of
London was begonne to make newe," says the
Chronicle of London.

It is pleasant to discover in the present buildings portions of the elder Hall. The vaulting
of the crypt, supported on slender shafts, is
remarkably fine. The great hall was paved with

THE GUILDHALL

Purbeck marble by the Executors of Sir Richard Whittington, while the windows were resplendent with his arms and those of distinguished Aldermen. The fires blazed on two hearths in the centre of the hall, and the smoke escaped through louvres in the roof, the gift of Sir William Harryot, Mayor. The Guildhall gradually grew and increased the number of its chambers and there was added a chamber for the Mayor and one for the Council, and finally an important feature of the establishment, the kitchens. These were completed in 1501 when Sir John Shaa was Mayor and since that time the Lord Mayor's Banquet on November 9th, the highest and crowning point of civic hospitality, has always been held in the world-renowned Guildhall. It was hung with tapestry by Sir Nicholas Alwyn, Mayor. In 1614, the new Council Chamber was added. In 1861 Wren's flat roof was removed and the present fine, lofty, high-pitched roof, with its crowning pinnacle, was substituted and added an appearance of dignity to the building. The " City Fathers " have always been eager to improve the condition of their Guidhall, the ancient home of the Corporation of the greatest city in the world.

The porch or Gatehouse has been already mentioned and I may point out here the ancient work set up in 1425, some of which, happily, was spared by the Fire. The two bays of groined vaulting remain, and deeply recessed, moulded

27

and traceried panels on the walls. If we wish to recall the former appearance we must imagine it adorned with seven statues ; on either side stood Discipline, Justice, Fortitude, and Temperance, to remind the citizens of virtues necessary to the perfecting of character and the full enjoyment of civic life. Law and Learning looked down upon them from above and the figure of the Saviour in the highest niche pointed out the claims of religion and the worship of God as the duty of all men. As we shall see presently, in the case of all the Companies religious observances played an important part in the life of the rulers of the city.[1] The Corporation had their Chapel on the north-east side of the Guildhall yard. There they worshipped and attended in state special services on many occasions in each year, especially just before the election of a new Mayor at Michaelmas, when they sought the wisdom and guidance of the Holy Spirit in the choice of the chief magistrate of the City. The Hall is a magnificent building and has been the scene of many historic events in ancient and

---

[1] The six statues were removed in 1789 and deposited in a cellar, and afterwards given to Thomas Banks, the sculptor, and subsequently sold. They were fine specimens of art, and it is unfortunate that they have vanished. The figure of the Christ has gone, too. It probably was taken down when the Puritans waged war against images and the iconoclasts were busy. A 16th century rhymer referred to this figure with its companions in the verse :

> " Where Jesus Christ aloft doth stand,
>   Law and Learning on either hand."

The city arms now occupy its place.

modern times. Over it the City giants, Gog and Magog (or as Mr. Fairholt calls them, Gogmagog and Corineus), keep watchful guard. These figures are about two centuries old and replaced two old wicker giants which were borne in the procession on Lord Mayor's day.

Strange scenes rise before our eyes as we stand in this ancient Hall. We see it crowded with a host of citizens in 1483 when the Duke of Buckingham and the Mayor were trying to espouse the cause of Richard, Duke of Gloucester, and to make him King. The citizens liked not the Hunchback, and save for a few of the Duke's servants at the back of the Hall, and a few noisy apprentices, received the proposal with silence. But the Duke of Buckingham chose to interpret the slight applause as an expression of the will of the people in favour of Richard, to the undoing of the nation and the promotion of much trouble. We see poor Anne Askew publicly examined and condemned to death for heresy because she upheld the Protestant principles of the Reformation. Tortured, racked and starved, she adhered to her faith and would not disclose the names of any confederates, and at length met her death at Smithfield by fire, with three other victims. These walls looked down upon the dramatic trial of Sir Nicholas Throckmorton, who was accused of participating in the insurrection of Wyatt in the time of Queen Mary. A full report of the proceeding is given by Holinshed. Shrewd and sagacious, impressive and irresistible, the prisoner pleaded for his life, overthrew the arguments of his accusers, convinced the jury, who, to their credit, refused to give a decision contrary to their consciences, and eventually obtained a verdict of innocence of the charges brought against him. It was a memorable trial, and not less dramatic than that of Father Garnet, the Jesuit, who was concerned in the Gunpowder Plot, and which ended in his conviction and execution. Poets, too, have here stood at the bar of justice. Henry Howard, Earl of Surrey (1517-1547), the introducer of blank verse into English literature, was charged with plotting for the Crown and lost his head, and Edward Waller (1606-1687), one of the founders of the Classical School of Poetry, during the Civil War period, was accused of being engaged in a plot to hold London for King Charles. He escaped with his life, but was heavily fined. In the Court of Common Council there is a memorial on a shield of the hasty visit of King Charles I to demand the Corporation to deliver up the persons of the five Members of Parliament to justice for resisting the authority of the Crown. This the Court refused, and the Sovereign had to return to Whitehall without gaining any satisfaction and with the knowledge that the city would be against him in the conflict that was soon to break out.

Many pages would be needed to describe fully all the contents and treasures of the Guildhall.

THE GUILDHALL

In Wren's building of the Court of Aldermen, you see in the ceiling the allegorical paintings of Sir James Thornhill. Monuments, paintings of City worthies and of those who have won the affections of London citizens appear everywhere —Nelson, Wellington, the Earl of Chatham, Lord Mayor Beckford and a host of others, who have done good service in their generations, upheld the honour of England, and promoted the glory and welfare of the city.

Such is a brief description of the Guildhall, in which the Gildsmen used to assemble, and take their part, in the government of London, and it thus is closely associated with the story of the City Companies which this book is designed to tell.

III. THE ORIGIN OF ⋗ ⋗
⋖ ⋖ THE COMPANIES

WE must go back to very early times in order to find the original conformation of the City Companies of London. Indeed some authorities trace a connection with the Roman Collegia and Sodalitates, but there is in this country a fatal gap between the departure of the Roman legions and the coming of the Anglo-Saxon tribes which no historical evidence is able to bridge. In France it was not so. According to Levasseur, in that country, " the cities preserved their Roman population, and even a portion of their ancient civil and political institutions." [1] The general opinion of all French writers on the subject shows the great probability of a virtual and direct descent from the Roman colleges and municipalities to the French trade gilds and communes of the Early Middle Ages. [2]

A capitulary of Charlemagne decrees the Corporation of Bakers shall be maintained in full efficiency in the provinces and an edict of 864 mentions the Gild of Goldsmiths. Lacroix and Seré assert that it would be possible to find traces of the Goldsmiths' Gild among the Gauls ever since the Roman occupation. [3]

---

[1] "Histoire des clanes ouvrières." Vol. I, p. 122.
[2] "Gould's History of Freemasons," p. 183. " Récits des Merovingiens " by Aug. Thierry.
[3] Ouin-Lacroix, " Histoire des anciennes corporations d'arts et metiers," p. 2.

ORIGIN OF THE COMPANIES

In England we have no such evidence, and for 200 years history is a blank, and reluctantly we must abandon any hope of proving that the Anglo-Saxon Gilds can trace their descent from Roman times. But these institutions found favour among the Anglo-Saxons, when they were settled on British soil, and made Britain English, and they probably brought the Gild system with them. There existed several Saxon Gilds in this country. The Saddlers' Gild, subsequently styled Company, was founded in pre-Conquest times, and the Weavers had their Gild, and Stow tells us of the Knighten or Cnihten Gild which held a tournament in London in the time of King Edgar, and was composed of " thirteen Knights or soldiers, well beloved to the King and this realm " who received a grant of land in the City which Stow carefully describes. Edward the Confessor confirmed their Charter, which is " fair written in Saxon letter and tongue."

According to the Letter Books of the London City Corporation the story was transcribed from the Chartulary of Holy Trinity Priory, and Canute, not Edgar, is stated to have been the founder. There are several elements of legend. The King is said to have granted the land to the Gild, on condition that each of the thirteen should victoriously fight three combats, viz., above ground, below it, and in the water, and afterwards on a certain day, in the field called East Smith-

33   c

THE CITY COMPANIES

field they should contend with lances against all comers.

These conditions were gloriously fulfilled, and on the said day the King invested them with the name Cnihten Gild. The Charter of Edward the Confessor granted that they might have their manorial jurisdiction (or Soke) and be as worthy of good laws as they were in the days of Edgar, Ethelred and Cnut, and that no man should wrong them, but that all should be in peace. William I, William II, and Henry I confirmed to the men of the "Cnihten Gilds" their Gild and land and customs as they had them in the time of Edward the Confessor. In 1125, "15 men of the ancient progeny of the Noble English Cnihts assembled in the Charterhouse of the Holy Trinity near Aldgate and gave to that Church and the Canons there of the land and Soke, for which donation they were admitted into the monastery."

There were Gilds of Knights in other places besides London. At Canterbury one existed in the reign of Ethelbert (860-866) as well as the Priests' Gild and the "Cheapmanne" or Merchant Gild.

Winchester too, in the time of Henry I, had a Knighten Gild which met in a chenietehalla (or Knights' hall) "where the cnihts (Knights) used to drink their Gild and had it in free tenure from King Edward (chenietehalla ubi chenietes potabunt gildam suam, et eam libere tenebunt

34

de rege Edwardo),[1] also another Hall held by
" cnihts " in the reign of Edward the Confessor
(Chenietes tenebunt la chenietahalla libere de
rege Edwardo).[2]   Again, the Doomsday Book
speaks of a Gild Hall (gihalla) at Dover.   Some
other examples exist.

The ordinances of the Gild of Knights at
Cambridge disclose some of the features of Gild
life in this period.   Each member had to take an
oath of initiation.   It was governed by a reeve or
warden.   The bodies of deceased members were
brought by the Gild to the church and a funeral
feast was held.   Each member gave a contribution
to the wergild.   Strict rules were framed against
members using abusive language and violence,
and the fine was usually a saxtarium of honey.[3]

A famous Gild existed at Exeter, of which the
rules survive.   The members met three times a
year, and the following ordinances are given :

Each Gild brother to bring two sesters of
malt, and each " cniht " one sester and a sciat
of honey, and say Masses for the living and the
dead.   At the death of a brother, each man said
six Masses and paid five pence, and at a house-
burning each man paid one penny.

If anyone misgreet another he was fined thirty
pence.[4]

Mr. Lambert also quotes the ordinances of

[1] Domesday Book, V.C.H. (Hants).
[2] *ibid.*
[3] Lambert, " Two Thousand Years of Gild Life," p. 47.
[4] *ibid.*

Orey's Gild at Abbotsbury, but these are too
lengthy to be repeated here. It is evident from
these authorities that Gilds were a well-known
institution among the Anglo Saxons.[1]

In Norman and Mediæval times the Gild
system extended itself throughout the country
and the number of these fraternities increased
enormously. They permeated civic and parochial
life, in towns and villages, and differed as widely
as the aristocratic Merchant Gild of London or
Winchester differed from the Ploughman's Gild
who kept the Ploughman's light burning in his
village church. In city or town or country village
the whole municipal, industrial or social life of the
Middle Ages moved in the circle of the Gild.
Much has been written about the meaning of
the word which I have ventured in this work to
spell " Gild " and not " Guild," which Professor
Skeat " pronounced to be as false as it is common." Either in its Anglo-Saxon or Latin form
the " u " has no place, and all the chief and most
authoritative writers on the subject have adopted
the spelling " gild," such as Dr. Gross, in spite
of many years' use of the other form. We usually
speak of the Hall of the Gild as the "Guildhall,"
and I suppose no amount of protest will change
the Guildhall of London into the " Gildhall."
Former writers seem to have satisfied themselves
that the word is derived from the Anglo-Saxon
" gyldan," which means " to pay," and with that

---

[1] "The Gild Merchant," by Dr. C. Gross.

the present writer was content to be satisfied. But subsequent scholars have thrown considerable doubt upon its accuracy. Dr. Gross declares that the word has various and different meanings, such as " sacrificium " or " adoratio," " tributum," or " societas." The members of a Gild were called by the Anglo-Saxons " Gegildan," and Kemble says that " the term represents those who mutually pay for one another, i.e., under a system of pecuniary mulcts, those who are mutually responsible before the law."

However, whatever the original meaning of the word, we know quite well what the Gilds were. They were voluntary associations formed for religious, social, or funereal objects and for the promotion and benefit of the profession or trade with which the members were specially concerned. There were religious Gilds, or " Gilds of the Calendar " as they were called, which were composed mainly of the clergy; social-religious Gilds, established for the performance of religious exercises often including other objects such as the protection of life and property ; trade Gilds which were separated into Merchant Gilds and craft or artist-Gilds.[1] From such associations the City Companies grew. They were instituted for the purpose of protecting the consumer or employer against incompetency or fraud of the dealer or artisan, and also for securing a maintenance to the skilful artisan

[1] Dr. Gross, p. 177.

preventing him from being undersold in a labour market by an unlimited number of competitors.[1] Each Gild was given a monopoly in its own particular trade. No one could interfere with its members, or start a rival business without becoming a member of the Gild, into which he was formally admitted and had to swear obedience and to preserve the secrets of the trade ; to conduct himself orderly with his fellow members, and to observe the rules and ordinances of the Gild. Each Gild had its master or wardens, its court or livery, assistants, yeomanry or bachelors, and apprentices. The Companies acted as domestic tribunals, arbitrating between master and man, and settling disputes, thus diminishing hostile litigation and promoting amity and goodwill.

They were also in the nature of benefit societies from which the workman in return for the contributions which he had made in health and vigour to the common stock of the Gild might be relieved in sickness or when disabled by age. This was greatly increased by the benevolence of the richer members of the Gild who contributed large funds for charitable purposes, built almshouses for their afflicted folk, erected great schools, and who had such confidence in the integrity of the ruling members of their company that they believed they could not find any better trustees. Hence arose the numerous charitable

[1] Report of Municipal Commission in 1834.

gifts and foundations which were entrusted to their care. They also possessed the character of modern clubs, in which feasting and social intercourse were regular features of their Gild life.

In old London, workers and traders, as we shall see presently, lived together in the same quarters, and there formed their Gilds. Each undertook the regulation of the trade with which they were associated. Overseers were appointed to inspect the wares produced or sold, and to see that their monopolies were not infringed. Each Gild had its " Ordinances " which were religious, social, charitable, and industrial. The religious ordinances referred to the attendances at the services of the Church, the promotion of pilgrimages, and the celebration of Masses for the dead. The social and charitable ordinances referred to their dining, meeting together for refreshment and amusement, and relief of their poorer sisters and brothers ; while the third class of regulations were concerned with the hours of labour, the wages of workmen and teaching the 'prentices the mysteries of their trade.

The Sovereigns of England at various dates granted to the Companies Charters by which they were incorporated and recognized by the State. They were thus permitted to hold land and other property and were obliged to carry out their by-laws and to apply their trust funds to the purposes for which they were bequeathed.

THE CITY COMPANIES

Very valuable considerations were given to the Crown for the granting of their Charters, and the national exchequer was much enriched thereby. The first Charters were granted by Edward III. Prior to that reign, the Gilds were styled adulterine or unauthorized, and an enquiry into their objects and conditions in 1179-80 showed that there were no less than nineteen, of which only four were trade Gilds,[1] namely, the Goldsmiths', Grocers' or Pepperers', Butchers' and Cloth Workers'. There was much riot and disturbance in London at this period, and the Gilds as secret societies, were regarded with some ill-favour by the authorities, and as an element of danger. All this was removed by the incorporation and approval of the Sovereign and they became " nurseries of charities and seminaries of good citizens."[2]

The privilege of becoming a member of these fraternities was obtained in three ways, by patrimony, apprenticeship and redemption. Thus the right of membership from time immemorial has always been hereditary. All lineal descendants of a freeman had a right to become freemen. The son of a Skinner can become a Skinner, although he may be a solicitor or follow any other profession or trade. Hence in course of time all the freemen may in no way

[1] *London, its Origin and Early Development*, by William Page, F.S.A., p. 101.
[2] Minute of the Court of the Grocers' Company, August 18th, 1687.

be connected with the trade which the name of the fraternity bears. From time immemorial admission may be gained by apprenticeship, and this can still be done. A suitable candidate for the freedom, though he follows some other business or profession, can serve a nominal apprenticeship for seven years, with someone who carries on the trade with which the Company is associated and then claim his freedom. The last method to obtain the freedom is by redemption, by paying a large or small amount of money for the privilege, but those who enter the gate by this method usually can say with the Roman captain who addressed St. Paul : " With a great sum obtained I this freedom."

It may be asked what is the relation of the City Companies to the City of London, and what is their share in its governance ? At one time they were absolutely the body politic, sharing with the Lord Mayor and Aldermen and Sheriffs the rule of the City. In the history of the Companies the Lord Mayor and Aldermen used to adjudicate and settle differences, but the Liverymen had power of election, by the Charter of Edward II, of the Chamberlain, the Common Sergeant, the Town Clerk, the Bridgemaster, the Ale Conners, and the Auditors, and in the Act (2 George I, c. 18) for regulating elections it is enacted that the elections of Mayor, Sheriff, Members of Parliament, Chamberlains, Bridgemaster, Auditors, etc., should be done by the liverymen thereof. The liverymen of the Companies alone are the " commonalty " who assemble in common Hall, and there discharge their functions as electors. They elect the Lord Mayor from among the Aldermen who have served the office of Sheriff, and submit two names for final selection by the Court of Aldermen. They do not now elect the Members of Parliament for the City.

CHARITY AND RELIGION

We have seen the livery in their gay clothing marching in procession through London streets, taking their stands in Cheapside, going to Court in their barges on the river, and performing their pageants for the amusement and recreation of the citizens.

But pleasure, pomp and pageantry were not the sole uses of these Gilds in olden days. A study of the preamble to their numerous Charters shows that to maintain the poor members of their Companies was one of their chief objects. The Fishmongers had a grant of power to hold land for " the sustentation of the poor men and women of the said commonalty " ; the Goldsmiths' Charter recites that " . . . many persons of that trade, by fire and smoke of quicksilver had lost their sight, and that others of them by working in that trade became so crazed and infirm that they were disabled to subsist but of relief from others ; and that divers of the said

42

City, compassionating the condition of such, were disposed to give and grant divers tenements and rents in the said City to the value of twenty pounds per annum to the Company of the said craft, to the maintenance of the said blind, weak and infirm." Legacies were also bequeathed to the Companies for the same object, and thus we find them in the fourteenth century administering large charities for the benefit of the poor of London, and with the help of the monasteries providing a system of relief and educational organization in the absence of any poor-law administration or State education.

These City Gilds were also of a distinctly religious character, and prescribed rules for the attendance of members at the services of the Church, for pilgrimages, and the celebration of Masses for the dead. Each Company had its patron saint, and maintained a chantry priest or chaplain. They founded altars in churches in honour of their patron saint, who was usually selected on account of his emblem or symbol being in some way connected with the particular trade of the Gild. Thus St. Dunstan who was a worker in precious metals, became the patron saint of the Goldsmiths ; the Fishmongers selected St. Peter, a fisherman, and held their services at St. Peter's church ; the Merchant Taylors venerated St. John Baptist, whose symbol is the *Agnus Dei*. In several cases, the saint to whom the church they were attending was dedicated was adopted as their own patron. Thus the Grocers called themselves " the fraternity of St. Anthony," because they had their altar in St. Anthony's Church ; the Vintners " the fraternity of St. Martin," from the like connection with St. Martin's Vintry Church. Indeed it has been truly observed that the maintenance of their arts and mysteries during several ages was blended with so many customs and observances that it was not till the times subsequent to the Reformation that the fraternities could be regarded as strictly secular. On election days when the master and wardens were chosen, the company marched in solemn procession to the Church of St. Laurence, to hear Mass. Stow tells of the Skinners going to the Church of St. Laurence, Poultry, on Corpus Christi day, with more than 200 torches of wax borne before them, costly garnished, burning bright, and about 200 clerks and priests in surplices and copes singing. The brethren were clad in their new liveries, the Mayor and Aldermen in scarlet, and on their return to the hall enjoyed a great feast. On the Sunday following the election day the brethren attended a Mass of requiem for their deceased members, when the Bede Roll was read and prayers offered for the souls of the departed members, as well as for those who still survived, each brother being mentioned by name.

ORIGIN OF THE COMPANIES

But the chief object of the existence of the Companies was the promotion of the prosperity of the trades with which they were associated. They were appointed by Charter " to settle and govern their mysteries," to elect officers, " to inquire of the concerns of their trade " and to correct and amend the same. They had the right of search through their respective trades, in order that each of them might detect dishonest practices in their own craft and punish offenders, and to keep out and suppress all " foreigners " who dared to carry on a trade and yet did not belong to the particular company which governed and regulated it. To preserve the secrets of the craft and to regulate apprenticeships were also some of the duties of the Gild. Each fraternity had its own duties to perform. Thus the Grocers had the oversight of all drugs, and their officers were ordered " to go away and assay weights, powders, confections, plasters, oyntments, and all other things belonging to the same craft"; the Goldsmiths had the assay of metals ; the Fishmongers the oversight and rejection of fish brought to London which they did not deem fit for the use of the people ; the Vintners had the tasting and gauging of wines. Many curious ¬and obsolete trades are disclosed in the records of the Companies. The Mercers were the *Mercatores*, or Merchants, no simple traders or

45

small tradesmen, but persons who dealt in a varied assortment of goods, such as linen cloths, buckrams, fustians, satins, jewels, fine woollen and other English clothes, drugs, cotton, thread and wool, silk, wood, oil, copper, wine, lead, and salt. The Grocer was one who dealt *en gros* —wholesale—as opposed to retail merchandise. The original title of the Gild was the " Company of Pepperers of Soper's Lane." The Drapers were makers of woollen cloth. The Fishmongers united into one body the two ancient Gilds of the Salt Fishmongers and the Stock Fishmongers. The title of the Merchant Taylors in the time of Edward I was the " Fraternity of the Taylors and Linen-Armourers of St. John the Baptist," and manufactured everything pertaining to armour, including the linings, surcoats, caparisons and accoutrements, Royal pavilions, and robes of State, tents for soldiers, as well as ordinary garments and wardrobe requirements, except only the actual metal-work. It may be observed how minutely the work of the trades was divided and sub-divided, and how zealously each craft was guarded, lest one tradesman or craftsman should interfere with the work of another. The whole system of the Companies was to form an absolute monopoly of each craft. A Universal Provider, or a man who " could turn his hand to anything " was unknown in the palmy days of the City Companies.

The Skinners, or Pelliparii, naturally dealt in

46

skins and furs, which, before the days of sombre black coats and tweed suits, were in great request, and were the distinguished badge of rank and high estate. The Haberdashers united in one Gild the Hat Merchants ; the Haberdashers of Hats including the crafts of the Hurriers or Cappers, and the Millianers or Milliners, who derived their name from the fact that they imported their goods chiefly from Milan. The Salters naturally dealt in that necessary article of consumption, and conveniently had their quarters near the Fishmongers. The Ironmongers were both merchants and traders having large warehouses and yards whence they exported and sold both iron and iron rods, and also had shops for the retail of manufactured iron goods. The Vintners, or Merchant wine-Tonners of Gascoyne, were divided into two classes—the Vinetarii, or importers of wine, residing in stately stone houses, built of stone brought from Caen in Normandy, adjoining the wharves ; and the Tabernarii, or keepers of taverns, inns or cook-houses. The Clothmakers combined the ancient Gilds of the Fullers and Shearmen.

The above twelve Companies are styled the Great Companies, and in addition to these there are sixty-two minor Companies, several of which are less only in name than their greater brethren. In point of numbers and wealth, some are equal to the less opulent of the Great Companies. The Armourers, Carpenters, Leather-sellers, and

47

THE CITY COMPANIES

Saddlers are especially wealthy corporations, and have fine halls, which are scarcely surpassed by any in the City. Some have no halls, and small incomes ; but there is scarcely a Company which has not an interesting history, or which does not have some attractive and interesting historical associations.

Sic tranſit gloria Mundi.

LonDon

THE GREAT FIRE

IV. THE VICISSITUDES
OF THE COMPANIES

FROM this brief record of the City Companies, and of the part each one played in the drama of the life of London, it will be gathered that most of these Gilds showed strong and vigorous growth in the fifteenth century, and were thoroughly established. Then came the period of the Reformation, which proved a time of storm and stress to the Companies. They held much property bequeathed to them for the endowment of chantries, for the celebration of Masses for the dead, and for other purposes which were deemed to be connected with " superstition." The Companies were rich. Greed and spoliation were rampant, and many powerful courtiers were eager enough to prove " superstitious uses " as an excuse for confiscation. Hence a very large amount of the property of the Companies, as well as of plate and other valuables, was seized by these robbers, and the Gilds were compelled to redeem their lands and wealth by paying down hard cash to the plunderers. It was a grievous time, but the Companies weathered the storm, and regained by much sacrifice their possessions. The system of forced loans instituted by the Tudor and Stuart monarchs also pressed hard upon the Companies. Henry VIII required of them £21,000—an enormous sum in those days—for his war with Scotland.

THE CITY COMPANIES

Philip and Mary demanded £100,000 for the war with France. The Mercers alone supplied Queen Elizabeth with £4,000 after the defeat of the Spanish Armada. Before the Petition of Rights put an end to these forced loans, Charles I extracted a loan of £120,000 from the City, and the Civil War made further demands on the funds of the Companies, both contending parties pressing them for money. It need not be added that little of this enormous wealth was ever returned to the Gilds, and they were much impoverished. Many of them were compelled to sell their plate and other valuables, and some were almost reduced to the verge of bankruptcy.

Another drain upon the resources of the Companies was the scheme of James I to establish the Ulster Plantation upon land forfeited to the Crown through a recent rebellion there. The King offered the land to the City Companies for a colony, pointing out the very great advantages which the land afforded. These were painted in very glowing colours, but scarcely answered the expectations of the colonists. The active citizens of London at once formed the Irish Society, raised £60,000 for the purchase of the land from the sagacious King, and each Company took shares. The old county of Derry was the chief scene of this enterprise, and in token of its new masters the chief town was rechristened London-Derry. The colony had scarcely been established when Charles I, with his strange arbitrariness,

removed the grant, but it was restored by
Charles II, and most of the estates still belong
to the energetic Companies, and have made
Ulster the most prosperous and loyal part of
the " distressful island."

But the greatest of all the misfortunes which
have befallen the companies was the Great Fire.
Hall after hall, replete with costly treasures
bequeathed by departed brethren of the Gilds,
with all their archives and documents, perished
in the hideous holocaust. All the wealth that
repacious kings and the troubles of the Civil
War had spared was engulfed in that awful
catastrophe. Again and again, when we try to
read the history of a Company, we meet with
the distressing intelligence that all its records
were destroyed in the Great Fire. Very few
escaped. The Leather-sellers, Pinners, and
Ironmongers were happily without the range
of the conflagration; "the Cloth-workers partially
escaped." All the books of the Companies
abound with graphic details of this calamity.
It melted their plate, burned their records, and
laid their property, from which they chiefly
derived their incomes, in ashes. At the same time
they were burdened with a load of debt, the
consequence of the compulsory loans to which I
have referred, and saw no means left of paying.
The clouds of smoke issued from the burning
ruins of their halls, but their English hearts
were not daunted, and bravely did they struggle

51

with their adversities. They immediately set to work to do what they could to save the relics of their fortunes. They first took steps to secure their melted plate from the ruined buildings. Then they set about the rebuilding of their properties. Extraordinary exertions were made. The wealthier members subscribed vast sums of money. The houses of their tenants rose like magic from the ruins, and it is remarkable that in no more than two or three years' time most of the halls of the Companies were rebuilt, and many shone forth with additional splendour. The reign of Charles II did not however conclude without involving the Companies in additional anxiety, occasioned by the King's arbitrary interference in their affairs by his *quo warranto* proceedings. He presumed to call into question the validity of the Charter of the City of London, and declared it to be forfeited ; and not only that, but also the Charters of all the corporations in England, including those of the City Companies. The whole business, when regarded in the light of history, seems farcical and absurd ; but the danger to the life of the corporations appeared very real and tremendous to the good citizens of London in the year 1684. They behaved in a most loyal and submissive manner, surrendered their Charters, expressed their fear that they had offended their sovereign, who, "in his princely wisdom," had issued a *quo warranto* against them, and earnestly begged to have their Charters renewed. The King granted them new Charters, which riveted strong fetters about the Gilds, placed them, bound hand and foot, at the mercy of the King, and reduced the City to entire subservience. James II showed no inclination to release the City and the Companies from their bonds, until the news of the advent of the Prince of Orange forced him to make an act of restitution ; the old Charters were restored, and the proceedings *quo warranto* were hastily quashed. One of the first acts of William and Mary was to renew the old Charters and declare that all the acts of the Stuart monarchs, with regard to the suppression of these ancient documents and the granting of new ones, were entirely null and void. This action endeared the new Sovereign to the citizens, and, doubtless, helped greatly to secure for him the English throne and the loyalty of his people.

Public confidence being restored, the affairs of the Companies began to improve. Though still hampered by the loss of much wealth, and by the misfortunes through which they had passed, their members were wealthy, and gifts and bequests were not lacking. It is true that their connection with the trades which they were supposed to govern was fast dying out—indeed, many of their trades had for a long time become öbsolete—but the corporations still cared for their poor members, managed their estates, promoted in some measure the trades with which

53

they were associated and took their part in the government of the affairs of the City. The value of their City property in recent years increased enormously, and raised them from poverty to affluence. This has enabled them to institute vast schemes of charity and munificence, which greatly benefit the whole country, and to maintain, preserve, and develop those magnificent educational and charitable establishments which pious benefactors have committed to their care. In the following pages I have told at some length their interesting history, and given an account of their charities and treasures, and how by wise schemes they adapted old bequests to modern needs, and how they maintain the hospitable traditions of the City of London. This generous hospitability of the Companies is well-known. It is founded on a tradition at least five hundred years old, though in hard times when funds were exhausted, or when grievous national troubles such as the late Great War, its course was interrupted. Members of these Gilds in former days bequeathed money for the holding of a feast and " dining lovingly together." After their worship of God in the church of their patron saint and the business of arranging and regulating their trade concerns, and the election of their officers, it was their custom to have some social enjoyment. In the history of the Merchant Taylors and the Skinners it will be noted later that a grievous dispute with regard to precedence between the

two fraternities was eventually healed by an order
issued by the Mayor that each should take
precedence in alternate years and that they should
dine together at each other's halls as a proof of
good fellowship, and although that arrangement
was made centuries ago it is still observed, a
pleasing incident that is depicted in the new series
of paintings in the Royal Exchange, setting forth
important events in the annals of the City.

The Companies have always recognized the
duty of entertaining guests, and extending the
hospitality of the City to distinguished servants of
the State and to visitors from other lands. Without their aid there would be no bodies in London
to perform such a duty. The Lord Mayor of
London personifies hospitality, but every distinguished person, every notable foreigner, cannot
always find room at his table in the Mansion House.
These feasts are of great service in bringing
together men of different classes and various
opinions on politics and other matters which tend
to arouse hostile feelings and acerbity. Great
statesmen such as Peel, Brougham, Lyndhurst,
Palmerston, Beaconsfield, Gladstone and their
modern successors, have been entertained in these
City Halls. Distinguished soldiers and naval
heroes, Colonial premiers and civil servants,
pioneers of Empire, the founders of the Colonies
and dependencies of the British Crown, have said
how they appreciated the welcome they received
from the Companies, and how greatly they were

encouraged in their hard and self-denying labours by the hospitality of London's citizens. And when distinguished foreigners come to our shores, who can give them such a cordial reception as these ancient fraternities in their great halls, or impress upon them the greatness, the power and the sympathy of England as the Companies ? Long lines of English sovereigns have honoured the Liveries by their presence and thought it not derogatory to their dignity to be members and free-men, and Emperors and Kings of almost every nation (in these days sadly diminished in numbers) have betaken of their hospitality, which smooths hostility, encourages friendship, and for which the Companies should receive the gratitude of the country for this kindly service.[1]

[1] Amongst the venomous attacks which were made against the Companies in the proceedings of the Royal Commission of 1880, Messrs. Firth, Beale and A. J. Phillips, the worthless initiators of the prosecution, had a great deal to say against this department of the Companies' service to the Empire. Their accusations were proved to be slanderous and totally untrue. They accused them of misappropriation of funds, of using money that had been left to them for educational or trade purposes, for dinners and entertainments. By the publishing of accounts and the calm statement of their case the Companies had no difficulty in vindicating themselves from such scurrilous attacks, and emerged from the trial triumphant, with their positions strengthened, having won the gratitude of all right-thinking Englishmen for their generosity, their wonderful bountiful schemes of charity, and their good works.

OLD MERCERS' SCHOOL

V. THE MERCERS' COMPANY

THE actual date of the foundation of the Gilds of London is often very difficult to ascertain. It is usually (according to the favourite expression among antiquaries) "shrouded in the mists of antiquity." Prior to their incorporation, i.e., before the granting of a Charter by the Sovereign, their history often is a little uncertain, but light perpetual shines upon them subsequent to their reception of that honour and privilege. The Worshipful Company of Mercers ranks high in dignity and importance. They are the first in precedence and their antiquity can be traced as far back at least to 1172, when about that period they became patrons of one of the great City charities, and a few years later one of their Company became Mayor of London in 1214; the title of Lord Mayor was not then established. The two earliest holders of that exalted office were Henry and Robert Fitz-Alwyn, who are also claimed by the Mercers as members of their fraternity.

The late Clerk of the Company, Sir John Watney, F.S.A., published privately a very interesting and exhaustive work (a copy of which he was good enough to present to me) on the connection of the Mercers with the Hospital of St. Thomas of Acon (or Acre), on the site of which their Hall now stands, some portions of the former building being incorporated in the present one. It was originally one of the houses of the military

57

THE CITY COMPANIES

order of the Knights of St. Thomas of Acre,
a small body of men who formed themselves into
a semi-religious order on the model of the
Templars. They took for their patron the
murdered Archbishop of Canterbury, Thomas
à Becket. The Order has an interesting history,
which Sir John Watney sets out in full detail,
and tells of their triumphs when fighting in the
Holy Land, of their trials and their escape when
they were spared the suppression and tortures
inflicted on their comrades in many a battle, the
Knights Templar. We are more concerned
with the Hospital in Cheapside, which was
founded by the sister of St. Thomas à Becket
about 20 years after his death. Near the Hospital
was a cluster of houses and shops where the
Mercers plied their trade and was called the
Mercery. Here was the house of Gilbert
Becket, a citizen of London and a Mercer, who
when, according to legend, travelling in the
Holy Land was taken prisoner by a Saracen
Emir, whose daughter, Matilda, fell in love with
him and enabled him to escape. By Becket's
persuasions she renounced her religion and
became a Christian.

Hence arose that charming romance upon the
truth of which we were glad to believe that
modern " Higher Criticism " had not raised
any doubt; of the fair Saracen maid, who knew
no English words but " Gilbert " and " London,"
following her lover to that city, and there dis-

58

covering him and being married to him and "living happily ever afterwards." But alas I I fear, though we can retain the story, we must abandon our belief in its truth. We are told that Gilbert Becket was a merchant of Rouen, who migrated to this country, and brought with him Rose, his wife, of burgess rank, from Caen, in Normandy.[1] So fades fair romance before the onslaught of historic truth. Gilbert Becket was a rich man and became Portreeve of London, an office equivalent to that of Mayor. By this fair Norman Rose he had several children, the eldest being the famous Archbishop, and amongst others Agnes, who married Thomas Fitz-Theobald de Helles, and with her husband founded the Hospital under the patronage of the fraternity of Mercers. The connection between the Hospital and the Company lasted for 300 years, and did not terminate until with all monastic institutions the former was suppressed. Sir John Watney states that :

"The church must have been a stately edifice, but it could not be seen from the street. In it our ancestors worshipped, and in its immediate vicinity they have held their feasts and dispensed their charity for nearly 700 years. In it, too, they were buried, and for many centuries their good deeds have been held in remembrance by their successors, animated by the same de-

---

[1] "London, its Origin and Early Development," by William Page, F.S.A.

votion to their Lord, the same loyalty to their Sovereign, and the same love to and care for their brethren."

What is the meaning of the name Mercer ? Herbert in his History of the London Great Companies states that originally a mercer in ancient times was a dealer in small wares, and merceries comprehended all things sold retail by the *little balance* or small scales, in contra-distinction to things sold by the *beam* or in gross, and included not only toys, together with haber-dashery and various other articles connected with dress, but also spices and drugs. In those early and simple times the Mercers chiefly kept the fairs and markets, and Herbert adds that the Mercers who in 1299 attended the French fairs, if they sat on the ground to sell their wares, paid a halfpenny toll, but if they occupied a stall they paid double. Childebert, King of France, as early as the beginning of the 8th century, enumerates merceries amongst other merchandise mentioned in the *Charta Mercatoria* of Edward I, and in various subsequent authorities, in all instances meaning nearly the same as pedlary. This description seems to indicate a lowly origin for a great Company; but all traders and mer-chants adopted the same mode of transacting their businesses. In much later times they attended such great fairs as that at Stourbridge, near Cambridge, set up their stall, as did the manufacturers of Kendal cloth, as well as the

THE MERCERS' COMPANY

traders from London, and many thousands of pounds were realized while the fair lasted. The business of the Mercers throve. A Mercer was no longer a simple pedlar or small tradesman, but a merchant who dealt in a varied assortment of goods, such as linen clothes, buckrams, fustians, satins, jewels, fine woollen and other English clothes, drugs, cotton, thread and wool, silk, wood, oil, copper, wine, lead and salt. In the year 1347 the Company was recognized, when a code of rules was drawn up at an assembly of " all the good people of the mercery of London."

The rules for the governance of the Gild ordained that there should be chosen every year four masters to preside over the community, that each member should contribute a certain fee, that strict regulations should be ordained for the governance of the apprentices, who were often very troublesome high-spirited youths who required much discipline. Here is an example of a curious method of punishment inflicted upon an apprentice for a *faux pas* of a particular nature. The wardens of the Company caused to be made two porters' frocks and two hoods of the same canvas, made after visor shape, with a space for the mouth and the eyes left open; wherein, the next court day, within the parlours two tall men having the said frocks upon them, because they should not be known (for otherwise the " bold 'prenticcs " would no doubt have effec-

61

tually prevented any more such kind attentions from the same quarter), "came in with two pennyworth of birchen rods and then in the presence of the said Master and Wardens, withouten any words speaking they pulled off the doublet and shirt of the said John Rolls and there upon him (being naked) they spend all the said rods for his said unthrifty demeanour."

Amongst the rules of the Mercers we find that an annual feast was arranged for the members for the promotion of good fellowship and the cherishing of unity among them after they had attended Mass in the church of the company; nor was charity forgotten. If any of the mystery should be undeservedly reduced to poverty by adventure at sea, debts, or feebleness of body, he should be relieved by the alms of the mystery. We may gather from their rules and regulations that the fraternity was an association of traders, that it was even then, in 1347, an important body, and both in numbers and income exceeded the other Companies of the City.

It is not often realized how much the country owes to these fraternities in general, and to the Mercers in particular, for the secure laying of the foundations of foreign trade. They established a trading company, the " Brothers of St. Thomas à Becket," subsequently known as the "Merchant Adventurers," who received their Charter from King Edward I in 1296, established themselves in Antwerp and promoted both export and

THE MERCERS' COMPANY

import trade in connection with the Mercers. Subsequently their powers were greatly increased by Queen Elizabeth, and they became a separate body, but cordial relations were continued for centuries. They had as their motto, *Dieu nous donne bonne adventure*, which has been adopted in spirit by many members of the Company of Mercers in old as in recent times. A relic of the connection between the two companies is preserved in the Master's hammer, which bears the Tudor arms and those of the Merchant Adventurers and the maidenhead of the Mercers.

Having served the City well the Company was incorporated by letters patent granted by Richard II in 1393, by the name of the Wardens and Company of the Mystery of the Mercers of the City of London.

The Charter recites that " Many men of the Mystery frequently by misfortune at sea and other unforeseen casualties fall into so great a poverty and want as to leave little or nothing wherewith to support themselves unless through the bounty of others, who pity and assist them, and that on that account the men of the said mystery had a wish and intention of constituting some certain provision by 100 marks paid into the Hanaper granting for himself and his heirs to his said liege subjects that they should be of themselves one perpetual community and that the said community might every year elect and

63

THE CITY COMPANIES

make four wardens to supervise, rule and govern
the said community and give licence to them to
hold lands, etc., for the support of poor men of
the Community and for the maintenance of a
chaplain to pray for the souls of the King and
Queen and of the members of the Mystery."
This was the first Charter, which was renewed
by many succeeding Sovereigns of England.

The silk trade brought great advantages to
the Mercers' business, though they were much
troubled by foreign silk manufacturers sending
their work to England and selling it there without
any regard for the Company. The silk trade was
fairly considerable during the reign of Edward IV,
Richard III, and Henry VII. It was considered
somewhat of a luxury, and the trade, although
discouraged by the Sumptuary Statutes of Queen
Elizabeth, had considerably extended itself; and
Camden records that " The people of the richer
sort wear silks glittering with gold and silver,
either embroidered or laced." Sir Baptist Hicks,
a member of the Company, created Viscount
Camden, obtained great wealth as a Silk Mercer.
Fortunately for him he was plying his trade when
James I came to the English throne, as he was
able to supply the Court with silk and rich
merceries " when that monarch and his bare
Scotch nobility and gentry came in." He built
a new Sessions House on Camberwell Green,
called Hicks' Hall, which name is preserved in
all the old road-books, as all the distances are

DEAN COLET

measured from Hicks' Hall. He retired to the charming district of the Cotswolds, and there raised at Chipping Camden a noble house, which was doomed to destruction by fire. Lady Camden, his widow, left a bequest to the Company in 1642 for the benefit of the young freemen who began business as shopkeepers, affording them a loan of £1,000. The Livery were excluded from this benefit. She wisely stated that " the shopkeeper of the Mercery should be preferred, and next the silk men, being of the Company and not of Livery. The Company can boast of many illustrious citizens, amongst whom is the famous Sir Richard Whittington, whose memory lives in children's books and gorgeous panto-mimes. Legend has woven many a story con-cerning his career, and mystery has clustered thick around him. He was no poor boy of lowly origin, but the son of a Gloucestershire squire, who, according to the custom of the time, sent his son to be apprenticed to some rich London merchant. We like to hear again the bells of Bow calling him back to his master's shop and promising that he should be thrice Lord Mayor of London. The story of his wonderful cat probably arose from the name of the vessel which earned his wealth. He became very rich and laid the foundations of many great charities. We find him devising laws for the governance of London; those contained in the *Liber Albus* are attributed to him. Among his benefactions was the founding of Whittington College and Almshouses, and these he placed under the management of the Company, the charge of which was not the least important of the duties entrusted to it.

Another great benefactor of the Company was Dean Colet, Dean of St. Paul's, the friend of Erasmus, who was a strong advocate for the reformation of the Church before the actual Reformation and plundering of the Church took place. He was the founder of St. Paul's School, which exists until the present day. Very noticeable in the history of the Companies is the great reliance its members placed on their integrity and watchful care of the benefactions entrusted to them. Their affection for these fraternities and loyal love for them induced them to believe that no better custodians could be found than these noble bodies to which they belonged. So as regard the Mercers, Sir Richard Whittington, Dean Colet and many others left their benefactions to the care of the Company. At the time of the Reformation the Company suffered heavy losses as regards their trust funds. Many of the benefactions which had been placed in their care contained some such clause as that they should appoint a chaplain to say Mass for the good of their souls, of the souls of the donor, his relations and ancestors, the King and Queen and others. These bequests were deemed to be " superstitious " at the time of the Reforma-

tion by some of the Reformers, who asserted
that prayers for the dead and Masses offered for
the good of their souls did not conform with
the Reformed Religion; hence chantries and
every so-called relic of " superstition " were seized
by King Henry VIII, or in the time of his son,
Edward VI, and confiscated with all their
endowments. Hence a very large part of the
properties of the Mercers was seized by the
Royal Commissioners, but the Mercers and nearly
all the richer Companies spent large sums re-
deeming these confiscated estates, which they
were able to hand down to future ages. As we
shall see presently, efforts were soon made to
rob them of their wealth.

While events were moving in the direction of
the Reformation, we hear of a letter sent to
Cromwell (not yet Vicar General) in 1535 by
Robert Ward who had attended service in the
chapel and had spied certain windows whereon
were depicted the life of St. Thomas of Canterbury and the punishing of Henry II. The
writer was distressed to see divers monks with
rods in their hands and the King kneeling naked
before a monk who was beating him before the
shrine of St. Thomas. Such pictures he deemed
a great hindrance to the contentation of the
King's subjects. The times were lawless. A
Mercer, Robert Packynton, M.P. for the City,
had in Parliament vehemently denounced the
depravity of the religious orders. As a result

67

he was foully murdered as he was going to Mass in the church of St. Thomas of Acon. His assassin was caught at Banbury and suffered the extreme penalty of this and other crimes.

Amongst other distinguished members of the Company was Sir Geoffrey Boleyn who was Lord Mayor in 1451 and father of Anne Boleyn, and great-grandfather of Queen Elizabeth. The Greshams were also distinguished members of the Company. Sir Thomas Gresham was founder of the Royal Exchange and of Gresham College which still continues its useful career.

In the midst of the disturbances of the time the King and his latest Queen (Anne Boleyn) intimated that they would come to Mercers' Hall on St. John's night to see the marching Watch, and the Company resolved to entertain their Majesties to a banquet. On several other occasions they repeated their visit.

We have already alluded to the plundering of the Companies by the exaction of forced loans by the Tudor and Stuart Monarchs. As a rich Company the Mercers were very heavily fleeced, and were obliged to sell their plate. Then the Civil War made a fresh demand upon the funds of the Company.

Another heavy charge upon the funds of the Company was the Irish Plantation Scheme propounded by James I, to which I have already alluded. The Mercers lost heavily by the

THE MERCERS' COMPANY

Royal device. Only the Monarch derived a profit.

The constant demands of the State upon the wealth of the Company impoverished it exceedingly. Then came the Great Fire which destroyed the whole, or nearly all of their very extensive London properties. As they walked along Cheapside wherein their Hall stood they saw a scene of fearful desolation, their house in ruins and their exchequer nearly exhausted and their debts amounted to £6,000, although by the benefactions of the members they were able to contribute half the cost of re-building the Royal Exchange which had been swept away by the Fire. At the beginning of the eighteenth century the Mercers found themselves practically bankrupt; they appealed for help to the State, pointing out the enormous sums that they had advanced to the Government in the troublesome times and that few of their loans had ever been repaid. Parliament granted them an annual sum of £3,000 out of the Coal dues of the City of London for a period of years. From this humiliating position the Mercers made rapid recovery. Their houses and lands in London increased enormously in value and they made excellent use of their increasing riches. When the Royal Exchange was again ~consumed by fire it was rebuilt by the Corporation of London and the Mercers' Company. As I have written elsewhere, the history of the

69

Mercers has been a chequered one, but it shows the energy, determination and perseverance characteristic of the English race; bravely did they face the troubles which threatened to overwhelm them, and all right-minded people will rejoice that they so successfully weathered the storm that pressed on them in the eighteenth century, and that they lived on to remind us of past glories of our civic life and to confer vast benefits on people of our own age and country.

THE HALL

The Mercers have never wandered far from the site of their earliest habitation. We have already stated the connection of the Gild with the Hospital of St. Thomas of Acre founded by Agnes de Helles, sister of the murdered Archbishop St. Thomas of Canterbury, and her husband, Thomas Fitz-Theobalt de Helles. It is thought that Gilbert Becket, the father of the Archbishop, citizen, mercer and portreeve of London, had his shop and home somewhere near the entrance to the present Hall. The founders gave to the Hospital all the land which belonged to Gilbert Becket and was in the parish of St. Mary of Colechurch. The story of the Hall in early days was mixed up with that of the Hospital, in which they held a small room for the transaction of their business affairs. They had also a chapel for their services, close

to the door of the church of St. Thomas, and
long before their incorporation the Mercers
were appointed by the founders patrons of the
Hospital. The Brethren of the latter used to
lend their hall to other Companies, besides
the Mercers. Henry III enlarged the premises
of the Hospital by granting to it some land
which he seized from an unfortunate Jew
named Benomye Martin which was in front of
Ironmonger Lane in the parish of St. Martin,
and two stone houses belonging to Moses
the Jew of Canterbury. The Hospital buildings
must have been a beautiful corner of old London,
consisting of courtyards, cloister courts, chapter-
house, and the church and churchyard of St.
Thomas, a large and imposing building consisting of nave, choir, and aisles. It became a
favourite place for the burial of illustrious
noblemen and citizens, and was adorned with
many beautiful monuments.

In 1511 the Company having become a
large important body found the " little room "
too strait for them ; so they began to build
a new hall and chapel. Sir John Watney discovered a Patent Roll of 1519 concerning this,
which narrates that the Mercers were building
" a right goodly chapel and also a house of
stonework adjoining to the church of St. Thomas
Acon to the enlarging and beautifying of the
said Church which house they intended, God
willing, should not only serve for them to keep

their courts and assemblies therein and at all times accustomed to have their common resort thither, to hold such counsel and recreations as of old times, for the politic order and governance of the said fellowship they had used to do, but also for the honour of the King and entertaining ambassadors and other noble personages coming into the city."[1] As the King's licence was necessary for the work to proceed, it was granted, and for three years the operations were carried on, before the chapel, which must have been a handsome and highly decorated building, was ready for consecration. Of this chapel Weaver informs us that " before the hospital towards the street was a fayre and beautiful *chappell* arched over with stone which stood before the *great old chappell* (St. Thomas's Church) and over which was the Mercers' Hall a most curious piece of work." A rough sketch of " this curious piece of work " is shown in Aggas's Plan of London which was published about 1560. The total cost of the building was £2,735 18s. 10½d. This was a large sum and there was some difficulty in raising it. Many had promised sums, but the collecting of it was not easy. A curious case arose concerning one Edmund Rede, one of those who had promised and then died, and whose widow was required to pay the money. This she refused to do and

[1] Pat. Roll. 2 Henry VIII. cf. " The Hospital of St. Thomas of Acre," by Sir John Watney, F.S.A.

SIR THOMAS GRESHAM

was summoned before Cardinal Wolsey then Lord Chancellor, for repayment. A full report of the proceedings is given in the minutes of the Court. The sum demanded was £518, and the widow was let off with £300 to be paid by instalments. Still money was wanted, but, as in all difficulties generous benefactors amongst the Mercers were always to be found, Sir John Aleyn came forward and relieved the Company from their anxieties. He also helped them again in the furnishing of the chapel, wherein the altar stood " naked " ; so they invited Walter Vandale, a carver of Antwerp, to carve a " platt " (altar piece). He demanded £50, and this, too, Sir John Aleyn paid.

In the meantime there were many changes in this group of buildings. The Dissolution of the monasteries had taken place and the King and his greedy courtiers had seized upon these magnificent buildings and appropriated the wealth. The Hospital of St. Thomas shared the fate of the other institutions and was purchased by the Company for £969 17s. 6d., together with the parsonages of St. Mary Colechurch and other property in the City. This purchase was carried through by Sir Richard Gresham, a Mercer, and a favourite of King Henry. Stow tells us that the church was again set open on the Eve of St. Michael, and is now called Mercers' Chapel wherein is kept a free grammar school as of old time had

73

been accustomed and had been commanded by Parliament. This Grammar School is one of the oldest in England and is known as Mercers' School. It was held in the chapel of the Hospital for some time, and though Henry VIII was rapacious and greedy of wealth, he had some regard for education and when he granted the Hospital to the Mercers he arranged that the school should be continued. He forgot to confer upon it any endowment, but the Mercers agreed " to find and keep a Grammar School within the City for ever." The school has had many migrations. It was first held in the chapel and then in the church of St. Mary Coleman, close to Mercers' Chapel, then on the west side of old Jewry, then to Budge Row. Subsequently it travelled to No. 20 Red Lion Court, Watling Street, and to College Hill, where it occupied an appropriate site, as it stood on the ground formerly occupied by the Almshouses erected by Richard Whittington, another great Mercers' benefactor. In recent time it has found a final home in Barnard's Inn, an ancient Chancery Inn at the north end of Chancery Lane.

The story of this interesting school has caused us to wander from Mercers' Hall and we must retrace our steps. We are informed by Wriothesley in his chronicle that Thomas Cromwell ordered the image of Thomas à Becket which stood at the high altar of the church to be taken down, and all the windows which told the story of the martyrdom were removed. Instead of the statue the figure of the Maidenhead of the Mercers was erected. The goods of the Hospital were carted off to the King's treasury when the master and brethren were expelled. Moreover, the King ordered that the murdered Archbishop Thomas should no more be called a saint, his festival to be erased from the calendar and all references to him in services and offices should be razed from all books, " to the intent that the King's subjects should be no longer blindly led to commit idolatry, as they had done in times past." The *Liber Albus* contained several references to him, and these were all struck out. The archbishop who bearded another King Henry would not be exactly a favourite of ruthless Henry VIII.

All the buildings of Mercers' Hall were destroyed in the Great Fire and need not here be particularized. Sir John Watney has gathered together from the Company's record a description of the property and of the church which consisted of a nave with aisles and a high altar and two side chapels in the choir. Six chapels are mentioned and five altars besides the high altar and numerous chantries. When Queen Mary ruled, the Roman Catholic services were restored and the Mercers were ordered to provide vestments and a mass-book, and 6d. for a "sakeringe

75

bell." An image of St. Thomas was placed over the street doorway, but this aroused some Protestant fury and it was broken in the night by " serten velyns " as Machyn in his Diary calls them. When Elizabeth reigned, the Book of Common Prayer was again used. Mercers' Chapel became the great resort of foreigners, especially Italians. Dr. Middleton went to Venice in the train of an ambassador to perfect himself in the language, and returned to act as preacher. He was succeeded by one Jeronius Farlitus, an Italian preacher, and other Italians. In James I's time a very fashionable congregation flocked here to hear the sermon of a notorious person, Marco Antonio de Dominis, Bishop of Spalato, who professed to be a convert to Anglicanism from Roman Catholicism. He was cordially welcomed by the King, who made him Canon of Windsor and gave him the rich living of Ilsley in Berkshire. He expressed warm attachment to the Church of England and exposed the errors of Rome. But he was undoubtedly a time-server and a lover of " loaves and fishes," and when increased preferment did not immediately come to him, he began to talk of returning to his allegiance to Rome, and was induced to go to Flanders to discuss the possibilities of this. There he was seized by Roman emissaries and conveyed to the Castle of St. Angelo at Rome, where he died not without suspicion of poison.

76

THE MERCERS' COMPANY

During the Civil War soldiers were quartered in the hall and church and the Company petitioned Parliament to be freed from this burden on the ground that the hall was too small and that sermons were delivered to the Lord Mayor and Aldermen and the Italian congregation in the chapel, that their school was held there, and by way of a climax that the roof was defective. The chapel and hall were lent to the House of Commons for a service of thanksgiving after the battle of Naseby. Nothing more is heard of the Hall until the Great Fire laid it low. There were great hopes that it would be spared. For a moment the fire stayed, as if unwilling to destroy so fine a building ; but it gathered force and then went on its relentless way raging along Cheapside. Pepys records in his Diary that he picked up a piece of glass of the Mercers' Chapel where so much more was so melted and buckled with the heat of the fire as to be like parchment.

After this overwhelming disaster the Company with wonted generosity began to repair the great public buildings of the City before turning their attention to their own misfortunes. The Great Cathedral of St. Paul, the Royal Exchange and their own school were first considered, and they then asked Mr. Jarman, who must have been quite as busy as Sir Christopher Wren, and whose name is connected with nearly all the rebuildings of the Companies' Halls, to prepare plans for

77

the re-edification of their Hall ; but he died
soon afterwards and his work was continued
by John Oliver. The whole cost of the rebuilding was £11,881 3s. 4d. and the Hall
then erected was the same as we see
it to-day. They used " Gresham College,"
which escaped the fire, for their meetings while
their Hall was being rebuilt. You enter it from
Ironmonger Lane, except on State occasions
when the front entrance door is thrown open for
reception of the guests.

Proceeding through the former we find ourselves in a small court which occupies the site
of the ancient cloister. This leads to the main
building and we enter upon an ambulatory
where formerly stood the nave of the Church
of St. Thomas. A series of Doric columns support
the upper floor. At the end of this where the
chancel stood is the present Chapel. In the
ambulatory is the monument of " Sir Richard
Fishborne, " Mercer and benefactor," which
alone escaped the Fire. He died 1623.

A fine staircase leads to the hall and court-
room, and there is on the left a stone staircase
protected by a wooden portcullis. The hall
is one of the noblest of London. It is richly
panelled in dark oak and has an ornamented
plaster ceiling, a cunningly carved screen, and
is a room of great architectural charm. It is
attractive when viewed in its ordinary garb,
but looks most gorgeous when the tables are

78

laid for a banquet, and the plate of the Company adorns the lofty screen at the back of the high table, and innumerable lights glitter on the richly furnished tables.

Many portraits adorn the walls of the Hall and court-room and drawing-room. Amongst them we notice an original portrait of Sir Thomas Gresham by Holbein, a fanciful portrait of " Dick Whittington " with his faithful cat ; Dean Colet, the founder of St. Paul's School ; Sir Lionel Duckett, Lord Selborne ; Thomas Papillon, master in 1698 ; Rowland Wynne, who gave £400 towards wainscoting the Hall after the Great Fire, and other worthies. Some account of their other treasures will be found in a subsequent chapter. And so we take leave of this premier Company which accomplished so much for the benefit of the country in general and of London in particular.

THE Grocers' Company is one of the wealthiest and most important and most beneficent of the City Gilds. At one time they ranked in the premier place of all the Gilds, not excepting the Mercers. They are rich also in their archives, as at the time of the Great Fire all their documents were stored in a tower which happily escaped the conflagration.   They seem to have risen from an amalgamation of other bodies, especially from the ancient Gild of Pepperers of Sopers Lane, which included the Fraternity of St. Anthony, the objects of which were social and religious, and from the Spicers of the Ward of Cheape.

Mr. William Ravenhill, who was Clerk to the Grocers' Company at the beginning of the eighteenth century, wrote a short account of the fraternity in 1689, and was anxious to prove the antiquity of the trade, tracing it back to Roman times.   He quotes from the Satires of Persius, who wrote of the merchants' journeys to the East under the rising sun, and fetching "rough pepper" (rugusum Piper) and cummin seeds for Roman wares. Far had they to travel to find the pungent spice ; traders brought it from the forests of Travancore and Malabar. No one knows who first discovered the pepper plant and its pungent qualities, but it is one of

THE GROCERS' COMPANY

the earliest spices known to mankind, and for many years formed a staple article of commerce between India and Europe. Curious it is to realize that Venice, Genoa and the commercial cities of Central Europe were indebted to it for a large portion of their wealth. Tribute has been levied in pepper. The Goths and Vandals loved it, and one of the articles demanded by the Conqueror Alaric in A.D. 408 as part of the ransom of Rome was 3,000 lbs. of pepper. In England we still speak of the peppercorn rent which consisted originally of an obligation to supply a certain amount of pepper, usually 1 lb. at stated times. The price of the spice during the Middle Ages was exorbitantly high, and this led the Portuguese to endeavour to discover a sea route to India. It was formerly taxed very highly in England, the impost in 1623 amounting to 5s. per lb., and in 1823 to 2s. 6d., and in fairly modern times, grocers announced over their doors, that they were licensed to deal in pepper together with " tobacco and snuff."

The ancient pepperer also dealt in drugs, another branch of the grocers' trade, and these can claim a Roman origin. The mediæval drug-sellers are allied by descent with the Roman *medicamentarii*. The first mention of pepperers as a fraternity occurs in the time of Henry II, when the *Gilda de Pipariorum* was required to pay sixteen marks as a fine, and doubtless they existed long before that period. They must

THE CITY COMPANIES

have been a Gild of importance, as early in the thirteenth century we find that their principal members occupied prominent positions in the City, and most of the pepper merchants seem to have been of Italian descent. Andrew de Bokerel, pepperer, Mayor of London from 1231 to 1237, was of the Bockerelli family. The family name was sometimes spelt Bochel, and Francisco Bochel in 1351 was allied with the Lombard merchants when the mercers of Old Jewry made a violent attack upon them. Another great pepperer of the latter part of the thirteenth and early part of the fourteenth century was Sir John de Gisor, who was Mayor in 1310, a member of the Gisorio family of Italian origin. He was appointed by King Edward II Constable of the Tower of London, and Stow tells of the story of his family. William Gisor was one of the Sheriffs in 1329, and Sir John had two sons, Henry and John, who had a son Thomas, and this Thomas died in 1350 leaving to his son Thomas his messuage called Gisor's Hall in the Parish of St. Mildred, in Bread Street. Stow tells us much about this house, "one great house of the time built upon arched vaults and with arched gates of stone, brought from Caen in Normandy.[1]

[1] Stow records that the name Gisor's Hall was corrupted to Gerrard's Hall, where lived, according to legend, a mighty giant, Gerrard by name, who had a great beam 40 ft. long and 15 inches in circumference as a justing staff, and a ladder of the same length, and a tooth weighing 10 oz. troy weight, and a skull which held 5 pecks of wheat, and a shin-bone six feet in length. But, adds Stow, " we can leave these fables."

THE GROCERS' COMPANY

The Gisors and the Bokerells are mentioned in conjunction with the Basings and other Lombard merchants in the Hundred Rolls and Inquisitions in the reign of Edward the Third. English people never loved foreigners, and it was not till 1283 that any encouragement was given to "Merchants Strangers" to settle in this country, on account of our national jealousy. These merchants were mainly Lombards and other Italians of Genoa, Florence, Lucca, Pisa and Venice, who supplied all the western countries of Europe with Indian and Arabian spices and drugs, as well as their own fine manufactures of silks and stuffs and the wines and fruits of Italy. These Lombards became great lenders of money both to the King and nobles and thus assisted trade. Lombard Street where the bankers had erected their great houses of business preserves their name, and the golden balls outside our pawnbrokers' shops constituted the arms of the Lombards.

Among the City records we find the statutes and ordinances of the Pepperers of the time of Edward II[1] styled " Ordinatio Piperorum de

---

[1] A remarkable event that occurred in the time of this monarch shows the power of the Mayor and the opposition of the City to the foolish Edward II. A grocer, Hammond Chickwell, occupied the mayoral chair. The King was, as history tells us, in opposition to the Queen and Prince Edward. Bishop Stapleton of Exeter rode with his retinue to the gates of the City and demanded the keys for the King; this Chickwell refused and ordered the prelate to be beheaded. He earned the gratitude of the Queen. He held the distinguished office

Sopers Lane," and are written in Norman French beginning : "Ces souent les Pointz que les bons genz de Sopers Lane del Mestier des Peveres." The first formal meeting for the formation of the Society took place at the Abbot of Bury's house in St. Mary's Axe where twenty-two of their members met together at a dinner and there committed the particulars of their formation into a trading community to writing. After enjoying their dinner they elected two persons of their Gild, Robert Osekyn and Lawrence de Haliwell as their first Governors or wardens, appointing a priest to act as chaplain to celebrate Masses for their souls. The ordinances are set forth in Norman-French mingled with Old English words and run " En le honr de Dieu et de son douche Mere et de sanct Antonin and de touz saintz, etc.," and may be translated thus: " To the honour of God and his sweet Mother, Saint Anthony and all Saints, the 9th day of May, 1345, a Fraternity was founded by the Company of Pepperers of Sopers Lane, for love and unity to maintain and keep themselves together, of which fraternity and sundry beginners, founders and donors, to preserve the said fraternity." This is signed by William de Grantham and twenty-two others.

It was agreed that no person should belong to the fraternity who was not of the craft, that is to

of Mayor six years, and was buried in a place of honour nigh the choir in old St. Paul's.

say, a Pepperer of Sopers Lane or a spicer of the Ward of Cheape[1] or other persons of their mystery wherever they resided. They called this feast a " Mangerie " or " first assembly." They agreed that each brother should pay 12 pence, that they should adopt a Livery, that the priest should begin his duty by singing and praying at the Festival of St. John, and Midsummer's day, then next ensuing for the same brotherhood and for all Christian people, and for the maintenance of the priest everyone paid 1d. per week, his wages in advance of the ensuing year amounting to 4s. 4d. each member's share. We learn " Que preste commenceroyt de chanter le III jour de Julu en l'an avant dict and recevroit cheskun semaigne 15d."[2]

The resources of the fraternity at this early date were not very large. In 1346 their money amounted to £6 16s. od. in silver and gold. However, it seemed to have progressed in the right direction. In the next year it was £14 7s. 9½d., in gold, in 1348 to £22 5s. 9d., and in 1349 to £31 19s. 7d. Afterwards it increased rapidly as the fraternity's trade extended far and wide. No one was admitted to the Gild who was not of " good condicion in the craft," and was required to pay 13s. 4d. entrance money " or the value thereof." The ordinances

---

[1] This rule was never adhered to, and forty years later conditions were specified for the admission of persons not of the craft into the brotherhood.
[2] " Some Account of the Grocers' Company," p. 46.

THE CITY COMPANIES

included the duty of keeping their trade secret, regulating apprentices, the uniting together in brotherly love and affection, and the due performances of their religious ceremonies. The blending of Religion and Life was much more thoroughly carried out than in subsequent ages. ⸲ The first use of the name " Grocer " was in 1373 and signifies that he was a trader *en gros*, that is to say wholesale, and a dealer in many articles of consumption and an endless assortment of domestic necessaries. These included spices, drugs, medicines, oils, ointments, confectionery, syrups and waters, and also pepper, ginger, cloves, maces, cinnamon, resin, rhubarb, senna, electuaries, turpentine, anise, ammonia, wax, spikenard, waters, plasters, powders. The third class of objects included green ginger, succade, cardamums, dates, almonds, canvas and alum. These were all imported from the early times from the shores of the Mediterranean, Asia Minor and from the East by the Pepperers and Spicers. In later times when the use of tobacco came into this country, not, as commonly reported, by Sir Walter Raleigh, the fragrant weed, called in the Oxford State Book, *Noxia herba Nicotiana Anglese Tobacco*, the Grocers were the purveyors. The early historian of the Company, Mr. Ravenhill, wrote, " the word grocer was a term at first distinguishing merchants of this society in opposition to the inferior trades, for that they usually sold in gross quantities by great weights, and it was on this account that they are supposed afterwards to have obtained the custody of the *King's beam*. In after times the word grocery became so extensive that it can now be hardly restrained to certain kinds of merchandise they have formerly dealt in ; for they have been the most universal merchants that traded abroad, and what they brought home, many artists of this country found out ways afterwards to change and alter the species, by mixture, confections and compositions of simple ingredients, by which means many and various ways of dealing and trading passed under the dominion of Groceries, and indeed this city and nation do in a great measure owe the improvement of navigation to merchants originally exercising their mystery, as trading into all foreign parts whence we have received certain spices, drugs, fruits, gums or other rich aromatic commodities . . . The Levants and other rich merchant companies sprang out of this."

Early in their career they were accused of a wrong committed against the public. These Grossiers were guilty of establishing a corner in their wares, a practice that is not unknown in these enlightened days of progress, especially in America. They would buy up all sorts of articles, and then suddenly raise the price, thus obtaining great profits to the disadvantage of the people.

The History of the Company has been written by Mr. Heath, and was published before Herbert wrote his valuable work on " The Twelve Great Companies." From this we gather much information with regard to the gradual progress of the Gild, recording unimportant events which need not here be chronicled. One or two items may be mentioned. The Company was careful to keep separate the affairs and business of the Company itself from the ventures and trading of its members. Thus the Governors and wardens were not allowed to adventure overseas, nor to lend any goods of the fraternity but at their own hazard. The number of members increased every year, and sisters were admitted as members. As yet they had no permanent hall, and used to meet at various great mansions in the City. Not only was a large number of members admitted to the Gild (between 1350 and 1375 they rose from 22 to 124), but their wealth rose in proportion, and civic honours were bestowed upon them. In 1383, sixteen grocers were Aldermen, and several were elected Lord Mayors. One of these, Sir Nicholas Brembre, was most ambitious. He wished to gain for his Company the control of the City, the usurpation of the rights of the citizens, and the monopoly by the Grocers of the office of Mayor. The Guildhall was " stuffed with men-at-arms over even, by ordinance and assert of Sir Nicholas Brembre for to choose him Mayor on the morrow ; and so he was." It is curious that the records of these high-handed proceedings were removed from the Company's

THE GROCERS' COMPANY

documents as the members were not proud of the forcible part they had played; but retributive justice fell upon the ambitious Brembre, who was suddenly seized by the enraged citizens and beheaded.

Among other distinguished names we find that of Nicholas Chaucer, who is said to have been a relative of the " Father of English Song," Geoffrey Chaucer. Another honoured name is that of John Churchman who obtained for the Company the joint custody with the City of "The King's Beam," and who was the original founder of the Custom House. Stow says of him that in Richard II's time " for the quiet of merchants and to prevent disputes about overweight, he built a certain house on the Key, called Wood wharf, to serve for the Troynage or weighing of wools in the port of London, and which Troynage had been before at Woolchurch Hawe. Churchman received a grant from the King that the said Troynage should be held and kept there in the same house with easements there for the same beams and weights, and a convenient place for the customers, controllers, clerks and other officers of the said troynage." Churchman transferred his rights to his Company, who thus became keepers of the King's Beam, a source of considerable profit. About this time they removed their habitation from Sopers Lane,[1]

---

[1] The name Sopers Lane or Soper Lane has disappeared from the map of London. After the Great Fire it was re-named Queen Street, a continuation of King's Street, leading to the Guildhall.

THE CITY COMPANIES

which was occupied mainly by cordwainers and curriers, to Bucklersbury and there established their Beam.

Another lucrative office was granted to the Grocers, that of the Garbeller of Spices. The Garbeller had the right of search and could enter the shops of tradesmen and examine drugs and garble them, *i.e.*, to cleanse and purify them. The following goods were said to be garbellable : nutmegs, mace, cinnamon, ginger, gauls, rice and currants, cloves, grains, wormseed, aniseed, cumminseed, dates, senna, and other things. The Grocers possess two documents which record the charges they were entitled to make on weighing and garbling goods, but the lists are too long to be quoted here. This jurisdiction extended not only over London, but to South-ampton and Sandwich and other places. Their commerce extended far and wide even as far as Greenland, as we find mention of a curious sub-stance named " Wa-loil " which is none other than " whale-oil." The extent of the trade of the Grocers knew no limit and extended from " Greenland's icy mountains to India's coral strand."

The first Charter was granted to the Company by Henry VI in 1429 incorporating " The Freemen of the Mystery of Grocers in the King's City of London," allowing them to elect annually three wardens. In the following year Henry VI confirmed the Charter, granting increased privileges, and again the same monarch, who seems to have had a special liking for the grocers, in the twenty-sixth year of his reign constituted William Westmale, Richard Hakedy and Thomas Gibbs, wardens, garbellers of spices on behalf of the fraternity, with ample jurisdiction and control, and the examination of drugs. This was confirmed by Philip and Mary, and Queen Elizabeth and James I. Charles I granted the Grocers a new Charter which confirmed all their ancient privileges. These Charters were followed by others granted by Charles II and James II, and also William and Mary who renewed all the privileges of which they had been deprived by the iniquitous *Quo Warranto* proceedings of the Second Charles and moreover increased the scope of the Company by embodying with them the trades of confectioners, druggists, tobacconists, tobacco-cutters, and sugar refiners and extended the Grocers' power of Trade Search over the whole, to the City and its liberties and suburbs within the circuit of three miles.

This power of search was often much needed. In the time of Queen Elizabeth there are records of " Some bags and remnants of some evil and naynte pepper " which were ordered to be conveyed oversea to be sold. Although they did not like to sell the stuff in England they had no objection to dispose of it to foreigners, but some dust of the evil pepper " syrnamed ginger," they ordered to be burned. We read of another

91

despicable villain though a member of the Company, who mingled starch with sugar in making " comfytes." His stock was put into a tub of water and so consumed and poured out. " Biskitts " also are mentioned, and those who made them had to enter into a bond of £20 that they would only use " clere " sugar. An apothecary was sent to prison for selling defective and corrupt apothecaries unwholesome for man's body, and had dared to dispose of some such stuff to the Prince's own apothecary. No wonder he deserved his fate.

In the time of Henry VIII a grant of arms was bestowed upon the Company which are as follows: argent a chevron, gules, between sex cloves in chief and three in base, sable ; crest and helmet and torse, a loaded camel trippant proper, bridled of the second ; supporters two griffins per fess gules and or ; motto " God Grant the Grace."

The story of the Companies illustrates the growth of the English language. In early times Norman-French or Latin was used in the writing of their records, and not until the reign of Henry V was English employed in the transcribing of documents. As in the case of other fraternities there were the two divisions, the aristocratic and the tradesmen who had their shops and stalls and sold groceries by retail. Lydgate in his poem " Thomas Lickpenny " describing the visit of this countryman to London, his many adventures, records that the spice

THE GROCERS' COMPANY

dealers of the grocery had their stalls in Cheapside.

> " One bade me come here and buy some spyce,
> Peper and sayforne they gan me bed,
> But for want of money I might not speed."

A member of the Company who became Mayor in 1466, Sir John Young, showed that he was a man of might and valour. The City was in dire confusion. The Bastard Falconbridge had attacked the City bent on loot and conquest. All the citizens were alarmed, but Sir John Young and another noted hero, Sir John Crosby, the builder of Crosby Hall, rode gallantly to the fight and drove him away, and both were knighted on the field.

Time passed speedily away and no great event happened to disturb the influx of trade and commerce, and the growth of influence, wealth and power, until the time of the Reformation, when the Grocers suffered, as did all the other fraternities, from the confiscation of their property which was deemed by the tyrant Henry VIII to be held for superstitious purposes. They submitted with patience to the exactions of the Tudor and Stuart monarchs by forced loans. An amusing correspondence took place between King James I's Lord High Steward, the Duke of Lennox, and two other great officers of the Household. It is addressed to : " Our Friends the Wardens and Assistants of the Company of Grocers. After our hearty commendations :

93

Whereas by the neglect of His Majesty's Purveyors his house is at this time altogether unfurnished with wheat for the service of his household we do therefore pray and desire you, that out of your stock His Majesty may be supplied with 30 or 40 quarters of your best and sweetest wheat, until his own provisions may be brought in, for which we do faithfully promise shall be paid into you again in November next, at the furthest, and because it is intended that, by the exchange thereof you shall lose no less, we have therefore committed the care thereof to Mr. Harvey, one of His Majesty's officers of the Green Cloth, who shall see the same duly brought into your granary by the time appointed; and so, not doubting your willing performance upon so present and needful occasion, we bid you heartily farewell. Your loving friends— Lennox, Thomas Edmond John Suckling [father of the poet], Whitehall, 27th September, 1622." Sweet words, and irresistible! Mr. Harvey, who was in attendance on the Court when the letter was read, being called in, promised " so to mediate, that 10 quarters should be taken in satisfaction of the whole demand," which were granted. Mr. Herbert adds with a laudable sense of the bare possibility of its return, "whether it was ever repaid does not appear." At the Fire of London the granaries were burnt and never afterwards restored.

The Grocers were also involved in the Irish

THE GROCERS' COMPANY

Plantation scheme of James I and continued to hold their property until the year 1872, when they were fortunate enough to find a purchaser to relieve them of their troublesome charge.

During the Civil War they were compelled to pay vast sums by the Royalists and the Parliament. Isaac Pennington, the Lord Mayor, demanded £50,000 from the Companies for the defence of the city in these dangerous times, and also all the armour stored in their halls for the arming of the auxiliary forces. So the Grocers were forced to sell their plate. A right royal welcome greeted Charles II at his coronation and they contributed £540 to the exhibition. They were very loyal, though their loyalty had been sorely tried, and for some time they observed with becoming festivity the escape of King Charles on Oak-apple day by hiding in the oak at Boscobel.

Some trouble arose in 1664, when the College of the Physicians was inaugurated by a Royal Charter, which assigned to that body several privileges formerly enjoyed by this Company in exercising trade search over drugs and other goods required by the doctors. The Grocers, druggists and all who were concerned in like occupation, resolved to petition Parliament ; but with what results I know not. The year of the Great Plague must have increased the sale of their medicines, but owing to the sadness of the times " they resolved to abandon their annual

95

election banquet." This reminds one of the terrible years of the Great War when all Companies' dinners ceased.

Much might be written concerning the pageants of the Grocers which seem to have eclipsed all others in grandeur and magnificence, but I have described these shows already, displaying their magnitude and gorgeous character, and need not depict too many, though each had its own particular characteristics, and told the story of the Company by classical symbolism and traditional legend. It is time that we should hasten to visit the Hall of the Company in Princes Street. We shall not trace antiquity in the present magnificent palace which was erected about thirty years ago.

THE HALL

In early days the fraternity was very migratory, and had no fixed dwelling-place. At first it met in the Town House of the Abbot of Bury in St. Mary Axe ; then they migrated to Rynged Hall in Budge Row, nigh to the Church of St. Anthony, and then to the Hotel of the Abbot of St. Croix, whence they removed to Bucklersbury at the Cornet's Tower. Afterwards they migrated to the Town House of Lord Fitzwalter in Old Jewry and in 1427 they built a new Hall which seems to have been very complete, as it contained a Chapel, Parlour and Chamber, Buttery, Pantry, Cellar and Kitchen, a tower in the Garden, and a set of Almshouses. The floor was covered with rushes which were a great danger of fire in the winter and noisome in summer, and so was boarded in 1631, and three dozen chairs were added, being of the best Raushe (Russia) leather.

It was often let to strangers for dinners and suppers, funerals, feasts and weddings. In it the Grand Committee of Safety met during the Commonwealth period, and Cromwell and Fairfax were entertained in great state. This Hall was destroyed in the Great Fire, which melted the plate, but the metal was recovered and sold for the relief of the distress. The Company found themselves almost ruined ; however, a wealthy member, Sir John Moore, advanced the money for the rebuilding of the Hall. It was used by the Bank of England from 1694 to 1734. A new building was erected in 1802, restored 1827, and now entirely replaced by the magnificent pile which is entered from Princes Street.

The Grocers have the honour of having had two Royal Masters, Charles II and William III ; in recognition of this it was ordered that three fat bucks from Enfield Chase should annually be given to the worshipful Company. They possess a very large amount of benefactions but little trust income. However, they have used their corporate wealth for the support of the institutions so splendidly endowed for the ad-

vancement of religion and promotion of very
numerous objects of public interest. The Grammar School and Almshouse at Oundle, North-
amptonshire, is one of their most important
benefactions, bequeathed to their care by Sir
William Laxton, Alderman of the City. They
have watched over the school and almshouses
with liberality and the greatest care and have
bestowed vast wealth upon it. It was founded
as a Free Grammar School for Oundle folk. The
Grocers have made it rank among the great
Public Schools of the country. Want of space
forbids a lengthy description of the extensive
charities of the Company. The Grocers have
the smallest trust income of any of the Gilds, and
a large corporate income which they spend with
admirable discretion for the benefit of the Nation,
the Church, and the City of London, especially
in educating the future citizens of England, promoting the study of scientific research and technical
education ; and in the densely populated districts
of the East End they have built no less than
three churches for the spiritual welfare of those
who are condemned to live in the slums and in
the dreary region of the Great City.

VII. THE DRAPERS' COMPANY

THE Worshipful Company of Drapers is a large, flourishing and hospitable institution. Well do I remember on several occasions being enabled to witness its ceremonies and being entertained by them in their noble Hall. On one such occasion I was invited by them to act as Chaplain, when they entertained nine Colonial Premiers at their feast ; and great was my disappointment when a private anxiety and sorrow prevented me from being present. It would require a long space to record their interesting history which dates back to a very early time ere they received their Charter. A Draper was not one who sold various and innumerable articles according to the modern acceptation of the term. He was a maker of woollen cloth, and here I am tempted to enlarge upon the history and interest of that industry. Time was when English folk were a nation of farmers and kept innumerable sheep whose rich fleeces were much sought after by foreign manufacturers of cloth, especially by the wealthy burghers of the Netherlands who wove them into cloth; so the fleeces returned to England in the form of clothing. There were certainly weavers in England, and one of the earliest Gilds of Weavers existed in London in the time of Henry I. Edward III considered it a wasteful business to impoverish his own subjects and to enrich the Netherlands; so he invited Flemish weavers to England and forbade the exportation of wool. Hence the foreign weavers came to England and a colony settled in Candlewick Ward. Moreover, life in the Netherlands was not always very peaceful or free from persecution and bloodshed; thousands fled and came to this country. In the town of Reading cottages were built by Queen Elizabeth for some of these refugees, attached to the wall of the Refectory of the Reading Abbey. These aliens enriched England by their art and skill. There were other trades associated with the Drapers, including the Weavers, the Tailors, the Shearmen, Fullers and Dyers.

The first mention of the Drapers' Company is as early as 1215, when Henry Fitz-Alwyn, Draper and first Mayor of the City, who lived in a fair house and nigh the Church of St. Swithin's, bequeathed to his Company his estate of St. Mary Bothaw, a small parish near Queen Hythe. The earliest Charter was granted to them in 1364. The preamble recites that it was shown to the King and Council that a great number of persons belonging to divers mysteries had not properly learned the trade of drapery according to the good and ancient custom of London but meddled therewith, and not only was the quantity of cloth offered for sale consequently uncertain but it was in the hands of interlopers and forestallers who enhanced prices. The Charter prescribed that " Hereafter no one should exercise the calling until he had served his apprenticeship to it and that the sale of cloth should be limited to persons of those mysteries save where it was purveyed to lords and others in gross and not for retail."

The Charter granted by Henry VI conferred on the traders the right to form themselves into a Company under the name of the " Master Warden, Bretheren and Sisteren of the Gild or Fraternity of the Blessed Mary the Virgin of the Mystery of the Drapers of the City of London."

The documents of the Company have happily been preserved and the Charter of 1503 sets forth the religious character of the Company, their objects being the worship of God and His Blessed Mother and all the Company of Heaven, to abate rancour and more highly to increase charity and to maintain love. In 1405 the Company met to examine the points and articles ordained of old time with regard to their government, principles and observances and they had to maintain two Priests for Divine service, to support altar lights, the giving of livery, to arrange meetings, to attend Divine service, to arrange about the election of wardens, the contributions to the annual feast, the payment of quarterage, etc. Some of the items are curious, including payments for attendance at fairs ; to minstrels for the charges for their food and entertainment ; for horse hire for some of the

Company to ride in the civic procession to meet
the Queen, and to appear on her entry into
London after the Battle of Agincourt ; and the
disbursements of table cloths and garlands for
the Lord Mayor's mess, his lordship, Sir Nicholas
Wotten, this year being a Draper. At the time of
the Reformation they bought back their estates
which had been seized on the ground of superstitious usages. They were involvéd in the
Ulster Plantation Scheme and the usual forced
loans. In times of the great rejoicing at the
restoration of the monarchy, General Monck
was entertained by them in their Hall in 1660.
Since the time of William and Mary the Drapers
have ceased to exercise any control over the
industry ; they have great estates and much
wealth but scarcely any member of the Company
is now associated with the trade. It must be
noticed that the son of a Draper is entitled to be a
member of the Company whatsoever may be his
profession or business: hence in this, as in other
Companies, the members no longer follow the
trade with which the Company is associated.

The Great Fire destroyed their Hall and
property, but the Company seemed soon to have
recovered from that great disaster and was quite
solvent, unlike many of its fellows. It is true
that in the latter part of the seventeenth century
the wool trade languished, but that does not
seem to have interfered with the prosperity of
the Drapers' Company. In order to promote

THE DRAPERS' COMPANY

the trade in wool the Act for burying in woollens was passed in 1678, much to the annoyance of many gentlefolk who preferred to attire the dead bodies of their relatives in linen. In many churches we find records of the working of the Act. There are books containing lists of persons who are certified that they were buried in woollen, and these lists are countersigned by two magistrates who were required to receive an affidavit from the parson that the Act had been strictly carried out. You will remember Pope's lines on the burial of Oldfield, the actress who was laid to rest in Westminster Abbey in a Brussels lace head-dress, a Holland shift with tucker, and double ruffles of the same lace and a pair of new kid gloves.

> " Odious ! in woollen ! 'twould a saint provoke ! "
> Were the last words that poor Narcissa spoke.
> " No, let a charming chintz and Brussels lace,
> Wrap my cold limbs and shade my lifeless face."

But the property of the Drapers' Company was not interfered with by the decline in the woollen trade. We notice at this time the rise into importance of the linen-draper, of which John Gilpin, " of credit and renown," was a well-known character.

THE HALL

The story of the Hall of the Drapers' Company is somewhat lengthy. The first abode of the Company was in St. Swithin's Lane nigh

103

the church dedicated to the same saint who is supposed to exercise some proverbial influence on the weather. This was the house of John Hend, Mayor of the City in 1405.

There the Company for about a century and a half held their feasts, transacted their business, " drank their Gild," and entertained their wives and daughters. The Drapers seem always to have been very hospitable to the ladies. We read of the Lady Mayoress entertaining the Aldermen's ladies and others at Drapers' Hall in 1479 when (in modern parlance if I may be allowed to use such an expression) " they did themselves very well." Two harts, six bucks, and a tun of wine were sent by King Edward IV to grace the board. Tapestry adorned the walls. Three hundred guests could seat themselves at the hospitable tables. As in modern city dinners some of the ladies dined alone, the matrons in the ladies' chamber while the " chekker chamber " was reserved for the " maydens."

The entertainments were unusually splendid and the company most select, including City magnates and their wives, bishops and abbots, priors, knights and squires and a goodly company, while the tables groaned beneath the weight of swans and " feasants," barons of beef and veal and mutton and brawn and mustard, capons briled, quails, pyke, venison baked and roast, jellies, pastry, sturgeon, salmon, and wafers and ipocras which were served up in five

ALMSHOUSES OF THE DRAPERS' COMPANY

THE DRAPERS' COMPANY

" messes " or courses. Strict order was preserved
in the arrangement and precedence of the guests
and members of the Company, and a careful
enumeration is given of the plate arranged on the
tables.

The Drapers were especially fond of bright
colours for their liveries, which were changed
almost at every election. In 1483 they appeared
in " violet in grayne cloth " for the gown, with
" crimson in grayne " for the hood. In 1495
half murrey and half violet ; in 1498 murrey
for the gown, and blue and crimson for the hood.
All the colours of the rainbow were introduced
at divers times. Attired in such clothing on
election day they would go to Bow Church or
St. Michael's, Cornhill, hear the Lady Mass,
and " abide till it was done," offer a silver penny
at the altar and attend again at Evensong to
hear the dirge for deceased members. On
the following day the services would be repeated.

The Warden's accounts reveal very clearly
the lives of the old Drapers. They received the
apprentices' fees called " Spoon money " ; the
charges include the cost of minstrels and drinking
when they went by water to Westminster in
accompanying the Sheriffs and on attending the
Lord Mayor's Show, and potations at Our Lady
fair at Southwark when they went to make the
trade search. Salaries of officers, pensions of
the poor, payments for obits and chantries, the

105

riding in processions on great occasions and the providing of men and money for the State in times of emergencies—all these entries reveal very clearly pictures of bygone times, the modes and manners of the men of the age, and also events in our national history. They celebrated with fitting ceremony the coronation of Sovereigns, their deaths, victories and triumphal entries into the City. Royal marriages enticed them forth in all their glory, and when riots and insurrections troubled the peace of the City and of the country, the Drapers in conjunction with the other Companies sent forth their quota of armed men to bring the rebels into subjection. They took part in fitting out a ship for the expedition of Sebastian Cabot to explore Newfoundland, which had already been discovered by that brave adventurer's sire.

Such were some of the deeds of the gallant Drapers. We left them feasting in their Hall in St. Swithin's Lane where they devised various pageants such as that of " The Goldyn Flees," which is not so bad as it sounds, as the scribe meant " fleece." The "Assumption " and a new pageant of " St. Ursula " were favourite plays.

In course of time the Drapers sought a new home and found one on the site of their present Hall in Throgmorton Street. Thomas Cromwell, the shameless tool of Henry VIII, the destroyer of monasteries, loaded with favours and honours by his unscrupulous master, the Earl of Essex,

THE DRAPERS' COMPANY

Lord Privie Seal, Vicar General, High Chamberlain of England, had fallen from his high estate and lost his Sovereign's favour. He had built for himself a fine house, large and spacious, in place of some old and small tenements near Austin Friars Church, and in extending his garden, and in removing the house wherein Stow's father dwelt, without any authority save his own will, he had roused the anger of the antiquary. Stow for this treatment of his father concludes the account of these proceedings by saying : " The sudden rising of some men causes them to forget themselves." But a just judgment fell on the perpetrator ; Cromwell's house was forfeited by his attainder, and after some negotiations was sold to the Company. The following is a description of it : " Imprimis, a fayre grete gate ; a fayre yard paved ; a fayre low gallery on the north side of the yard, and a grete wyndyng steyr with bay glass windows leading into the hall.

" It^m, over the steyr fayre leads. It^m, a fayre hall ; with ij bay windows and clere stories wth a butterye, a pantrye, and a seller for wyne, ale and bere to the same. It^m, a dark chamber, wth lattis wyndowes over said butterye and pantrye to look down into the hall. It^m, a fayre grete p^{r}lo^r (parlour) with bay glass windowes, and a fayre chimney. It^m. a butterye with a clere story belonging to the same, and a jewel house within the said butterye. It^m, a fayre kitchyn wth ij grete

107

chymnies, dressing boards, and a grete cestern of led, wth conduite water coming thereunto and ij clere stories. It^{m}, a pastry house with iij fayre ovens, moulding boards and shelves and a clere story. It^{m}, a scullery house wth a chymney and a clere story. It^{m}, ij larder houses, wth clere stories. It^{m}, a cole house. It^{m}, a wynding ster from the kytchyn into the hall and over the same fayre leads. It^{m}, on the est syde of the great gate ij low chambers the one wth a chymney and an office to weyte in, and iij clere stories, and the other with a clere story, under the pantrye. It^{m}, in the ij^{d} story and a fayre chamber for the ladies seeled and matted wth a chymney. It^{m}, in the iij story, iij lytle chambers wth bay windows, and one chymney. It^{m}, a garret over them. It^{m}, under the grete stayre a lytle dark roome. It^{m}, under the grete parlour a fayre cellar, paved for wyne and ayle. It^{m}, the grete garden and an entrye thereto."

Such was the dwelling which Thomas Cromwell reared for himself out of his share of the spoils of monasteries. Unscrupulous tools usually manage to contrive that some of the wealth wrongly obtained should cling to their fingers. In Aggas's Map of London there is a rough sketch of this building. After long negotiations the Drapers purchased this property for their Hall. It was all destroyed in the Great Fire. Some of the plate was saved, having been deposited in a sewer. The Hall was rebuilt by Jarman, the builder of

THE DRAPERS' COMPANY

Fishmongers' Hall, in 1667 ; but fire again played havoc with the edifice when it was again partially rebuilt. However, in modern times it was not considered large enough and fine enough for the great Company and the present Hall was built in 1870, replacing that which Mr. Herbert so graphically described in his book.

Drapers' Gardens are well known in the City. A large part of the old gardens is now covered with buildings, the offices of stockbrokers and other City men. They were formerly very extensive, and on the north there was open country, and fine views were obtained as far as Hampstead and Highgate. Members of the Company were greatly annoyed by the spoiling of their gardens by persons " drying of naperye clothes " which destroyed " their knotts and borders of herbs " ; so stringent rules were passed prohibiting such use. The garden still exists and it is strange to find this oasis in the heart of London, this pleasant plot of ground neatly planted and laid out, where peace and rest may be obtained amid the busy scenes in Throgmorton Street and Avenue within the purlieus of the Stock Exchange. In spite of the enormous value of land in the City, long may it continue, and also its owners, the benevolent Company who make such good use of the wealth bequeathed to them by pious benefactors !

VIII.   THE FISHMONGERS'
🐟   🐟   COMPANY

A VISIT to Billingsgate Market is always interesting. It is the greatest market for fish in the country. The adjoining wharf has been used from very early times, and perhaps before the ninth century as a landing place for fishing-boats. In spite of the story of Dr. Johnson and the fish-wife, the idea that there you will find the use of the choicest and most virulent language imaginable has long since passed into the domain of point-less slander, though " Billingsgate " is still used as a term for foul language. Into this market come every day certain officials and inspectors, who enter it in order to discover any unsound and rotten fish, and if so, to condemn it as unfit for human food. These officials are provided by the Fishmongers' Company according to the ancient rules of the fraternity to which is consigned the duty of protecting the public from purchasing bad fish.

Their Hall is nigh at hand, whither we are wending in order to discover some records of that interesting Company's history. It is a fine palatial building erected in 1831, at the same time when new London Bridge was built and replaced. The Hall was erected by Mr. Jarman, who as we have seen was responsible for the raising of the old Drapers' Hall after the Great Fire, and of several others. On entering, we see a grand staircase and in the

FISHMONGERS' COMPANY

vestibule there stands a large statue of Sir William Walworth carved out of oak by Pierce, and beneath there is the following inscription :

> " Brave Walworth, Knight, Lord Mayor, slew
> Rebellious Tyler in his alarums.
> The King therefore did give in lieu
> The dagger in the City arms.[1]
> Fourth year of Richard, 1381."

This story is generally credited, but it is inconsistent with historical truth. The weapon in the City arms is not a dagger, but a sword, which first occurs in the arms of the City in 1380, a year before Wat Tyler was slain and Sir William Walworth knighted. It is the symbol of St. Paul, the patron saint of London's City, and has nothing to do with " Brave Walworth's " deed. His dagger with which he slew the rebel is preserved in the Hall and many treasures far too numerous to be mentioned here. The pall of the Company has been preserved, which is said to have been made prior to 1381 by some nuns, and to have been used at Walworth's funeral, but it is probably not earlier than the sixteenth century. There are not many of the Companies who have retained their pall which was used at the funeral of their members. We shall meet with a few others in the course of our pilgrimage. A large number of most interesting portraits are

---

[1] For a full account of the history of the Arms of London, see " Memorials of Old Trade," Vol. i, p. 232, containing a chapter on the subject by the late F. Tavenor-Perry.

hung in the Hall, which we cannot now particularize.[1] They have a very graphic representation of an ancient pageant performed in former days of old-time splendour, which gives a good impression of one of London's old scenes of civic state, and also a noble Master's chair made out of stone and wood taken from the foundations of old London Bridge.

This fraternity was one of the earliest of the City Gilds and has had a long and interesting history. Their trade and industry extended back to very early times and British oysters are said to have first tempted the Romans to cross the Dover Straits and conquer Britain. There was vast fishing on the Norfolk coast whence herrings were brought to London and elsewhere, the fish being sold by the last, which signifies 10,000. Lampreys were sent to the King's household and John died from a surfeit of them. They are a species of eel and were brought from Gloucester. Our ancestors were very fond of eels, especially in the monasteries. They were caught in traps called *anguitonia* which were set up at convenient places on the chief rivers. Salted salmon, haddock, mackerel, and sturgeon, are mentioned in the list of pontage dues at London Bridge in the time of Edward I, and whales caught upon our coasts when salted furnished a succulent dish. In the time of the

[1] cf. "The City Companies of London and their Good Works," by P. H. Ditchfield, pp. 63 and 64.

First Edward you could have bought a dozen soles for 3d., the best turbot for 6d., mackerel at 1d. each, and oysters 2d. per gallon, and 25 eels for 2d. During Lent in the Middle Ages fish was the universal diet, and also on Fridays all the year round. When fasting became less observed in post-Reformation times it was enacted that fish should be taken as food on Fridays for the benefit of the fish trade.

The Gild was in existence before the reign of Henry II, and the Fishmongers received Charters from Edward I and also Edward II and Edward III. This last, which was written in Norman-French (it is too long to be quoted here) granted a monopoly of the trade to the Company, forbidding anyone who did not belong to the mystery to intermeddle with their industry and directing them to elect four persons to oversee the buying and selling of fish " for the common commodity of our people." The Charter of Richard II who favoured so many of these Gilds is the most important of all. Prior to his time it appears there were two separate communities, the Salt-Fishmongers, and the Stock-Fishmongers. By his Royal Charter they were united into one body corporate, and the Fishmongers were granted leave to sell their fish in Stock-Fishmongers' Row as well as in their other places of sale, viz., Bridge's Street, Old Fish Street, and the Stock Market, where the Mansion House now stands. This Charter was renewed by Henry VI, but in that of Henry VII the two Companies were again separated, only to be again united by the Charter of Henry VIII, which was granted in 1536, into one body, their Hall to be but one, in the house given to them by Sir John Cornwall, Lord Fanhope. There was good reason for this, as it appears there had been much strife, contention and debate, between the rival Companies. From henceforth it was determined that all such quarrels should cease, and their houses and estates should be held together as plate, jewels, money, charters, writings, goods and chattels, and all brought together into Fishmongers' Hall for the joint use of both fellowships.

Very minute are the ordinances for the governing of the Company and the members thereof in the conducting of their business. The apprentices were kept very strictly and the rules stated that " vicious and unruled apprentices, and using dice, cards, or any such games, or haunting, resorting to taverns, or for other misbehaving," should be punished, probably in the manner that has already been described. Their rules and regulations are somewhat lengthy and tedious and need not be recorded here. There seem, however, to have been some prodigious youthful scholars in those days, as these ordinances and regulations were copied out and embellished with elaborate and fanciful initials by a boy only 12 years old, the execution thereof doing him great credit. Thus does he write *finis* to his labours :

FISHMONGERS' COMPANY

" Here yndyth the Book of Rules and Ordinances belonging to the fellowship of fysshemongers, written by me richard felde, the sone of Maister Jho'n felde, then being Warden, and I, ye saide rycharde being of the age of xij years at the fynishing hereof."

The Charters were renewed by Queen Mary, Elizabeth, James I, and Charles II, and need not be further recorded here. It is more interesting, I venture to think, to try to discover the lives of the Fishmongers. Herbert, in his history of the Companies, took great pains in investigating the site of the hall, or rather halls, for at one time there were six, before the amalgamation of the two branches. He traces their former ownership to one John Lovekyn, stock-fishmonger and four times Mayor. Sir William Walworth was at one time owner. He was an apprentice and executor of Lovekyn, and rose to knighthood by his historic deed. There were other owners including Thomas Botiller, Sir Thomas Sackville, Lord Fanhope, until at last it came into the possession of the Company. They were always careful to discharge their religious obligations and we find that in 1499 they built the chapel of St. Peter and St. Sebastian in the parish church of St. Michael (spelt in the record St. Meghell), in Crooked Lane.

The Great Fire found plenty of combustibles in Thames Street, which it is stated was the " lodge of oil, hemp, flax, pitch, tar, cordage,

hops, wines, brandies," and other inflammable
substances; moreover all the wharfs for coal,
timber and wood, lay along the river bank.
Pudding Lane as is well-known was the place of
its origin, whence it shot forward to the church
of St. Magnus, and all along the Thames bank,
and Fishmongers' Hall was the first great
building it attacked. The picture in the Royal
Exchange affords a graphic view of the tragedy.
Strange to say, though all the buildings were
reduced to ruins, the shell of Fishmongers' Hall
escaped, but the large hall itself which stood at
the back of the building was entirely destroyed.
The Court books record the energy and speed
with which the damage was restored, and how
carefully they guarded their properties, lest
others should build upon the foundations of
destroyed dwellings. It speaks well for the
goodwill and spirit of fellowship that prevailed
in London at the time of this common disaster
that there was no encroaching on each other's
properties, not a single lawsuit between owners,
when so much confusion must have reigned.
The architect, Mr. Jarman, seems to have been
most helpful in mapping out the ground, and
rebuilding, and in 1671, five years after its
destruction, it is recorded with an air of triumph
that " the Hall was completely finished," and
was let to Alderman Dawes, Master of Customs,
" who had been drank to by the Lord Mayor
at the Bridge House, according to custom as one

of the Sherriffs for the ensuing year," for his use for the service of the Sherivalty.

The Hall, built by Mr. Jarman, though sometimes attributed to Sir Christopher Wren, appears in many prints of Old London, and this, as I have said, gave way to the present structure which was erected in 1831, just in time to be mentioned by Mr. Herbert, whose history of the twelve Great Companies was published in 1836, and who gives it a strong eulogium. He wrote, " In delightfulness of situation, elegance of design and finishing, and above all capaciousness and convenience, extending not only to its state apartments, but to its offices, kitchen and cellarage—none of the other Companies' Halls can hope to eclipse, and will be complimented by saying that they equal the new Fishmongers' Hall."

In the history of the City Companies, we often find them sharply divided according to the interest of their trade, and struggling for the mastery of London with whole-hearted ferocity, or fighting for precedence, or quarrelling for some trifling cause. It is pleasant to find that perfect amity seems to have existed between the Worshipful Company of Fishmongers and the Goldsmiths. This was shown in a peculiar manner. They yearly exchanged and wore each other's new-made livery in token of their friendship.

The old custom of electing the Wardens annually by placing a garland or cap on the heads of the newly elected was duly observed. This custom prevailed, I believe, longer than in most of these fraternities, amongst the Girdlers. The garland or cap was placed on the heads of sundry persons present, and the members shouted "No fit," but when it ornamented the heads of those who had been duly elected, the company cried "Good fit," and the Wardens were installed in their office. It is interesting to follow the engagements of the court during a whole year, which show that the members were not idle. We will take the doings of a year when George the Third was King. They met early in January for binding apprentices, and transacting various business connected with the Company and marched to St. Paul's to hear a sermon on "King Charles the Martyr." In February a court was held to admit freemen, and also divers committees. On March 22nd the anniversary of the day on which Archbishop Whitgift founded the Hospital that bears his name (so often threatened, but still happily surviving), they went to Croydon, to deliver some gifts which had been entrusted to their care by Dr. Barlow and Lady Ann Allott. The former provided for the preaching of a sermon, and a dinner to the inmates of the Hospital, to the poor-box for the distribution of legacies, and the almsfolk in St. Peter's Hospital. I will not record the engagements for every month, noting only the following: to hear a sermon at St. Paul's on " The Restoration of Charles II," to go to St. Michael's church in Crooked Lane, hear a sermon, and afterwards dine at their Hall, to attend at Guildhall to elect the Sheriffs, chamberlains, etc., to distribute £100 among the poor of the Company out of the profits of Sir Thomas Knesworth's estate. It will be remembered that this knight was a worthy patriot in the reign of Henry VII, who was imprisoned in the Tower for resisting the extortions of Empson and Dudley, the tools of that monarch in his financial exactions.

In August they had the pleasant duty of starting the Waterman's race for Doggett's coat and badge. This race was instituted by one Doggett, a comedian and a member of the Company, who left a bequest for the arrangement of the water contest which still takes place annually. To St. Paul's they wend again to hear a sermon on the " Anniversary of the Fire of London " (September 2nd). On the 29th the court and livery were summoned to the Guildhall, and then go to the church of St. Laurence Pountney, hear a sermon and then to the Guildhall to elect a Mayor, and afterwards dine. On the anniversary of the accession of the King they heard a sermon at St. Paul's, and also on November 5th (Guy Fawkes' Day). Then as now they assembled on Lord Mayor's day on November 9th, but not to ride in carriages ; they went in the Company's barge to Westminster and afterwards enjoyed the Lord Mayor's banquet.

On another day they distributed various gifts
to the poor, and coats and gowns to the almsfolk,
to each one of whom they gave a glass of wine,
teetotalism not being then a thriving cult.

There have been some noted pageants performed by the Fishmongers, one of which has
already been recorded. The modern crowd which
lines Cheapside and Ludgate Hill would be
astonished to see, as the leader of the procession,
a figure clad in armour riding a horse, with a
dagger in his hand. This represented Sir William
Walworth, while before him another rode bearing
the head of the rebel, Wat Tyler, carried on
a pole.

The Fishmongers are a benevolent society and
have charge of many important trusts. Moreover they keep pace with the times and encourage
by liberal donations all movements in any way
connected with their original trade. As I have
said, they appoint and pay the " fishmasters " in
Billingsgate Market, who protect the public
from buying unwholesome fish. They support
the Biological Laboratory at Plymouth for the
study of marine life, and carry on the National
Sea Fisheries Protection Association. They have
three notable almshouses to control and sustain,
the Jesus Hospital at Bray, which is very well
known to me, the Harrietsham almshouses
founded by Mark Querted, and St. Peter's
Hospital, Wandsworth. They are also the trustees
of a large and important school at Holt, Norfolk,

FISHMONGERS' HALL

FISHMONGERS' COMPANY

founded by Sir John Gresham, in 1554. No scheme for the benefit of mankind seems to have been forgotten by this bountiful Company. I have given a long account of their benefactions in my story of the good works of the Company which need not be repeated here. As I have said before, " Time has not dimmed their power of usefulness nor checked the flow of their generous sympathy and charity."

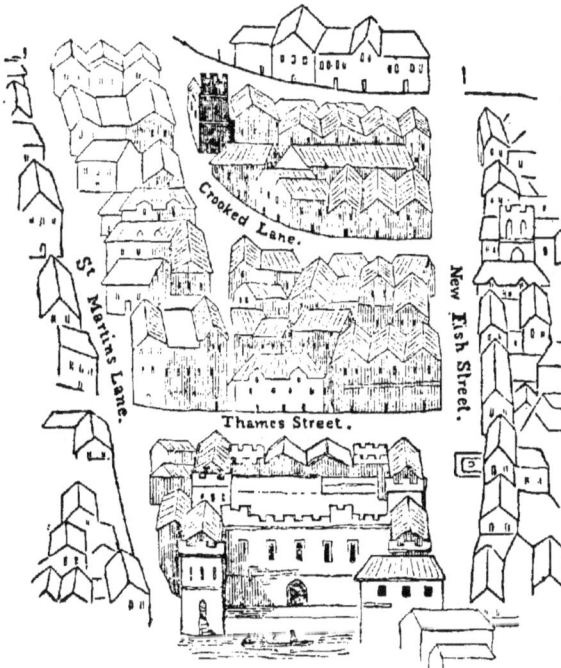

FISHMONGERS' HALL
in the sixteenth century

IX. THE GOLDSMITHS' COMPANY

"TO God only be all glory" is the pious motto of the ancient arms of the Company, which has a long history telling of a very antique and honourable trade. In the Royal County of Berkshire we have the manor of Shottesbroke, which was held in the time of William Rufus by one Alward who was Goldsmith to the King, and whose father held it under King Edward the Confessor by a singular species of Grand Sergeantry, viz., by the service of providing charcoal to make the crown and other regalia for the King's coronation. The art flourished in early times, as when St. Wilfrid had a golden case made for the church of Ripon of pure gold set with jewels for the holding of a copy of the Gospel ; and Alfred's jewel is a wonderful example of Saxon art. During Norman times the goldsmith's craft flourished. St. Dunstan, the patron saint of the Company, was a famous worker in metals, and Edward I had a ring with a sapphire of his workmanship.

No one can point to the exact date of the foundation of this fraternity, but certainly it was one of the earliest as the *Gilda Aurifrabrorum* was in existence before 1180, and in that year it was amerced for being "adulterine," i.e., it had not obtained the special licence of the King. It was incorporated by Edward III, by letters

122

THE GOLDSMITHS' COMPANY

patent in 1327, and styled " The Wardens and Commonalty of the Mystery of the Goldsmiths of the City of London." He seems to have been very partial to the Gild, as he granted to it three other confirmation Charters. In early times, as I have said, particular trades were carried on in certain fixed places in the City and the Goldsmiths have never wandered far from the locality wherein their present Hall is situated, that is to say, in the Parish of St. John Zachary and St. Vedast, Foster Lane. Goldsmiths' Row was on the east side of the latter lane; it became one of the chief sights in the City on account of its magnificent display of the gold-workers' art, and was much admired by foreign visitors to England.

The number of Charters granted to the Goldsmiths is almost bewildering, and need not be recorded here ; but special privileges were assigned to them. They had the right of search for defective work and to condemn any gold or silver ornaments, vases and other products of their art, if found to be badly wrought and apparently to confiscate the goods. They were appointed assayers, and all workers in precious metals had to bring their goods to their Hall to be assayed by the officers of the Company. An assay master was appointed to superintend the management of the assay office. The statute of Edward I originally vested the right of assay in the Company, and directed that no vessels of

gold or silver should leave the maker's hands till
they had been tested by the Wardens and stamped
with the leopard's head. Later on they had the
power granted them of fining and imprisoning
all defaulters. To the work of the Company we
owe the markings on plate which enable us to
discover the actual age of each piece in our
collection, or of the Church plate kept in safes
in the custody of each rector and his wardens.
The leopard's head is the earliest assay mark and
is maintained in the statute of 1300 as *une teste
de leopart*; and then we have the maker's mark,
first made compulsory in 1363, at first consisting
of some symbol, as an animal, fish, crown, star or
rose, and later on a single or double letter forming
the initials of the maker. There is the date letter
which has been in use since 1478 until the present
time, the various alphabets each composed of
twenty letters regularly succeeding each other.
St. Dunstan being the patron saint of the Goldsmiths, until the Restoration the annual letter
was always changed on his festival (May 19th).
All standard gold and sterling were marked with
the lion passant in 1598, which was called by the
Company " Her Majesty's Lion." Then we
have the head of the sovereign in profile, and
other varieties, the shape of the shields and much
else that is included in the lore of the subject.
In 1700 five new provincial assay offices were
started, but out of every 100 pieces of plate we
are indebted to this London Company for assaying

at least ninety-nine, and for this service the public should be most grateful.

Another great service the Goldsmiths render, and that is " the trial of the pix " by which all new coinage is tested. The " pix " is the box containing the new coinage brought by the Master of the Mint, and this is tested by an elaborate process before a jury appointed under the precept of the Lord Chancellor; and when the latter is informed that all is well the Mint Master receives a record stating that the trial is satisfactory and goes on his way rejoicing.

Returning to old times, manners and customs, we have remarked on the amity which existed between the Goldsmiths and the Fishmongers. But this friendship did not always persist between the fraternities. A great conflict arose between the former and the Merchant Taylors in the year 1226. So great was the quarrel that each party and their friends met upon a certain night to the number of 500 men completely armed, and proceeded to settle their difference in fierce conflict. Many were killed and wounded on both sides ; nor could they be parted till the Sheriffs with the City *posse comitatus* came and stopped the fray and arrested the ringleaders, thirteen of whom were executed.

The Great Plague, or Black Death, wrought havoc among the leaders of the Gild and all the Wardens are reported to be dead in 1350 and there is a tale-telling gap in the reports of the pro-

125

ceedings of the Company. The chroniclers tell us that 50,000 persons were carried off by this terrible pestilence in London and buried in the Charterhouse precincts. However, the members of the Gild seem to have recovered their position before long, and were bidden by Henry VI to welcome his Queen, Margaret of Anjou, in becoming state, as he knew how well they had acquitted themselves on former occasions, in conjunction with the Mayor, Aldermen and other crafts. Their appearance must have been very striking, as they all had " bawderykes of gold about their necks, with two hangers behind or three as they liked; with short hoods of scarlet jagged." On several other royal occasions when there were " ridings in the Cheap " they distinguished themselves no less gloriously, and when there was trouble in the City with the " Kentish men " and " the Northern men " they all turned out, not in gorgeous dress, but in " jackets of one suit and defensible armour " to defend the City.

The City watch was kept on the vigils of St. John Baptist and SS. Peter and Paul, and on these occasions the Goldsmiths' troop took their part, bearing bows and arrows " clenely harnessed and arrayed in jakkits of white with the armes of the said City." In ancient times as in modern this Gild with the rest of the Companies was very generous, and was often invited to help necessitous persons and communities. When the Black friars wanted to glaze a window in their

126

THE GOLDSMITHS' COMPANY

cloister and the nuns of St. Clair by Aldgate desired to build their nunnery, which had been burned, they appealed to the Goldsmiths for aid, and were not disappointed. Individual members were asked to subscribe according to their means, and if the required sum was not obtained by this means, the rest was given out of their corporate funds.

In his conduct to this Company King Henry VIII manifested his mad arbitrary nature and greed for pelf. He accused them for some faults in regard to the assay, ordered them to appear before him, insulted them by appointing a Haberdasher and a Grocer to be assay masters, and inflicted a fine of £3,000. The troubles of the Reformation pressed hardly upon them, and the first victim was St. Dunstan, their patron saint, whose silver-gilt image was ordered to be broken and also a cup surmounted by his figure. Moreover they had to pay an embroiderer to " amend " the Company's funeral pall, that is, to remove all figures and emblems that were deemed " superstitious," and also give up all the lands and property to which were attached " superstitious " usages, such as the payment of priests to say Mass and obits for departed brethren, the keeping of lights and lamps before images and altars. These properties they redeemed out of their own funds, but were compelled to sell some tenements to enable them to do this.

So the life of the Company went on. They

had much trouble with fraudulent workers and
tricksters who were ingenious in their deceits.
They carved tin so subtly that it could be scarcely
distinguished from fine silver, and in bracelets,
lockets and rings they set divers colours, cleverly
counterfeiting genuine jewels. These fraudulent
artificers used to work in tenements situated in
obscure turnings, by-lanes, alleys, in old London,
of which there were many, and these favoured
the designs of the nefarious craftsmen. The
precincts of monasteries which had the privilege
of sanctuary were their favourite resorts, and
many curious stories do the records tell of the
searchers after these secret workers. Representatives of the Company used to attend the great
fairs at Smithfield, and as far away as Stowbridge,
nigh Cambridge, in order to search for defective
work ; but inasmuch as they went in great
state and dignity, it was easy enough for the
culprits to hide their base wares, and escape
any penalty.

We find the Goldsmiths very busy and gorgeous
in their robes at the coronation ceremonies of the
Tudor and Stuart monarchs. During the Commonwealth period their Hall was the exchequer
of the Parliament, where the wealth which the
Roundheads gathered from the sequestration of
the estates of the Royalists was stored and given
as rewards to their adherents. Doubtless the Goldsmiths rejoiced when the last of these meetings
was held and the Cromwellian faction were

THE GOLDSMITHS' COMPANY

forced to leave, when the Londoners were throwing up their caps and welcoming their lawful King. Just after the Restoration in 1660 a great entertainment was given to General Monk and the Council of State by the Company in Goldsmiths' Hall and a " speech " was made by T. Jordan. It seems to have been part of a pageant, and is described in a broadside as " After a song in four parts at the conclusion of a Chorus, enter a Sea-Captain " who it may be assumed was the orator himself who addressed the guests.

When the Great Plague ravaged London the Gild contributed to the help of the sufferers and then in the following year their Hall perished in the Great Fire. The Wardens' Account records the efforts made to remedy the disaster. A brief account of the Hall may here be given.

THE HALL

The Goldsmiths have never wandered from their original home. There is no record to state when their first Hall was founded, but it was in existence in 1366. At the beginning of the century the site was owned by Sir Nicholas de Segrave, brother of the Bishop of London, and was bought by the Company together with the mansion, which was used as a meeting place of the Gild. Some years later, in 1407, Sir Drue Barentyn began to build a new Hall which must have been a large building containing Chamber, Hall, Armoury, Granary, Assay Office, Vaults,

129   I

Chapel, courtyard, with an entrance gate. The hall was adorned with tapestry which depicted the story of their patron saint, St. Dunstan. Stow describes a feast that is supposed to have taken place here, and rather ridicules the idae of its being able to accommodate a hundred guests and to furnish " Messes and dishes, the paled park in the centre of the Hall furnished with fruit trees, beasts of venery," and other things for which Westminster could scarcely have sufficed. But some very satisfactory feastings did certainly take place in this Hall, as on St. Dunstan's Day, A.D. 1518, when the following constituted the menu : eight dozen chickens, four and a half dozen geese, two dozen capons, six herons, and numerous quails, rabbits, pigeons and eggs. The fish course contained " conger eels, turbot, lampreys, and salmon " and the butcher provided " surloyne of beef, mutton, veal, marrowbones, lambs, ribbs of beef and a neats tongue." Our forefathers were evidently good trenchermen, and the viands were washed down with ale, red wine, claret, malmsey, and other drinks.

During the Great Fire the Hall seems only to have been partially destroyed and severely damaged, and the archives of the Company were happily saved by the forethought of Sir Charles Doe who obtained the keys of the Company's treasury and transferred all their riches and documents to a house at Edmonton, for which prudent act he was cordially thanked by the

THE GOLDSMITHS' COMPANY

Wardens. Until the Hall was restored the house in Grubb Street was leased by the Company. Mr. Jarman was again employed by this Company as by several others and undertook the repairs. The buildings were of a fine red brick and surrounded a square court which was paved, the front being ornamented with stone corners wrought in rustic, and a large arched entrance which exhibited a high pediment supported on Gothic columns and open at the top to give room for a shield of the Company's arms. The livery or common hall which was on the east side of the court was a spacious and lofty apartment, paved with black and white marble and very elegantly fitted up. The wainscoting was very handsome and the ceiling and its appendages richly stuccoed, and an enormous flower adorned the centre, the City and Goldsmiths' arms with various decorations appearing in its four corners. A richly-carved screen with Composite pillars, pilasters, etc., a balustrade with vases terminating in branches with lights, between which were displayed banners and flags used on public occasions and a buffet of considerable size with white and gold ornaments formed a part of the embellishments of this splendid room. The balustrade of the staircase was elegantly carved and the walls exhibited numerous reliefs of scrolls, flowers and instruments of music. The Court Room was another richly-wainscoted apartment and the ceiling very grand, although perhaps somewhat loaded with embellishments. The chimney-piece was statuary marble and very sumptuous.

This building was replaced in 1835 by the present palatial edifice, which is perhaps the most imposing of all the Companies' Halls.

A magnificent marble staircase leads from the ground floor. Monolith pillars support the roof, and the bust of the Founder of the Company, Edward III, faces the entrance. Two fine sculptures of the story of Libian Sybille and Cleopatra adorn the vestibule. The Hall is a splendid building and the Court Room is wainscoted with oak panelling from the old Hall. It contains a painting of St. Dunstan, and the original arms of Sir Hugh Middleton, a portrait of Mr. Wothy (1544) and also of Sir Thomas Viver, Sir Martyn Bowes, three times Lord Mayor, and a bust of Walter Prideaux, Esquire, who occupied for thirty years the honourable post of clerk to the Company, and who was succeeded by his son, Sir Walter Sherbourne Prideaux, the present clerk. This room contains also some most perfect specimens of modern art. A magnificent silver vase and shield by Bechte which were exhibited in the Exhibition of 1851. Not the least interesting of the contents of the Court Room is a small Roman altar, discovered while the foundations of the Hall were being laid. It has the honour of being mentioned in the Ingoldsby Legends in the

THE GOLDSMITHS' COMPANY

Lay of St. Dunstan, which begins with the words of the bard :

" Of course you have read that St. Dunstan was bred
  A Goldsmith that never quite gave up the trade.
  The Company richest in London 'tis said
  Acknowledge him still as a patron and head."

There is a fine collection of antique silver Elizabethan chalices. A unique collection of Apostles' spoons, the ancient Badge of the Company's Barge Master and other objects of interest. The plate of the Company is very fine and includes Queen Elizabeth's cup used by Her Majesty at her coronation. Magnificent salt cellars, a helmet cup and candelabras from the Duke of Buckingham's collection at Stowe made from designs by Flaxman. In one of the rooms there is a painting historically interesting representing several worthies who had been Lord Mayors of London drinking in secret the health of the Pretender in the year 1752. At the back of the Hall is the Assay Office.

Under the will of Sir Edmund Shaa they are bound to contribute £10 a year to a college at Stockport ; instead of only expending this small account they have made this old Grammar School a large and flourishing institution, expending on its construction in 1830 £9,000, while the annual cost of the school then amounted to £500 a year : in 1859 to £1,000, the total outlay being £39,000. They then presented the

133

school to the Corporation of Stockport and endowed it with £300 a year. In the same liberal way they have treated the school at Cromer, and a school at Dee, Cumberland. They have several almshouses, and a large number of the freemen belonging to the artisan class are objects of the bounty of the Company, in sickness, age and want of employment. The Goldsmiths have taken the foremost place in promoting technical education and have done most extraordinary work in establishing a technical and recreation institute at New Cross entailing an expenditure of not less than one hundred thousand pounds. Without mentioning other munificent schemes I may mention a great contribution to the housing of the poor when they made a grant of £25,000 for dwellings to be erected in Clerkenwell, for the poorer classes of workmen engaged in the several branches of the trade. No greater benefit could be conferred on them than this and the Company is to be congratulated upon the conception of this bountiful scheme which shows not only their generosity but the wisdom which guides their benevolence.

X. THE SKINNERS' COMPANY

THE Skinners were the fur merchants of old times, and then, as now when fashion or the delicacy of ladies has decreed an elaborate and all prevailing use of furs, they plied an enormous trade. At one time they were a badge of dignity and by a statute of Edward III the wearing of furs was confined to royalty and to bishops, earls, barons, knights and ladies and " to people of the Holy Church who might expend £100 to their benefices at the least." It is hardly necessary to refer to early times, to our prehistoric ancestors, who clad themselves in the skins of the animals they had slain, nor to Saxon shepherds' sheepskin coats or gloves made from the same material. Goats and lambs lent their skins for the wardrobes of Edward I, and in the time of the third Edward the furs of minever,[1] bison and stradling[2] are mentioned. Edward III took so much interest in the subject that he incorporated the fraternity of the skinners in 1327 and styled them the Master and Wardens, Brothers and Sisters of the Gild or Fraternity of the Skinners of London, to the honour of God and the precious body of our Lord Jesus Christ." Armed with this grant the Skinners began their

[1] Minever—the fur of the ermine mixed with that of the small weasel. The white stoat is called minefer in Norfolk.
[2] Stradling, or stranling, the skin of the squirrel between Michaelmas and winter.

135

THE CITY COMPANIES

corporate career and in subsequent years obtained several Charters from successive Sovereigns.

When trade with foreign countries extended, the skins of several other animals were introduced into commerce, and were mentioned in the Charter of Henry VII. These were the skins of ermine, of sables, marten, foyns[1], minever (pure), scaged grey, foin grey, linsey grey, fur of the liveries of the Companies including beaver skins, pople[2], fur of bethes (in English, livery furs), boggs[3], leggs, etc. Although beavers existed in England in early times, it was not till later that their skins are mentioned and presumably this was imported. Strype says : " This Company flourished in former times when sables, lucernes, and other rich furs were worn for tippets in England, which were princely ornaments," and adds " of which Henry Lane in a letter to Richard Hackluyt, the collector of the English voyages *anno* 1567, thus spake: ' That it was a great pity, but it should be renewed, especially in courts and amongst magistrates, not only for the restoring of an old worshipful art and Company, but also because they are for our climate wholesome, delicate, grave and comely, expressing dignity, comforting age and of long continuance, and better with small cost to be preferred than those of new silks, shags and rags, wherein a

[1] Foyne, foine, or foone—fur of the stone-marten or fitchet.
[2] Pople, the back of the squirrel in spring.
[3] Boggys or boay—lambskin with wool inside.

GOLDSMITHS' HALL

great part of the wealth of the land is hastily consumed.' "

Strype states that the skin of the homely rabbit, or coney, and other furs of the breed of this realm were in these times " by such as had them of their own breed, and such as gathered them—as pedlars and such like—ordinarily.bought and offered to be sold to the Skinners ; and the Skinners bought them at reasonable rates and then, out of such skins and furs, chose out and culled what was fit for wear within this realm, and caused them to be dressed, and set the poor to work ; and so had by choice and plenty wherewith to serve the nobles, gentlemen and other subjects of England. The residue of the skins so come to hand they vended to every man as fitted his trade ; and to the merchants as were fit to be sent beyond seas. But afterwards, almost the latter end of Queen Elizabeth's time, the Skinners were much disabled, it being common for the wealthy merchants, English and strangers, to send abroad into the shires and counties of the realm, and draw into them the pedlars, petty chapmen and other gatherers of skins and thereby procured skins which they sent beyond sea ; and so engrossing them into their hands, the Skinners were exceedingly hindered in their trade."

"However, we have wandered far from the beginning of the Company who after their incorporation became a powerful body, jealous of their privileges, which soon brought them into collision with the Fishmongers. In the early years of the fifteenth century, there was much strife amongst them " as to who should be accounted the greatest." There was an absurd rage for precedency as to the position each Company should occupy when there were " ridings in the Cheap " on Lord Mayor's Day, and when the Gilds set out to welcome their King on his return from the wars, or at his coronation and other State functions. In these quarrels some of the ladies seem to have been worse than the men. On one occasion two ladies named Grange and Trussel began fighting and actually carried their quarrel into the Church of St. Dunstan in the East, inciting the members of the rival Companies to fight. We know not whether these valiant dames proceeded any further than shrieking at each other, scratching faces and pulling hair ; but unfortunately their husbands joined in the fray ; swords were drawn and in the melée a Fishmonger, one Petwardin, was slain and several others wounded. The sanctity of the church having thus been violated, they were excommunicated, and the chroniclers tell of a riot which the magistrates were forced to quell, some of the offenders were seized, and then the followers and apprentices of the other side shouted " Rescue ! Rescue ! " and Thomas Hansart and John le Brewer ucceeded in liberating the prisoners, wounded the officers and ill-used the Mayor, Henry Darcie. Such turbulence could not be tolerated ; so the two men were seized, tried, condemned at the Guildhall, and executed in Cheapside *pour l'encouragement des auteurs.*

The peace of the city was often disturbed by such violent contests. Stow, whose chronicles are so invaluable to us in our endeavour to conjure up the life and scenes of Old London, tells us that in the first year of the reign of Edward III, the bakers, tavern-keepers, millers, cooks, poulterers, fishmongers, butchers, brewers, chandlers, and divers other trades and mysteries, together with the loose sort of people called malefactors, were the chief mischief-makers in the tumults, also broke open the houses of citizens, and spoiled their goods, imprisoned their persons, wounding some and killing others. No wonder the King grew alarmed at these frequent encounters, and the Mayor was ordered to take strong methods for the repression of the turbulent citizens.

A very memorable contest was waged between the Skinners and the Merchant Taylors concerning the subject of precedence, to which allusion will be made in our account of the latter Company. The dispute ran high, blows quickly followed, and at last it was decided that the matter should be settled by an appeal to " the Rule and Judgement of Robert Billesdon, Mair, and Aldremen of the said Cittie of London," who decided that each Company should have precedence in alternate years, and that they should dine together every year and thus cement this sensible and amicable arrangement. With only one exception the two Companies have thus dined together ever since the first year of the reign of Richard III and have thus pledged each other in the following toast : " The Master, Wardens, and Court of Assistants drink health, happiness and prosperity to the Master, Wardens and Court of Assistants of the Merchant Taylors' Company, Merchant Taylors Skinners, Skinners and Merchant Taylors root and branch, and may they continue for ever."

This happy conclusion is commemorated by a picture of this loving feast on one of the panels of the Royal Exchange, which set forth some of the chief events in the annals of London's City.

In the Edwardian Wars we find the Skinners contributing to their share of the cost of the expeditions. During their early history the Skinners were divided into two fraternities, one at St. Mary Spital and the other at St. Mary Bethlem, the former situated on the East side on the North End of Bishopsgate ; the latter hospital between Bishopsgate and Moorfields. The two branches were united in 1395, under the rule of Richard II. It seems to have been the privilege of the Skinners to provide one of their members as chief butler on the coronation of a Sovereign. John Pasmer, Pelliparius (Skinner) acted

140

THE SKINNERS' COMPANY

in that capacity at the coronation of Richard III,
and a beautiful rose-water dish in the possession
of the Company bears witness that John Moore,
a member of the Company, performed the like
duty when George IV was crowned. We may
presume that other Sovereigns have found their
chief butler amongst the members of the Skinners.

The part of the City wherein the Skinners
resided was in the neighbourhood of St. Mary
at Axe, and St. Andrew Undershaft, and subsequently removed to Bridge Row and Walworth.
Their market was at Leadenhall. The laws were
very strict with regard to pelterers or Skinners.[1]
"No pelterer shall make a set of furs of less than
fifty skins, that so the same be of six tiers[2] in
length, and that of one manner of workmanship,
and not intermingled, that is to say greywork[3]
by itself ; red porlayne[4] by itself, and roskyn[5] by
itself ; all squirrel skins to match ; nor shall
anyone work new skins intermingled with old.
And he who shall do otherwise and shall thereof
be attainted shall be set upon the pillory."

Such defects the officials of the Company
were called upon to detect and to punish offenders,
and they were ordered to make search for defective goods at the fairs of St. Botolph, Windsor,

[1] Liber Albus, p. 243.
[2] A tier, or timbre, was a breadth containing a certain number
of skins.
[3] According to the Liber Horn, grey work was the back
of the squirrel in winter.
[4] The fur of the dark squirrel of Poland.
[5] The fur of the squirrel in summer.

141

Winchester, St. Ives, Stamford, St. Edith, and at other fairs in the realm.

The Company, which was soon to hold a position of the highest state among the Gilds, employed numbers of poor workmen, called " Tawyers " in the dressing of coney skins and others of home growth, which were collected round the country by the poor country people who possessed them, from whom the Skinners bought them at reasonable rates. The Skinners employed the Tawyers to dress what were fit for nobles, gentry and others in England and sold undressed or exported the remainder. The *Liber Albus* records many writs and ordinances for the government of the Tawyers lest they should charge exorbitantly.

The Skinners' Company was founded on a strong religious basis, as its title shows, the Gild or Fraternity of the body of Christ, the patron saint of the female members being St. Mary the Blessed Virgin. The festival of Corpus Christi is the date of their election feast and in former days of a solemn procession. It may be well to draw a picture of the proceedings of the Skinners when they shone forth in all their mediæval glory :

" It is the morning of the festival of Corpus Christi ; and the Skinners are rapidly thronging into the Hall in their new suits or liveries, and falling into their places in the procession that is being formed. As they go forth and pass along

142

the principal streets, most imposing is the appearance they present. Scattered at intervals along the line are seen the lights of above a hundred waxen torches 'costly garnished'; and among the different bodies included in the procession are some two hundred priests and clerks, in surplices and copes, singing. After these come the Sheriff's servants, then the clerks of the counters, the Sheriffs' chaplains, the mayor's sergeants, the common council, the Mayor and Aldermen in their brilliant scarlet robes, and lastly the members of the Company, which it is the business of the day to honour, the Skinners, male and female. The Church of St. Lawrence in the Poultry is their destination, where they all advance up to the altar of Corpus Christi, and make their offerings and then stay while Mass is performed. From the church they return in the same state to the Hall to dinner. Extensive are the preparations for so numerous a Company. Besides the principal and the side tables in the hall, there are tables laid out in all the chief apartments of the building for the use of the guests and their attendants, the officers of the Company occupying one, the maidens another, the players another, and the minstrels a fourth; and soon plate is glittering on every side; the choice hangings are exciting admiration; the materials for the pageant suspended from the roof attract many an enquiring glance, the fragrance of the preserved Indian sandalwood

143

THE CITY COMPANIES

is filling the atmosphere though not altogether to the exclusion of the still more precious exhalations which come stealing up to the nose and thence downward to the heart of the anxious epicures, who you may perceive looking on with a sort of uneasy abstracted air, whilst the true business of the day, the election of the Masters and Wardens, is going on in the great parlour, whither all the assistants (the executive of the Company) have retired. The said epicures know, if you do not, how many accidents flesh is heir to in the kitchen, how easily the exact point of perfection between too much and too little done may be missed in the roasted swans or the exquisite flavour of the mortrewes degenerate into coarseness or insipidity, if the cook swerves but a hair's breadth from the true proportion of the materials. The guests now seat themselves, the ladies according to their rank, at the different tables, but in the best places at each the lady Mayoress with the Sheriff's ladies sitting of course at the principal board with the distinguished guests of the day, the noblemen and others with the reverend priors of the great conventual establishments of London, St. Mary Overies, St. Bartholomew and Christ Church. Of the dinner itself what shall we say that can adequately describe its variety, profusion and costliness, or the skill with which it has been prepared ? The boars' heads and the mighty barons of beef almost seem to require an apology for their introduction amidst the delicacies that surround them in the upper division of the table (the part above the stately salt cellar) where we see dishes of brawn, fat swans, conger and sea-hog, dishes of 'great birds with little ones together,' 'pork pounded in a mortar with eggs, raisins, dates and sugar, salt, pepper, spices, milk of almonds and red wine, the whole boiled in a bladder,' and we know not how many other dishes of similarly elaborate composition. Whilst the 'subtleties,' so 'marvellously cunning wrought,' tell in allegory the history of the Company and of the Saviour as its patron, and after the dinner while the spice breads, hippocras and comfits go round, the election ceremonies take place. The Master and Wardens enter with garlands on their heads, preceded by the minstrels playing, and the Beadle ; then the garlands are taken off and after a little show of trying whose heads among the assistants the said garlands best fit, it is found by a remarkable coincidence that the persons previously chosen are the right wearers. The oath of office is then administered, beginning in the case of the Wardens with an injunction that they shall well and truly occupy the office, that they shall "arear" no new customs nor bind the commonalty of the said craft to any new charges, nor yet discharge any duty to their hurt ; and that they shall not lay down any of their good old customs

THE CITY COMPANIES

or acts written without the assent of the said commonalty. With renewed ceremony a cup is next brought in, from which the old Masters and Wardens drink to the new Master and Wardens, who finally assume their garlands and are duly acknowledged by the fraternity.

"The play is now eagerly looked for; the tables are cleared away, the pageant is let down from the roof; the actors, nine in number, approach, and the entire audience is speedily engrossed in the history's of Noah's flood."

Such is the description of the Skinners' festival on Corpus Christi day, as given by Charles Knight in his book on the annals of London, and if not true in all its details and perhaps coloured a little by the writer's powerful imagination, still it remains without doubt a fair representation of the lively scenes that took place at a City feast in mediæval times.

. Parliaments and County Councils do not concern themselves with the regulations of costumes and the decrees of fashion, but our ancestors had to bow to the decisions of Sumptuary Laws which were passed at divers times for the suppression of luxurious habits and unwonted displays of dress. In the matter of the use of furs restraining laws were passed. Thus in the reign of Henry IV the wearing of furs of ermine, lettice, pure minevers or grey, by the wives of esquires was prohibited, unless they themselves were noble or their husbands warriors

THE SKINNERS' COMPANY

or Mayors of London. The Queen's gentle-women and attendants upon a princess or duchess are likewise prohibited from wearing the richer furs. In the first half of the fourteenth century common women were not allowed to array themselves in clothing furred with burge or wool, and women of evil life could not wear goods that were furred except with the wool of lambs or the fur of rabbits.

EARLY COURT BOOKS

The Skinners possess a very remarkable set of Court Books, which are beautifully illuminated and written on vellum. They are fine examples of the illuminator's art, the first volume relating to the mystery or craft of the Fraternity of Corpus Christi being what is now called the worshipful Company of Skinners ; the second is the Roll of the Fraternity of Our Lady. Prior to the Reformation we see each year's record of the names of Master and Wardens, headed by representations of the Chalice and Host and sacred monograms IHS and XRS, with other rich illuminations, and the words :

" These be the names of the bretheren and Sisteren of the ffraternite of Corpus Xri of the Crafte of Skynners of London, entered att the ffeast of Corpus Xri the yeare of Our Lorde God MCCCCXXXV, Maister William Martyn, Alderman, than being

Maister of the selde ffraternite and crafte; Richard
Swan, Olyur Caston, Thomas Busselcon and Roger
Swanloft, than being Wardyns."

After the Reformation the Chalice and Host
are superseded by the Royal Crown, but all
through the Puritan régime the Crown and Lion
and Prince of Wales' feathers appear boldly
illuminated, testifying to the continued loyalty
of the Company. It is interesting to note that
the highest persons in the land were enrolled
as members, including :

"The Queen Margarete Sutyme Wyff and Spowse
of kyng harry the Sexthe,"

of whom a beautifully illuminated portrait is
given, depicting her praying, holding a book
at a faldstool, on which lie her crown and
sceptre, and attended by a lady in waiting, on
her knees a book of prayers. There is a gold
background with stars.

In the time of Henry VII there seems to have
been a great increase in the trade, and the Company
was very prosperous. The skins then principally
in use were those of the badger, beaver, otter,
cat, calf, coney (black and grey), elk, fox, genet,
kid, lamb, mosker, rabbit (distinguished from
the coney, but I know not wherein they differed),
sheep and squirrel. The Continent and far-
distant lands were then laid under contribution
for the English market.

THE SKINNERS' COMPANY

The Skinners' Gild for many years looked after the trade indicated by its name, but many members were not engaged in the trade, and not resident in London. As I have already indicated, members were admitted to the privileges of the Gild by patrimony ; hence the son of a Skinner who had embraced some other calling was still enrolled as a member. As early as 1445, we find included in the list a doctor, gentleman, butcher, dyer, joiner, grocer and silkwife, and members who resided at St. Albans, Bristol, Salisbury, Aldenham and Godstone. Besides those who appeared on the livery, there were numerous artisans, tawyers who worked on the skins ; and the history of the Company shows that on several occasions these working men had several grievances against the governing body, and alleged that owing to the want of representatives their interests and rights were neglected and unrecognized. They brought their grievances before Parliament and obtained an Act (3 James I) entitled "An Act for the relief of such as follow the trade and craft of Skinners," and then gained the ear of James I, who in granting a new Charter to the Company introduced certain democratic features which were not in accord with the wishes of the oligarchical court. The Company refused to acknowledge the new Charter and lodged a petition against it ; in consequence of which it was cancelled, and the court maintained its

149

ancient constitution. In the middle of the eighteenth century this struggle was renewed. The artisans presented a petition to the court, and not obtaining satisfaction they carried the matter before the Court of King's Bench, but with no better success ; after a long trial they were again defeated.

The Skinners' trade did not flourish during the Puritan régime, as that party liked not fine clothes. Moreover, by a very arbitrary Act, Charles I obliged the Company to surrender all their possessions and securities, which were not restored to them till the Long Parliament ordered them to be relinquished. By such tyrannical acts the ill-fated monarch lost the affection and confidence of his subjects. In 1667 they obtained a new Charter from Charles II, which revealed the fact that the trade had greatly revived ; doubtless the gorgeous dresses of the gay courtiers of Charles's court, both male and female, contributed greatly to the restoration of the trade. In conjunction with other fraternities, the Skinners suffered from the arbitrary acts of the *Quo warranto* proceedings instituted by Charles II and his brother James, and their ancient Charters and privileges were not restored until William III came to the throne.

The Skinners were, like the rest of their confrères, very fond of pageants. When Sir George Waterman, a member, was Lord Mayor in 1671, they had a great and very splendid show, one of which is worth describing. It represented a wilderness consisting of various trees, bushes, brambles and thickets, inhabited by divers wild beasts and birds, of various kinds and colours. In front were two negro boys, mounted on panthers, bearing the banners of the Lord Mayor and the Company's arms. In the rear was a figure of a pyramid with four triumphal arches. In the front arch stood Orpheus playing a lyre, and on each side was a satyr. Another satyr played on a hautboy, and all the beasts and satyrs danced, curvetted and tumbled. A performing bear added to the amusements of the show.

On the arrival of William III and his Queen the City of London was *en fête*, and the Companies wearied by the tyranny of the two last Stuarts, showed great honour to the two new Sovereigns. Sir Thomas Pilkington, a Skinner, was Lord Mayor during the first year of his rule. He had had a stormy career. He belonged to the Protestant Party, and was bitterly opposed to Charles II and his Royal brother. He is said to have declared at the Court of Aldermen that Charles " had burnt the City and had now come to cut the people's throats." For this he was fined £100,000, and subsequently sent to the Tower. He was popular with the people, who welcomed him warmly when he was elected Lord Mayor. His pageant represented the wilderness, first described, and in addition to the other beasts, there were " wolves, bears, panthers, leopards, sables and beavers, together with dogs, cats, foxes, and rabbits, and which latter tost up now and then into the balcony, fell oft upon the Company's heads, and being by them tost again into the crowd, afforded great diversion."

The Companies and City kept their poets, such as Elkanah Settle, who wrote their pageants and the merits of the fraternities. One of them, Taubman by name, wrote the following address to the Skinners on the occasion of Sir John Pilkington's pageant : " There is not a Company in this famous City (though yet more ancient) has arrived to the dignity you have done ; you have the honour to have six Kings members of your Society, and this year a King and Queen for your Royal guests, in the first year of their reign, and the first year of your deliverance from arbitrary and tyrannical impositions. There is yet another honour worthy to be recorded, the deserving patriot of his country, Sir Thomas Pilkington, Lord Mayor, signalised by his suffering, you have most decidedly exalted from a prison to the pretorical (Prætorian) Chair. This will be your applause for what is done, etc."

THE HALL

The home of the Company has for centuries been situated on Dowgate Hill; wherein, says Strype, " for the convenience of it the Mayors of London sometimes keep their Mayoralty, and lately here also the new East India Company met and kept

their general courts before their incorporation
with the old Company, paying a rent of £300
yearly. It hath a large quadrangle paved with
freestone. That was after the Great Fire." Prior
to that Stow informs us that Skinners' Hall
was a fair house, sometime called Copped Hall,
in the parish of St. John upon Wallbrook, and
was held by them as early as the reign of Henry
III. By some means it was alienated from them
and was held by Ralph de Cobham, the brave
Kentish warrior who, having made Edward III
his heir, caused the King to reinstate the Skinners
in their former dwelling. Pepys noted that
General Monk was here entertained at the
Restoration of the Monarchy. As I have said,
this Hall was destroyed by the Great Fire, and
soon rebuilt. In the " New View of London "
(1708) it is described as " a noble structure on
the West side of Dowgate Hill, built with fine
bricks and richly furnished, the Hall with right
wainscot and the great parlour with odoriferous
cedar." This cedar-scented chamber still exists.

Since that time there have been many alterations. The front was erected in 1790 by the
architect Mr. Richard Jupp, and is of the Ionic
style. Six pilasters support the entablature and
pointed pediment, on the tympanum of which
are the Arms of the Company. A courtyard
separates this new part from the old, which
contains the Hall and other chambers. This
Hall was much altered in 1847 by the architect

of the Company, Mr. George Moore, and the handsome fireplace is specially noteworthy. This fine but rather small chamber was redecorated in 1891 and is very handsomely embellished with the Arms of past Masters, benefactors and distinguished members. The motto of the Company " To God only be the Glory," is painted on the wainscot. The Court Room contains portraits of departed worthies, amongst whom we notice Sir Thomas Smythe, Sir Thomas Pilkington and Sir Joseph Causton. Sir Andrew Judd, the founder of Tonbridge School, was a notable member. He was Lord Mayor in 1550, and six times Master of the Company. If space permitted I should like to tell the story of this wonderful school founded by Sir Andrew Judd during his lifetime in 1553, and by his will in 1558 entrusted to the care of the Skinners. He drew up the rules of the management of the School which he submitted to Alexander Nowall, Dean of St. Paul's, for his correction and approval. " The Dean of Paules " was of a lenient and kindly disposition, and made sundry alterations in the rules which show that he was in favour of mild discipline. Owing to the generous management of the school by the Skinners it is a large and flourishing institution, endowed with several scholarships at the Universities. Moreover, there is a large middle class school as part of the foundation, and another at Tonbridge Wells, and a girls' school at Stamford Hill. This is a notable instance of how these City Companies manage the charitable institutions committed to their care by pious benefactors.

The Company possesses some valuable and interesting plate. Among other pieces there are five silver-gilt loving cups in the form of cocks, of which the head must be removed for the purpose of drinking. These were bequeathed by Mr. Walter Cockayne in 1598, who thus was guilty of making a pun on his own name. They are used on the occasion of the election of the Master and Wardens of the Company. There is another loving cup in the shape of a pea-hen with two chicks given by the wife of John Peacock and there is a silver snuff box in the shape of a leopard, the crest of the Company.

There is much else to be recorded concerning the wonderful Skinners, but want of space forbids. I would like to describe the Company's barge which figured largely in the favourite water pageant on the Thames, and to cross the sea and visit their Irish Estate, appropriately called " The Manor of Pellipar," but I must resist the temptation. If fashion plates are to be trusted, the costumes of our ladies studied, and the length of our bills for the clothing of our women-folk carefully examined, it may be safely concluded that the trade of a Skinner is in no danger of immediate dissolution. But that does not concern the Company, the functions of which as a trade Gild, owing to the altered circumstances

of trade, have long become obsolete. Less than
half of the livery men have any connection with
the business. But although time has wrought
many changes the Company maintain their
ancient conditions and privileges, and in the able
management of their corporate and trust properties have many duties to perform, which they
discharge with wisdom, carefulness and fidelity.

XI. THE MERCHANT ✦
✦ TAYLORS' COMPANY

I T is difficult to know whether this worshipful Company is to be placed before or after the Skinners on our record as a great strife for precedence arose between the two Companies as far back as 1484, when bitter fights ensued, not without bloodshed. However, after this contention, by the action of the Lord Mayor, a peace was concluded which has lasted ever since. The wise decision of the chief magistrate being that each Company should take the first place in the procession in alternate years, and as a pledge of this mutual understanding the Companies agree to dine with each other in their respective Halls. To this allusion has already been made in a previous page, and also to the picture in the Royal Exchange representing the two Companies dining lovingly together.

The Merchant Taylors' Company, anciently known as the Taylors and Linen Armourers, was constituted by Letters Patent of Edward IV in 1466, but many of the members being great merchants, Henry VII, who was made a freeman of it in the 18th year of his reign (in 1503), re-incorporated the same by the name of "The Master and Wardens of the Merchant Taylors and the Fraternity of Saint John " in the City of London. It is a very honourable and distinguished Company. Numbering amongst its ranks are at least ten Kings, and many Princes, Bishops and Dukes, Earls, Lords and Lord Mayors. From the very early period of their history to the present day they have ever shown themselves to be an earnest and religious body, patrons of learning and helpers of the poor. We have already mentioned the various combats which took place between the Goldsmiths and the Taylors in 1267, which shews they were in existence at an early date and can therefore claim as ancient an origin as most of the other Companies. At the time of the granting of their Royal Licence by Edward I, they used to manufacture everything pertaining to armour, including surcoats, caparisons and accoutrements, royal pavilions and robes of state, tents for the soldiers, as well as ordinary garments, and wardrobe requirements, except only metal work which was done by other companies. Through the reign of Edward III they were great importers of woollen cloth from Flanders, and were responsible for the interior lining of armour ; and as both Edward I and Edward III were engaged in great wars both at home and abroad the members of the Company must have been extremely well employed, and had a lucrative trade. It appears that there was in existence in 1180 a Gild of Pilgrims which may have been the ancestor of the present Company, and it is noticeable that the master who was a pilgrim was a traveller for the whole Company and

THE MERCHANT TAYLORS

arranged its business both at home and abroad.
Not only for the men they provided lining for
armour and civilian dress, the making of gowns
for the livery companies, but also apparel for
ladies, and inasmuch as iron or steel armour was
used for the protection of horses, a linen armourer
had much work to do which required artistic
skill and constant employment. The name of
the street wherein their Hall is situated, Thread-
needle Street, was derived from the presence of
the Taylors in that part of London. They seem
to have had a habitation in Birchin Lane where a
story is told of his Satanic Majesty which gave
rise to the legend of " The devil amongst the
Taylors." The devil, the hero of the tale,
" knowing by his experience that every taylor
hath his Hell to himself under the shop board
(where he damnes new sattin) amongst them he
thought to find his best welcome, and therefore
to Birchin Lane he stalks very mannerly, Pride
going along with him and taking the upper hand.
No sooner was he entered into the ranks of the
linen armourers (whose weapons are Spanish
needles) than he was terribly and sharply set upon.
Every 'prentice boy had a pull at him, and he
feared they had all been serjeants because they
all had him by the back. Never was a poor devil
so tormented in Hell as he was amongst them ;
he thought it had been St. Thomas his day, and
that he had been called upon to be constable,
there was such bawling in his ears."

159

Edward III who renewed and extended his grandfather's grant states in this later charter that they had existed time out of mind. This was renewed by Richard II and all the customs touching the aforesaid Gild, as also Henry IV and Henry VI, Edward IV, Henry VII and the other Tudor and Stuart monarchs.

They were very strict in observing good manners amongst themselves, for in the ordinances of James I, I find "that any person of the Mystery presumptuously, obstinately, rudely and without reverence speaking unseemly words, rebuking and reviling another or otherwise misbehaving himself or any persons of this or any other Mystery, in any matter before the Master and Wardens, whether it be within the Common Hall or whether in any other place or open audience within the precincts of this City, shall be required to forfeit twenty shillings sterling if able to bear the penalty which should not in any case exceed five pounds. No apprentices of the Mystery were allowed to carry any weapons "invasive or defensive" in this City without reasonable cause being assigned. A fine was inflicted on any man who enticed away another man's apprentice.

The Company enjoyed the right of search and measuring cloth which was considered an important privilege. The Merchant Taylors possessed the silver yard upon which the Company's arms are engraven, and armed with this their

THE MERCHANT TAYLORS

officials attended Bartholomew and other fairs
to see that the cloth was measured rightly. On
one occasion a woman was committed to prison
for an unlawful yard found in her possession during the search. When the Company entertained
James I what was called a delightful song of the
four famous feasts of England was sung, showing
how seven Kings have been free of the Company
and how lastly it was graced with the patronage
of the " Renowned Henry of Great Britain."
This song is somewhat lengthy, and I will
content myself with quoting a portion thereof :

(To the tune of Treason's Joy.)

England is a Kingdom
Of all the world admired.
More stately in pleasures,
Can nowhere be desired ;
The court is full of bravery,
The City stor'd with wealth,
The law preserveth unity,
The country keeps it health.

The Merchant Taylors Company,
The fellowship of fame,
To London' lasting dignity,
Lives, Honoured with the same,
A gift King Henry VII gave,
Kept once in three years still ;
Where gold and gowns be to poor men
Given by King Henry will . . .

Then let all London Companies
So Highly in the renown,
Give Merchant Taylors name and fame

161   L

To wear the laurel crown.
For seven of England's royal Kings
Thereof have all been free,
And with their lives and favours graced
This worthy Company.

The Merchant Taylors must have been very
gorgeous in appearance when they attended
their feasts and festivals with gowns made of a
scarlet and red, a crimson and blue, and sometimes
a scarlet and crimson and other striking colours.
The life of the Company is reflected in its
documents which have been admirably presented
in Mr. C. M. Clodes' memorials of the same.
The fraternity is fortunate in possessing a great
store of ancient books which reveal its triumphs,
trials, vicissitudes. They tell us of the trade
rivalry which existed between their old opponents
the Drapers who were engaged in a somewhat
similar line of business. They opposed the election
of Robert Clopton as Mayor of the City, main-
taining the right of one of their own members
Ralph Hollands in 1442. So vehement was
the contest that some of the leaders were sent to
Newgate prison. Clopton revenged himself by
questioning the legality of their Charter ; but
this matter was happily settled by King Edward
IV who allowed himself to be enrolled as a
member of the Gild and granted them a new
Charter, containing all their ancient privileges.
The religious character of the Company is
shown by their possession of a chapel in St.

162

THE MERCHANT TAYLORS

Paul's Cathedral which they maintained and frequented at certain times of the season, and when this was too small to accommodate the Company they erected a Chapel in their own Hall, and a Bull was obtained from the Pope, authorizing them to hold their services there.

They added to their dignity by receiving a grant of Arms from Sir Thomas Holme, Clarencieux King of Arms in 1480, which consist (after some subsequent alterations) of argent, a tent royal, between two parliament robes, gules, lined ermine, on a chief azure, a lion of England ; crest, a holy lamb, in glory proper. Supporters, two camels, or, motto, *Concordia parva res crescunt.* The original crest was "A pavilion purple garnished with gold, being within the same ' Our Blessed Mary ' the Virgin in a vesture of gold sitting upon a cushion azure, Christ her son standing naked before her, holding between his hands a vesture called *tunica inconsutilis* (seamless). His mother working upon that, one end of that same vesture broidering wreath gold and azure, the mantle purple, furred with ermine." A curious mistake of the scribe is noted when he records that two loving brethren were sent to talk with the " King of Harolds " (Heralds) concerning the crest of the Company's arms.

The usual events which followed the Reformation as we have seen in other Companies, occurred with the Merchant Taylors who had

163

to compound for their properties held for
" superstition " purposes, the saying of obits in
their chapel in St. Paul's and elsewhere.

The frequency of the plague in London is
recorded in several entries, which inform us
that owing to the departure into the country of
their members " for avoiding the infection and
sickness of the plague that so sore continueth
amongst us," meetings could not be held. One
entry concludes with the pious prayer " May God
for his Christ's sake cure it and withdraw his
heavy wrath from us." This was in 1563. A
few years later Nicholas Fullchamber, clerk of
the Company, was carried off by the same
infection. At this time the Merchant Taylors
had amongst their members several bountiful
benefactors, chief amongst whom was Sir Thomas
White who founded the famous Merchant
Taylors' School and St. John's College, Oxford.
In the former he was greatly assisted by Richard
Hilles. The School was first established in the
mansion of Sir John de Pulteney in Suffolk Lane,
in the Parish of St. Laurence Pountney ; the
buildings were much damaged by the Great Fire,
rebuilt by the Company, and when Charterhouse
School removed to Godalming, the Merchant
Taylors' School found a home in the abandoned
buildings. Hilles also erected some almshouses
on Tower Hill for the poor of the Company in
addition to the set at the Hall.

In the days of " Merrie England " which

THE MERCHANT TAYLORS

some locate in the reign of Queen Elizabeth, the Merchant Taylors took part in the festivities of the time. There were " Mayings " at Greenwich and the Company sent 188 men " in military costume, 94 provided with corselets and pikes, 36 with corselets with halberds, and 58 with kalivers and morryens for a shew." It was usual that only " handsome men " should present themselves. The Company were often required to furnish men for less peaceful occasions, when war threatened for the defence of the realm when the Invincible Armada dared to attack England's sea-girt isle, and together with the Vintners they were required to watch each of the gates of the City every tenth day; foreigners usually received no kindly welcome to the city. The term foreigner was generally applied to anyone who set up his trade in London and was not a freeman of the Gild to which his particular trade was attached ; he received no mercy from his co-traders. But during the French wars of religion in the time of Elizabeth, when Catholics and Protestants were contending with each other in dire conflict, and the Bartholomew massacre was an incident in the terrible persecution, many French refugees fled to England for refuge, and the Queen thought it necessary to issue an order " to use the French strangers well and quietly. So the Merchant Taylors were directed to appoint " two discreet of their members " to attend daily at Aldgate in order to see that Her Majesty's

165

order was duly executed. Moreover, the Company were to be assembled in their Hall and warned to demean themselves courteously to the strangers, and to direct their apprentices and servants to behave well to them, "doing nothing towards them in deed, word, or countenance, or other occasion of unkindness." Offenders were to be sent to prison. These injunctions were coupled with the threat " Fayle youe not as youe will answer for the contrary and at your peril."

Besides raising much money by forced loans from the Company, the Queen devised another means for extracting pelf, and that was to establish a lottery, the first taking place in 1567. It was not very satisfactorily conducted as the payment of prizes was a little uncertain. However, another attempt was made in 1585, and our Company was recommended to "try their fortunes in ye said lottery." The prizes were to be armour. Gifts of plate were promised to the Lord Mayor and Sheriffs for helping forward the scheme. But our Merchant Taylors were not very keen in making the "Adventure" and scornfully wrote in their book the motto :

> " One byrde in the hand is worth two in the wood,
> If we get the great lot it will do us no good."

The Company deserve credit in their encouragement of historical research. John Stow, the indefatigable collector of all details of the history of London, to whom every writer on the City

is extraordinarily indebted, was a member **of**
the fraternity, to which he presented his "annals."
This historian received little gratitude for his
arduous labours, and his monument in the
Church of St. Andrew Undershaft was raised
by his widow; so little appreciation of his service
was shewn by the men of his generation. It is
refreshing to know that the Merchant Taylors
gave him an annuity of £4 which was subsequently
raised to £10, a modest enough sum, but of
course much more valuable in those days than
in these. John Speed was also a member and
gave to the Company his famous maps.

A notable event in their history is the entertainment given by the Merchant Taylors to
James I on his arrival from Scotland. The royal
procession took place on March 15th, 1603, and
is recorded by Decker, Harrison and Ben
Jonson and is almost too magnificent to be described. There were six triumphal arches named
the Device called Londinum; the Italians
Pegnme, the Pegnme of the Dutchman, the new
Arabic Felix, the Garden of Felix, the New
World, and the Temple of Janus. The members
of this Company and of the others lined the
streets on June 7th, the King, accompanied by
the King of Denmark, dined in splendour in
Merchant Taylors' Hall, the feast costing them
no less than £1,000.

About the King's scheme for the Ulster
Plantation enough has been said already in the

THE CITY COMPANIES

records of previous companies, but the Merchant Taylors were induced to subscribe to another scheme, the colonization of Virginia. All kinds of attractions were held out to would-be adventurers and emigrants. They were promised "meat, drink and clothing, with a house and garden for the maintenance of a family and a portion of land likewise for their posterity of 100 acres each." The Company responded to the invitation to the sum of £200, and individuals also contributed £587 13s. 4d. on their own risk. The old animosity between this and the Drapers' Gild burst forth afresh even in the spacious days of the first James, when the latter tried to deprive the former of their rights of search at Bartholomew Fair. It was an old dispute long ago settled by a lawsuit, and the clerk of the Merchant Taylors had no difficulty in pointing out the error of the Drapers' way in trying to deprive them of a right when they had enjoyed it for more than a century and a half.

The trade of England had made rapid progress during the time of Queen Elizabeth and James I, who had established and granted Charters to the Merchants of Elbing, the Muscovite Company, the Levant or Turkey Company, the Virginia Company, the African Company, the Merchants of East India, the Merchants of Spain. Far and wide the ships of England sped and brought trade and prosperity to English merchants and increased influence to our home-

MERCHANT TAYLORS' HALL

land. A proof is seen of this in the little fact that the Company was requested to allow a door to be opened into their garden from the adjoining house. This house was occupied by no less a person than the Persian Ambassador, and one of the City Aldermen asked the Company to permit this Eastern magnate to walk in their garden for his recreation, and that for his convenience a door from his house might be constructed. Of course the Company was delighted to oblige the exalted person and moreover invited him to one of their feasts, which doubtless he thoroughly enjoyed.

But the troubles of the Civil War were at hand. King Charles extracted £5,000 from their funds for the Northern Army. The Mayor demanded 40 barrels of gunpowder, matches and bullets. This took place in 1640. The idea of a great Civil War seemed far away when in the following year the King was met in great state on his return from Scotland, and this Company was requested to provide " 34 persons of the most grave, tall and comely appearance, well harnessed and apparelled in their best array and furniture of velvet and plush or satin and chaines of gold, each to have a footman with two staff torches to wait and attend on him in readiness, and substantially horsed and apparelled and appointed as aforesaid, to meet the Lord Mayor and Aldermen in Cornhill by one o'clock on the Thursday following, to escort His Majesty

from St. Leonard's Shoreditch Church to
Guildhall, and thence in the afternoon to his
palace." It all seemed very loyal and magnificent
and peaceful, but behind the ranks of the gay
Companies there were scowling faces as the
King rode by, and black-robed Puritans were
muttering together and biding their time. The
Royal Standard was raised at Nottingham, and
we need not follow the course of the War. The
Company was fleeced again by Parliament. The
Puritan factions prevailed upon their brethren to
deface the " superstitious pictures in the Hall";
later on the fine chamber suffered greatly by the
quartering of soldiers therein, until General
Fairfax as a special favour relieved the Company
from that grievous and destructive burden.

They were then required to erect in their Hall
the arms of the Commonwealth, to take down and
destroy the Royal Arms and also the portraits
of the King. Doubtless with sad hearts these
injunctions were carried out by many secret
loyalists of the Company, though at that time
most Londoners were on the side of the Parliament.

At this time the Merchant Taylors were very
hard pressed. They had lent a very large sum of
money on account of the shameless forced loans
extracted by several sovereigns. Parliament
had not been behindhand in requiring much
wealth for the war. So they were compelled to
sell some of their landed property and rentals,

THE MERCHANT TAYLORS

but they again showed themselves liberal in the
support of literature, and gave to their member,
Ogilvey the poet, £13 6s. 8d., who had, at much
study and expense, translated Virgil into English
metre, and likewise Æsop's Fables, and had
presented copies to the Company's library.
The Company stood with its fellows in the
miserable *quo warranto* proceedings of Charles
II which need not be again mentioned.

THE HALL

Merchant Taylors' Hall is one of the most
interesting in the City of London, not only
because it possesses the finest banqueting room,
but for the reason that it is practically the same
building which existed in mediæval times. The
Great Fire destroyed the roof, but the walls were
fortunately spared, and a few years ago the
learned Clerk of the Company told me that on
removing some outbuildings they found some
Gothic recesses or windows blocked up, which
testify to its antiquity. It is not the first Hall
owned by the Company. Pennant informs us
that the old Hall was situated about the back-
side of the Red Lion Inn in Basing Lane in the
ward of Cordwainer Street. Then in 1331, they
migrated to the present site, having received a
grant of the land and house of a worshipful
gentleman named Edmund Crepin made to
John of Yakley, the King's pavilion maker.
They also owned some shops and the advowson

171

THE CITY COMPANIES

of the Church of St. Martin Outwich, granted to
the Company by the family of Oteswich. whereupon they began to build a new Hall together
with seven almshouses for their poorer brethren.
William Goodman in 1599 drew a plan of these
buildings and of the church, which is preserved
in the vestry of the Church of St. Martin Outwich.
I have not seen this plan, but Herbert in his
book describes the Hall as " a high building
consisting of a ground floor and two upper
storeys. It had a central pointed arched gate
of entrance, and was enlightened in front by nine
large windows, exclusive of three smaller attic
windows, and on the east side by seven. The
roof is lofty and pointed, and is surmounted by a
louvre or lantern with a vane. The almshouses
form a small range of cottage-like buildings,
and are situate between the Hall and a second
large building which adjoins the church, and
bear some resemblance to an additional hall
or chapel." This was probably the chapel which
the Company prayed the Pope to grant to them
when they found their chapel in St. Paul's too
small for their increasing numbers. He records,
too, the trouble which the strewers of rushes
got into for using " divers indecent words, not
fit to be repeated," and unseemly behaviour to
the Master. Not long before the Great Fire, the
Hall was wainscoted. A new roof was erected
in 1584, and coats of arms painted on the glass
of the windows.

THE MERCHANT TAYLORS

Costly tapestry adorned the Hall depicting the history of John the Baptist, and there was a screen supporting a silver image of the Saint. Armorial bearings were depicted in the windows ; the floor was strewn with rushes, but later on as these were a danger from fire and somewhat noisome at times, tiles were laid down. Silk flags and streamers hung from the roof. The Merchant Taylors dined at trestle-tables covered with fine linen and glittering with plate.

Outside the Hall was a shady garden, alleys and terrace. It was found in 1557 that the south alley was noisome on account of the rain, so it was paved with Purbeck stone. The members were careful of their privileges and directed their tenant of the old Hall not to look out upon their garden, in which was a bowling green, and also a banqueting house over which the Company deemed it most convenient to store their powder. There were many chambers in the building and a treasury in the garden for storing their plate, securities and other valuables. The Bachelor's room, the long gallery, rich with the portraits of benefactors, the parlour hung with tapestry and old paintings given by Mr. Vernon in 1616, a portrait of Sir Thomas White, the founder of St. John's College, Oxford, a picture of Gerard Dow deemed so valuable that a silk curtain hung before it, and some old maps, probably those presented by Speed. Moreover, there was the King's Chamber, richly furnished for the reception of sovereigns who honoured this Company more than any other, the Drapery Place, where they stored their table cloths which were of damask ; and the armoury which contained a good supply of coverlets, muskets, pikes, long bows, halberts, flasks, touch-boxes, swords and daggers, and other things which completed a military equipment. In addition we find a Council Room and adjoining chamber wherein were placed the three hearse-cloths used at the funeral of the brethren, and various banners, the silver yard-measure used by the searchers when they examined the measures of the traders in Bartholomew Fair, and the Silver Mace.

Heavy were the hearts of the poor Merchant Taylors when they saw the flames leaping up and destroying their magnificent home ; but with courage characteristic of their race they faced their difficulties and began to make arrangements for its re-building and for the restoration of their other properties in the City. The fierce fire melted their old plate, and we can imagine the members searching among the ruins collecting the silver, of which they saved about 200 lbs., and this they sold in order to start a sum for the raising of their Hall. Happily, as I have said, the walls of the mediæval hall were strong and some parts of them were left standing, and ere three years had passed the members were able to dine in their newly-raised dwelling, though much remained to be done in erecting the

THE MERCHANT TAYLORS

various chambers, council room, etc. The Company was much impoverished by their heavy losses, and used to let their Hall for various purposes. It was rented by the East India Company for some years ; and the South Sea Company, of infamous memory, met here. To a Freemason it is endeared by the fact that Grand Lodge often held their functions here before they erected their palatial Hall in Great Queen Street. The Festival dinner of the Sons of the Clergy Corporation has always been held in this Hall since 1676-7, and on the last occasion the writer was present. The Archbishop of Canterbury, H.R.H. The Duke of Connaught and Stratherne, and other leaders in Church and State, supported the institution by their presence and speeches.

The Hall is a very noble chamber, large and spacious. It tells the story of the past life of the Company, with the names and coats-of-arms of the Masters emblazoned on the wainscoted walls, its grand screen of the Corinthian order with minstrel gallery at the west end, and on the east is a large buffet and screens which look very magnificent when on festal occasions the Company's plate is exhibited upon it. The windows have stained glass showing the arms of benefactors displayed upon them, beginning with Thomas Sibsay in 1404-5, John Churchman (1405), Peter Mason (1412), and following down to a later date. These same walls have witnessed

175

THE CITY COMPANIES

many gatherings : the administration of justice, the consideration of the affairs of the Gild, and that the time of the suitor should not be wasted or " should not pass unprofitable " the Master and Workers decreed on October 30th, 1578, that " the Bible in the new form (which was Parker's or the Bishop's Bible) then lately printed by Christopher Barker, should be bought and set up in their common Hall." This Bible is still in the possession of the Company, and is preserved in the Library.

Much space would be needed wherein to describe all the treasures of the Merchant Taylors, and some of these will be recorded in a subsequent chapter. They are very rich in portraits, royal and otherwise. We must notice here that of a prominent benefactor, Sir Thomas White, the founder of St. John's College, Oxford, which is closely allied with the famous Merchant Taylors' School which was founded, supported and upheld by the Company. It has no endowment, and when Charterhouse School migrated to the country they purchased the deserted buildings, spending no less than £90,000 upon them. It occupies a very prominent position among the great public schools of England. A very worthy member was Sir A. Renardson, Master in 1640 and Lord Mayor in 1648, who refused to proclaim in Cheapside the order of the Commons " for abolishing the King's office," and when summoned before the Bar of the House, pleaded his oath of allegiance. As a result of his loyalty he was degraded, fined, and imprisoned in the Tower ; but like a brave man he stuck to his oath.

A curious part of the Hall is the crypt through which I wandered on one occasion by the courtesy of the Clerk of the Company, Mr. Nash, who had so long and so ably presided over its affairs, to inspect the plate. We passed through this crypt, which is 12 feet below the surface of the outside street. It is vaulted and has heavy arched ribs of simple style, without bosses, springing from corbels with grotesque heads. What its object was can only be conjectured. Possibly it was a passage from the street, when its level was much lower than at present, to the chapel that was built in the garden in 1455 with the approval of Pope Calixtus ; but Mr. Philip Norman, F.S.A., is of opinion that it dates from the earlier part of the fourteenth century, and perhaps formed part of Crepin's house, occupied by Sir Oliver Ingham. The crypt now leads to the strong room where the plate is stored, and to the kitchen which is an interesting and lofty apartment of mediæval date, wherein I presume are prepared the materials for the splendid feasts for which the Merchant Taylors are celebrated. It was with much regret that I heard of the death of Mr. Nash which has recently occurred.

Many illustrious persons have been freemen of the Company. Amongst these is Sir John

Hawkwood, a mighty warrior and free-lance,
born in the reign of Edward III, the son of a
tanner. He had great military genius and splendid
courage, and became captain of a band of mer-
cenary adventurers, called *condottieri*, who fought
for hire, and let themselves out to fight for any
side which paid them well. He distinguished
himself as a soldier in France and Italy, especially
at Pisa and Milan, and Galeazo, Duke of Milan,
gave him his natural daughter, Domitia, in
marriage. He died at Florence, full of years
and military fame, in 1394, and had the character
of being the best soldier of his age. Some myths
have been woven around his memory, but there
seems to be little doubt about the genuineness
of the main facts of his history. Another famous
freeman was Sir William Fitz-William, Sheriff
and Alderman in 1506, who began his prosperous career by being a servant to Cardinal
Wolsey. When the latter retired in disgrace he
was faithful to his former master and received
him at his house. Henry VIII was angry and
sent for him, but his quiet reply to the charge
of having entertained so great an enemy to the
State, " that his only reason was that Wolsey
had been his master, and partly the means of
his greatest fortune," pleased the King, who said
that he had too few of such faithful servants.
So he knighted him, and made him a Privy
Councillor, and Fitz-William became treasurer
of the King's Household, Lord High Admiral

THE MERCHANT TAYLORS

and Earl of Southampton, while other honours were heaped upon him. His best standing cup was bequeathed to his brethren "in friendly remembrance of him for ever." He became the ancestor of the noble house of the Earls Fitz-William. Another notable Freeman was Sir William Craven, who came to London from Yorkshire, a poor man's son, became an apprentice and by his diligence and frugality rose to the Mayoralty in 1611. His son, Sir William, became a famous soldier, and devoted servant of the unfortunate Queen of Bohemia, daughter of James I, whom it is believed that he married. This is one of the greatest romances in history. He was created an earl by Charles II, and became the founder of the present noble family. The Merchant Taylors rank amongst their freemen more royal and noble personages than any other Company. All the sovereigns from Edward III to Henry VII, except, of course, the youthful Edward V, and subsequently Charles I and James II, some foreign potentates, and princes, earls, bishops and barons galore. Amongst the long list of benefactors is the name of Robert Dowe, who left a bequest to the Clerk of St. Sepulchre's, Newgate Street, for the tolling of the bell on the morning of an execution at Newgate Prison, so that people may be led to pray for the soul of the criminal who was about to die at the hands of the hangman.

It were vain to attempt to enumerate all the

THE CITY COMPANIES

worthies of the Company, the long list of Lord Mayors belonging to it, the remarkable number of benefactors who have bequeathed gifts for the support of numerous worthy objects, the promotion of education, the teaching of science, the relief of the poor, the building of churches, and countless other worthy schemes which the Company promotes ; but enough has been written to prove the greatness and importance of this munificent fraternity, and to cause every one to wish it as long a life and prosperity in the future, as it has enjoyed in the past.

XII. THE HABERDASHERS'
🙠   🙠   COMPANY

WHAT is a Haberdasher? This word has caused our antiquaries much trouble. Lexicographers inform us that he is a seller of small wares, such as ribbons and tapes, and that his name is connected with the Icelandic *hapartash*, meaning " things of little value "[1]; but on the principle that " every little makes a mickle," the haberdasher oft became a wealthy and important person, occupying a distinguished position in London's fair city, while his Company grew wealthy and honourable, and worthy to rank high among the twelve Great Gilds. Perhaps in his youth he sang with Autolycus :

> " Lawn, as white as driven snow ;
> Cyprus, black as e'er was crow ;
> Gloves, as sweet as damask roses
> Masks for faces, and for noses."

or

> " Will you buy any tape
> Or lace for your cape,
>
>   .   .   .   .   .
> "Any silk any thread,
> Any toys for your head ? "

And then being more advanced in age and worthiness he set up his shop in " the Cheap " and did good business.

[1] This is a little doubtful. There is a word *habertas* which occurs in the list of charges on goods imported from Spain, and may be the origin of " haberdashers."

181

THE CITY COMPANIES

As we walked along Cheapside you will remember that we admired the shops of the mercers and close behind them we found the stalls of the Haberdashers, who offered to sell us laces of red leather, bright-coloured ribands, caps of divers hues, and other small articles of dress which the Mercers' stalls no longer provided or sold. Lydgate in his ballad of Thomas Lickpenny places the Mercers' and the Haberdashers' shops as close together. The titles and ancestry of this fraternity are rather difficult to trace. They have borne several names. Sometimes they are styled Hatters, or Hurriers ; or Cappers and Hurriers, or Hatter Merchants, until the time of Henry VIII when the Court of Aldermen ordered the Chamberlain to deliver and pay " to the wardeyne of the Haberdashers xl marc^s st'ling towards the costs and charg^s susteyned and made to the King's Grace, and his Councell for their newe corporation by the whiche corporation their name ye changed from the name of Merchant haberdashers unto ye name of Haberdasshers." It appears from the *Liber Albus* that a hure was a shaggy rough cap, and certain judgments were pronounced upon the inferior or defective work of such articles. In the above-mentioned book there is a list of " judgements of pillory for lies, slanders, falsehoods and deceits, as also, other judgements, imprisonments, forfeitures, fines and burnings of divers things," and amongst them there are

182

HABERDASHERS' COMPANY

judgments upon, and burnings of, false caps and hures, and false hats with the infliction of fines. This same precious White Book records the ordinances of divers mysteries and handicrafts, and amongst them appear the ordinances of Cappers, Hurriers and Hatters, recorded in a folio volume.

In early times there were two distinct branches of the trade, and each branch had at first its own Gild, one dedicated to St. Catherine, and the other to St. Nicholas. These were certainly in existence as early as 1371 A.D. when their by-laws were drawn up. One branch of the trade was carried on by the Haberdashers of Hats, and these were divided into two crafts (according to the usual laws of the subdivision of labour as they existed in mediæval times), the Hurriers, or Hures, or Cappers, and the Hatter Merchants who, as I have said, until Tudor times maintained their separate individuality. The other branch of the trade was composed of the haberdashers of small wares, styled also Millianers or Milliners, because they chiefly imported their goods from Milan, in Italy. In these modern days, my Lady who often frequents her milliner's shop, is in entire ignorance that the name of the trade she is patronizing has anything to connect itself with the Italian city. Our ancient Milliners imported such things as ouches, broches, agglets, spurs, capes, glasses, etc.

The Company was incorporated by Letters

183

THE CITY COMPANIES

Patent of the 26th of Henry VI, 1447. This was confirmed by Henry VII and Henry VIII, Philip and Mary, and by Queen Elizabeth, who invested the Company with the usual powers and privileges. Arms were granted to them by Robert Cook, Clarencieux, King of Arms, in 1570, and which are thus described : " Barry nebule of six, argent and azure, on a bend gules, a lion passant, gardant or, crest on a helmet and torse, two arms supporting a laurel proper and issuing out of a cloud argent. Supporters two Indian goats, attired and hoofed, or ; motto, ' Serve and Obey.' "

Amongst other wares which constituted a part of the haberbashery of the early years of their existence were pins, before the introduction of which the English ladies are said to have used points or skewers made of thorns or bone or metal for the purpose of fastening their gowns and other garments. These must have been extremely inconvenient and troublesome, and I claim the sympathy of our modern ladies for their sisters in ancient times. However, some of them got over the difficulty of a lack of pins by using brooches and bodkins, often made of silver or gold. I know not who was the inventor of pins, but the making of these certainly was an old industry in the town of Reading in Berkshire. They were not the useful, delicate, sharp, elegant little implements in the early stage of their development, but clumsy-looking things

184

HABERDASHERS' HALL

with twisted wire forming the head ; at any rate they were better than thorns. There existed a voluntary Association of Pinners as early as 1376 which seems to have been united to the Girdlers by Queen Elizabeth. The Haberdashers found pins a very lucrative part of their trade ; and £50,000 annually is said to have been paid to foreigners on account of it in the early years of Queen Elizabeth ; yet long before her death they were made in England in large quantities. The makers of pins, therefore, became a large and important body of craftsmen, too large to be included in another Company, and eager to have a Charter of their own. So they approached King Charles I who willingly granted their request, and the ancient craft Gild blossomed out into " the Master, Assistants, and Commonalty of the Art or Mystery of Pinmakers of the City of London." Their early home was in Addle Street, but in 1619 they migrated to another Hall at St. Mary at Hill. Here they lived and worked until the early part of the eighteenth century, but the sun of prosperity soon set. While the retailers, the Haberdashers, flourished, the makers died out. You can still see in the City, Pinners' Court and a label recording Pinners' Hall, but it is a false direction. Pinners' Hall has long ceased to be.

The Company was at the height of its glory at the coronation of Queen Anne Boleyn in 1533, when one of their number was Lord Mayor.

185

THE CITY COMPANIES

On that occasion there were " marvailous cunning pageantes," in which Apollo with the Muses, and St. Anne with her children, had conspicuous places. The Three Graces stood in Cornhill, and the Cardinal Virtues in Fleet Street ; a fountain of Helicon, with courteous inconsistency, ran Rhenish wine, and its rival, the conduit in the Cheap, foamed forth claret. The Show on the river was magnificent. All decked with teeming banners and bannerets the barges proceeded from Greenwich to the Tower, and thence to Westminster, the Lord Mayor's barge at their head, having divers instruments of music that played continually, followed by fifty barges of the Company, and then by those of the other Gilds. Before the Lord Mayor's barge was a raft on which was a great red dragon, continually moving and casting forth wild fire, and round about were terrible, monstrous wild men, also casting forth fire and making a hideous noise. With such shouts of joy and rejoicing was the young Queen hailed ! Only three years later, on Tower Green, many of the same joyous crowd beheld her fair head struck off by the axe of the executioner, and mourned her speedy downfall. *Sic transit gloria mundi.*

The unhappy Queen's famous daughter, Elizabeth, favoured the Company by granting them another Charter which confirmed all the privileges granted to them by her predecessor, and allowed them to have a Hall within the city.

HABERDASHERS' COMPANY

They had power to apprehend, arrest, and commit to prison all persons who should be found faulty in anything with regard to their trade, and also such as were stubborn and resisted their directions. Strype has much to say concerning the shops of the Haberdashers, which made a very gay show in Cheapside owing to the various foreign commodities with which they were furnished ; and by the purchasing of them, he says, the people of London, and of other parts of England, began to expend extravagantly, whereof great complaints were made amongst the graver sort. There were few of these Milliners' shops in the reign of Edward VI, not more than a dozen in all London ; but in 1580 every street in Westminster embraced the business of woollen-drapers, cutlers, upholsterers, glass and earthen-ware men, perfumers, and various other dealers, eastwards, until the whole town became full of them. They sold, amongst other wares, French and Spanish gloves, and French cloth or fri-zarde (frieze), Flanders-dyed kersies, daggers, swords, knives, Spanish girdles, painted cruses, dials, tables, cards, balls, glasses, fine earthen pots, salt-cellars, spoons, tin dishes, puppets, pennons, inkhorns, toothpicks, silk, and silver buttons. "All which made such a shew," says Strype, " in passengers' eyes, that they could not help gazing on and buying these knick-knacks."

187

THE CITY COMPANIES

Churchyard in his " Challenge " (1593) tells
the same tale of fine shops and extravagance :

" Fine shops and sights, fine dames and houses gay,
Fine wares, fine words, fine sorts of meat is there,
Yea all is fine, and nothing grone they say,
Fine knaks cost much, cost spoils us everywhere.
Spoil is a worme, that wealth away will weare
A cancker crept, in Court for some mens crosse,
That eates up lands, and breeds great lacke and loss."

Stubbes and other contemporaries pour scorn
on the vanities of the Elizabethan age, and
another marvels that " no man taketh heed of it
what number of trifles cometh hither from beyond
seas, that we might either clean spare or else make
them within our own realm ; for the which we
either pay inestimable treasure every year, or
else exchange substantial wares and necessaries
for them, for the which we might receive great
treasure." Perhaps some of us in modern times
when we wander along Bond Street might be
inclined to utter the same sentiments.

A curious arrangement existed between the
Haberdashers and the Fishmongers, whereby
the right of search and interference in government was exercised by the former over the latter,
who seem to have submitted calmly to this
strange ruling. This Company suffered severely
together with their confrères in the troublous
times of the Civil War, being compelled to
contribute to forced loans levied both by the

188

King and afterwards by the Parliament ; so much so, that they lost no less than £50,000 which is, I believe, still owing to them, and may with certitude be written off as a " bad debt."

The Haberdashers were not so fortunate as some of the other Companies in saving their old books and records, which perished in the Great Fire. They were forced to surrender their Charters and privileges by the arbitrary demands of Charles II, who in his treatment of the Gilds certainly conformed to the judgment which the rhymer passed on him :

> "He never said a foolish thing
> And never did a wise one."

but James II, alarmed at the approach of William and Mary, hastily restored them, and when the latter came to the throne their ancient rights were firmly established. Since that time the story of the Company has been uneventful, and the Haberdashers have spent their days in managing their extensive trusts, which are of immense service to the nation, and in carrying out the duties entrusted to them by many benefactors.

THE HALL

The Hall is situated in Maiden Lane nigh Goldsmiths' Hall, and its site was bequeathed to the Company during the reign of Edward IV, in 1478, by William Bacon, citizen and haber-

THE CITY COMPANIES

dasher, together with various houses and premises attached. The ground covered by these buildings is about half an acre in extent, the value of which at the present time may be conjectured as enormous, when a square foot of land in the City is worth thousands of pounds. A plan of this is preserved among the archives of the Company, but no description of the ancient Hall is in existence, as the whole of it fell a victim to the Great Fire. The Hall must have been a large room as it was chosen by the Parliamentary Commissioners for their meetings during the Commonwealth period.

With the usual characteristic energy of the citizens of London they immediately set to work to rebuild their home, and employed for this purpose London's celebrated architect Sir Christopher Wren. It cannot be said of this, as of St. Paul's Cathedral, " *Si monumentum requiris, circumspice,*" as a second fire attacked the building in 1840, the only portion that escaped the flames being the court room and the drawing-room, the former retaining the fine ceiling designed by Wren. In this room, also, is a large wooden figure of St. Catherine, the patron saint of the Company, which was formerly the figure head of their barge.

In studying Mr. Herbert's History of the Company, I fancy that he was rather offended with the Haberdashers, and took umbrage because he was not allowed to examine some of their documents. Of the Hall, as it stood in his day, in 1836, he remarks that " it has nothing to merit description ; indeed, it much needs rebuilding." He adds that " there are some good portraits which need not be noticed here, being mentioned in most of the histories of London." I think that his feelings must have been a little ruffled.

The building erected in 1840 had a courtyard in the centre, but space in London is now so valuable that this has been built over and warehouses are more profitable than paving-stones. The present hall itself was not erected until 1864, and is a handsome room adorned with the arms of the past Masters. Here are seen two royal portraits of George I and Queen Caroline, which for some unaccountable reason wandered away into Devonshire and were not recovered until recent years, when they found their way home. I must not omit to describe some of the many fine portraits, as Mr. Herbert did. These are as follows :

George Whitmore, Lord Mayor in 1659.

John Banks (1716) who, anxious about his descendants, bequeathed £200 a year in trust to the Company for their benefit.

William Bond (1671).

William Jones, Merchant Adventurer and Haberdasher, who in 1614 founded the noble Grammar School at Monmouth. The story is told of him that having amassed great wealth he visited *incognito* his native place, Newland, in Gloucestershire. Unfortunately for them his old neighbours did not afford him a very hospitable reception ; he therefore proceeded to Monmouth, and bequeathed a large portion of his wealth to that town, which funds the Company administer. He built and endowed the Grammar School and twenty almshouses. The property has greatly increased in value and this has enabled the Company in recent years to spend £17,000 on the Grammar School at Pontypool. The inhabitants of Newland must have long regretted their inhospitable welcome to their former friend and neighbour.

Thomas Aldersey (1594), founder of the Company's School at Bunbury, in Cheshire, whose descendants still inhabit the mansion, Aldersey Hall (or did so until twenty years ago and I hope still hold their ancestral property).

Thomas Skinner, Lord Mayor in 1795.

On the walls of the handsome staircase I noticed the following portraits :

Robert Aske.

William Adams.

Sir Hugh Hammersley, Lord Mayor in 1776, First Colonel of the City, President of the Artillery Gentlemen, Governor of the Company of Russian Merchants.

Jerome Knapp, formerly Clerk of the Company, by Gainsborough.

HABERDASHERS' COMPANY

Queen Charlotte, and George III, by Sir Joshua Reynolds.

This Company is remarkable for the small amount of its corporate funds as compared with the very large trust funds which pious benefactors have entrusted to its care for administration. Its whole income is now less than £50,000, out of which the Haberdashers have to expend £41,000 upon its trusts. They have been foremost in promoting education. As early as 1552 the Court offered to give £5 yearly (a much larger sum than is represented in modern currency) towards the finding of a poor scholar at the University "so that the rest of the xij worshipfull companyes of the cittie doth like"— a good example to which doubtless the others responded. I have already referred to the Grammar Schools at Monmouth and Bunbury. They have also the charge of the Grammar School at Newport, Shropshire, founded by William Adam in 1656, a free school at Cripplegate founded in 1663 by Throgmorton Trotman ; a school and almshouses at Hoxton founded in 1692 by Robert Aske and another at Hatcham. In all these cases they have spent large sums out of their corporate funds to supplement their trusts, enlarging schools, building new ones, so that the original benefactions were only germs from which have arisen gigantic schemes for educational purposes for executing the plans and schemes of the first founders. They possess

193   N

THE CITY COMPANIES

the advowsons of thirteen benefices situated in seven counties besides London, and have contributed largely to the building of new churches. Such in brief is the record of this beneficent fraternity, which has proved itself worthy of the great trust reposed in them by worthy citizens of London and generous benefactors in days gone by.

XIII. THE SALTERS' COMPANY

SALT is a symbol. Its preservative qualities were understood by the ancients to make it a peculiarly fitting symbol of an enduring compact and fellowship —such as binds together the members of such a fraternity as the Salters' Gild. Amongst ancient people and Orientals down to the present day every meal that included salt had a certain sacred character and created a bond of piety and friend-ship among the participants. The Bible speaks of " a covenant of salt," and an Arabian proverb tells how friends swear an enduring bond of union by the saying " There is salt between us," and if a friend proves himself disloyal and ungrate-ful he is said to be " untrue to salt." Well may it be regarded as a necessity of life by many nations, though primitive man knew little of it : but when he fed only on milk and ate his food raw this mineral was unnecessary.

England has been greatly favoured in possessing salt mines and springs. The latter have been utilized from time immemorial and were well known to the Romans, but the discovery of rock salt is of comparatively modern date. The rock salt in Cheshire was accidentally found in 1670. Much salt was extracted from the sea in ancient times, and the place-name *wich*[1] usually denotes the former existence of salt-

[1] Inland places ending in *wich* derive their names from the

195

THE CITY COMPANIES

works. The brine springs at Droitwich are
mentioned in the year 816, and several *salinæ*
or salt-works are recorded in the Domesday
Survey. The workmen engaged in these primitive
salt-works were termed *salinarii*, wallers or boilers
of salt. It was boiled in " plumbi " or leaden
vats, and was heavily taxed and yielded a large
income for the Crown. It was measured by
ambra, four bushels ; *mita*, ten bushels ; *summa*,
horse loads ; and *sextarii*. Lymington supplied
the greatest quantity of marine salt, but East
Anglia must have run with it a close race. There
were three salt pans at Goleston, near Yarmouth,
when the Domesday Book was compiled and
another at Beccles, which town paid a rent of
60,000 herrings to the Abbey of St. Edmund.

Our forefathers required a very large amount
of salt for preserving their provisions. It was
their custom—the beneficent use of cold storage
had not then dawned upon mankind—to fatten
their beasts in the autumn and kill and salt the
flesh for winter use. This necessitated a large
amount of this mineral, and fish was much eaten
in royal and noblemen's households, especially
in Lent, as well as in the houses of the gentry,
farmers, tradesfolk and workmen, and in monasteries. Though there were stew ponds in the
gardens of every manor house, fresh fish could

Anglo-Saxon meaning a house or village, but those on the coast
from the Norse signifying a bay or creek, wherein the Vikings
had their stations, and where salt was obtained by evaporation
of sea-water.

not always be obtained. Hence it had to be salted. The household expenses of Edward I have been published, and these show the large sums that were expended upon a fish diet provided for the royal table, including the wages of the salter's man for salting fish during Lent which was made into a kind of bread (*piscum in pane coquend*). Various sorts of fish were in use, such as " salmon salis," valued at 8d. each ; durus piscus, grossus piscus, red herrings, etc. The cost of salt was 2s. 6d., 2s. 8d., or 3s. 2d. per quarter. The common provisions of the household of the Duke of Northumberland in the reign of Henry VII included stock-fish, salte fysche, whyt herring, rede herrynge, salt salmon, salt eels (it is to be hoped that these were not salted alive, as was the custom in some houses) and these formed part of every meal. For " my lord and lady's table " there was provided " ij pecys (pieces) of salt fische, vi beconned herryng, iiij white herring on a dish of sproots." These and other references show the enormous amount of salt fish that was consumed, not only in Lent but throughout the year, and the monks and nuns in conventual establishments required a very large supply. The port of Sandwich in the time of the Domesday Survey paid annually 40,000 herrings to the monks, and Dunwich 60,000 to the King. In 1302 Yarmouth furnished for the King's table ten lasts of herrings, a last being 10,000 herrings, and in 1338 the King, Edward

197

THE CITY COMPANIES

III, obtained 40 lasts, i.e., 400,000 herrings, for food for his army in Flanders. One wonders how the sea could yield so rich a harvest. We can well understand, therefore, that the salt manufacturers and merchants were in great request, and performed for society many useful functions.

The fraternity was in existence in London in early times, but does not appear to have been licensed by Letters Patent until the 37th year of Edward III, when it formed one of the Twelve Great Companies, and during the same reign they did their share in the governance of the City and were permitted to send two of their numbers to the Common Council. As we have seen with regard to other Gilds, Richard II took much interest in the welfare of the Salters and gave to them a Royal Charter constituting them a Livery Company, at the same time renewing the powers and privileges granted to them by his grandfather, Edward III. Other sovereigns have granted to them Charters in confirmation of those I have just mentioned, namely, Henry VI, Edward IV, Queen Elizabeth and James II. The Charter of Richard II stated all their rights and powers as traders and in the exercise of their monopoly as salt-merchants with power to make search and destroy that which was defective and bad, and also on the religious side of their Gild, permitted them to be a fraternity in honour of the Body of our Lord Jesus Christ in the

THE SALTERS' COMPANY

Church of All Saints in Bread Street in the City of London. Thither they resorted to hold their services and appointed a priest to say masses for the repose of the souls of their dead brothers.

The Salters' abode in Bread Street near to the location of their kindred tradesfolk, the Fishmongers, was a very natural arrangement, as the latter needed salt for the preservation of their fish. In the year 1454, Thomas Beamond, citizen and salter, left to the Wardens of the Brotherhood of the Gild of the Body of our Lord Jesus Christ in the Church of All Saints, Bread Street, and their successors for ever, certain lands in Bread Street, whereon had recently been erected Salters' Hall, together with other property, out of the rents and profits of which he directed that the Hall should be repaired and rebuilt as occasion might require. This Will also gave direction that obits should be offered for the repose of his soul and of his relatives, and for the support of poor Salters in almshouses. Some litigious persons some years later endeavoured to prove that the Company and the Gild were separate bodies, and that the Gild alone was entitled to the bequest of Thomas Beamond. As we should have expected, after examining so many of the constitutions of these fraternities, the Law decided that the Company and the Gild constituted one sole body, indivisible and identical. This decision was

199

entirely in accordance with the whole structure of the Gilds, the religious and social sides and the protection of their trade, being all united together in the work of the Company.

The Salters received a grant of arms in the twenty-second year of Henry VIII, Anno Domini 1530, by Thomas Benolt, Clarencieux, the crest and supporters being added by Robert Cooke, Clarencieux, in 1587. Their armorial ensigns are: per chevron azure and gules, three covered salts, or, springing salt proper. On a helmet and torse, issuing out of a cloud argent, a sinister arm proper holding a salt as the former. There seems to be some divergence of opinion with regard to the supporters. According to the " New View," they are given as two otters argent platter, gorged with ducal coronets, thereto a chain affixed and reflected, or : motto *Sal sapit omnia.* In "A Short History of the Company," however, the otters are rejected and ounces or small leopards are substituted. In a pageant of 1684 these beasts are called lions. The supporters are thus described : " Two ounces besants, gorged with crowns and chased gold." *Quot homines tot sententiæ* seems to be a solution of the problem ; but if one may hazard an opinion, I should prefer to cling to the otters. There is no possible connection between ounces and the trade of the Salters. For more than a hundred years the otters have held sway and been recognized as the correct supporters. Moreover, they have some connection with fish, the salting of which constituted a great part of the business of the salters. Indeed, it has been stated that otters have been trained to drive fish into a net and thus help the fishermen and benefit the salter. ·

The Salters took a leading part in raising money for the forced loans required by the Stuart monarchy, and a namesake and distant connection of the present writer was much concerned in collecting the sums. His name was Captain Edward Ditchfield, citizen and salter. I was permitted to examine the books of the Company on one occasion when I visited the Hall, and there found several records of large amounts paid to him. In consideration of the money lent to him, King Charles assigned to Captain Ditchfield, Hilord and two others, several manors in different parts of the country, and we constantly find in tracing the history of manors their names recorded, such as the Manors of West Derby, near Liverpool, the Chiltern Hundreds, Caversham, near Reading, a parish in Wales, etc. The inhabitants of West Derby objected to having their manors handed over to these gentlemen, and threatened to bring the matter before a Court of Law ; but when they found that they were in opposition to the City of London with all its power and wealth, they abandoned proceedings.

THE CITY COMPANIES

The Salters have been very migratory with regard to their home. As we have already stated, their first Hall was in Bread Street. In mediæval London, traders engaged in a particular industry lived together, and Bread Street was the location of the Salters not far removed from their kindred tradesfolk the Fishmongers of Old Fishmarket in Knightrider Street. There on ground bequeathed to the Salters by Thomas Beamond, a member of the Company, in 1451, they erected Salters' Hall, with a set of almshouses. Fire has been inimical to the property of the Company, and in 1533 this first Hall of theirs was destroyed according to the statement of John Stow, who wrote : " there was a great fyre at Salters' Hall in Bred Street, and much harm done." They rebuilt or repaired the Hall, which may be described as their second hall, according to a statement in the will of Sir Ambrose Nicholas, Lord Mayor in 1578, who described " the common hall of the said wardens and commonalty, called Salters' Hall in Bread Street," and we learn from Stow that there was an almshouse " for poor and decayed brethren of that Company." Twenty years later this was again damaged or destroyed by fire. It must have been repaired and made habitable, as in 1641 it was used by the Parliament where a discussion arose about increasing the army and raising more regiments of Horse and

Foot preparatory to the breaking out of the great Civil War which they felt was bound to come. Having lost two Halls by fire, perhaps animated by some superstitious fears, they resolved to seek a new home, and purchased a mansion which before the Dissolution of the Monasteries had been the town house of the Priors of Tortington. It was situate at the east end of the church of St. Swithin, London Stone, which stone, as is well known, was a Roman milliarium, and the centre of Roman London, and which is now embedded in the south wall of the church facing Cannon Street. Stow states that this house formerly belonged to the Earls of Oxford, and was called Oxford House, and then to Sir John Hart, Alderman and Lord Mayor, a member of the Company, and also that Sir Ambrose Nicholas, Salter and Alderman, a benefactor of the fraternity, kept his mayoralty there. John Stow also mentions two other fair houses there that looked into the garden of the Prior's lodgings, one of which was owned by Edmund Dudley and the other by Sir Richard Empson, Chancellor of the Duchy of Lancaster, in the time of Henry VII, whose ready tools they were in extorting money for that avaricious monarch. " Either of them," adds Stow, " had a door of intercourse into this garden, wherein they met and consulted of matters at their pleasure," doubtless devising many schemes for wringing money from the King's over-

THE CITY COMPANIES

taxed subjects. This Oxford House, sometimes called Oxford Place, passed into the hands of Captain George Smith and Katherine his wife, who sold it to the Salters for their Hall, doubtless adapting it to their needs.

And so it remained until the Great Fire, the third from which the Salters suffered, when it was entirely destroyed. Undaunted, they again set to work and rebuilt their Hall together with the wall of their great garden, and some adjoining buildings which belonged to them. It was built of brick and was of no great size, and Herbert states that "the entrance opened within an arcade of three arches springing from square pillars fluted. The parlour was handsome and there were on the premises a few original portraits." Mention is made of a Salters' Hall Meeting-House adjoining the garden, which was let to a congregation of Protestant Dissenters.

This, the fourth Hall, lasted for a century and a half and then not quite satisfied with the size and dignity of their home, the Salters having prospered and grown fairly wealthy, determined to erect a new palace for themselves. They resolved to make a clean sweep of their old buildings and to sell everything, the materials of the Hall and the adjoining houses and the meeting-house by public auction. So they posted their bills of sale, and crowds flocked to the doomed edifice on the 29th and three following days of August, 1821, and doubtless the bidding

THE SALTERS' COMPANY

was keen and good prices realized. Then they set to work to clear the site for the erection of the fifth and present Hall, and ordered their Surveyor, Mr. Henry Carr, to draw up an accurate plan of the site. Great care was exercised in the selection of an architect. They advertised and offered prizes for the best plan, and Herbert informs us that no less than sixty-two competitors contested. At length after much debate and divers consultations, the best was selected, and on October 16th, 1823, the first stone was laid with becoming pomp and ceremony, and in four years the present building was completed. It is a very striking and magnificent structure ; the large open space in front adds greatly to its imposing appearance, the entrance being especially fine, and creditable to the architects of the age which was not very remarkable for architectural triumphs. Four handsome Corinthian columns support the entablature, on which are carved two salts with covers and surrounded by scroll work, and the date " MDCCCXXIII," and above are the Arms of the Company, the supporters representing, we regret to say, the two leopards and not the otters.

Amongst the treasures of the Company are the original grant of Arms by Thomas Benolt, Clarencieux, in 1530, an old map of their Irish estate (the Salters were compelled by James I to join with the other Companies in his Irish scheme for developing the lands in Ulster

THE CITY COMPANIES

devastated by war), and a finely executed drawing of their lands at Maidenhead, Bray and Cookham, in Berkshire. The Master's chair in the Court Room is interesting, as it belonged to an early period of the history of the Gild, having been saved from destruction when their fourth Hall was destroyed in the Great Fire, the portraits of Charles I, William Robson and Barnard Hyde, having also been rescued and preserved. The dining-hall is a fine and beautiful chamber, highly decorated and adorned with portraits. Those of Queen Charlotte and George III are supposed to have been executed by Sir Joshua Reynolds.

The Salters have always realized their duty in providing for their aged and infirm members. Their almshouses have been removed to Watford and accommodate eighteen poor salters. Besides these, they have a liberal scheme of pensions for the assistance of those who are in pecuniary difficulties. They have also almshouses at Maidenhead founded by James Smith, citizen and salter, in 1661, and supplemented by George Pearce. I have in my previous book recorded the numerous benefactions of the Salters, for education, exhibitions and scholarships, hospitals, and religious and missionary objects, and need not repeat them here. Moreover, they continue, as their fathers did, to exercise bountiful hospitality in their hall, taking part in giving entertainment to distinguished guests according to the custom of the City of London.

THE SALTERS' COMPANY

It is interesting to notice the following menu of the Company's feast at the beginning of the sixteenth century. It was discovered amongst the documents in their Hall, and I am glad, by the courtesy of the Clerk, to possess a facsimile copy, which runs as follows :

BILL OF FARE FOR FIFTY PEOPLE OF THE COMPANY OF SALTERS, A.D. 1506.

36 Chickens	4–6	Bacon		6
1 Swan. 4 Geese	7–0	Quarter of a load of		
9 Rabbits	1–4	Coals		4
2 rumps of beef-tails	2	Faggots		2
6 Quails	1–6	3 Gallons and a half		
2 oz. of pepper	2	of Gascoyne Wine	2–4	
2 oz. cloves and mace	4	1 Bottle Muscedina	8	
1½ ounce saffron	6	Cherries and Tarts	8	
3 lbs. Sugar	8	Salt	1	
2 lbs. Raisons	4	Verjuice and vinigar	2	
1 lb. Dates	4	Paid the Cook	3–4	
1½ Comfits	2	Parfume	2	
¾ hundred eggs	2½	1 Bushel and a half		
4 gallons Curds	4	of Meal	8	
1 ditto gooseberries	2	Water	3	
2 dishes of butter	4	Garnishing the Vessels	3	
4 Breasts of Veal	1–5			

This feast was probably enjoyed by the Salters in their first Hall in Bread Street. Herbert reprints the following interesting recipe for making a Christmas pie, which recipe was discovered among the documents of the fraternity, and informs us that the cook who practised his art in 1833 when Herbert's history was written, constructed a pie after the same recipe and it was pronounced to be excellent. If any of our readers would like to try the same experiment, the recipe is here set forth :

207

THE CITY COMPANIES

" For to make a mooste choyce Paaste of Gamys to be eten at ye Feste of Chrystemasse.
(17th Richard II, A.D. 1394)

" Take Fesaunt, Haare, & Chykenne, or Capounne, of eche oone : w^t ij partruchis, ij Pygeonnes, & ij Conynggys : & smite hem on peces, & pyke clene awaye p'fro[1] alle p^e[2] boonys p^t[3] ye maye, and p'wt[4] do hem ynto a foyle[5] of gode paste, made craftely ynne p^e lykenes of a byrde's bodye, w^t p^e lynowes & hertys, ij kydneis of shepe, & farcys[6] & eyren[7] made into balles. Caste p'to[8] poudre of pepyr, salte, spyce, eysell,[9] and funges[10] pykled ; & panne[11] take p^e boonys & let hem seethe ynne a pot to make a gode brothe p'for,[12] & do y^t ynto foyle of past, & close hit uppe fast, & bake y^t wel, & so s'ue[13] yt forthe : wt p^e hede

(1) therefrom.
(2) the.
(3) that.
(4) therewith.
(5) Foyle—a shield or case of rolled paste.
(6) Farcys—seasoning or forced meats.
(7) Eyres—eggs made into balls.
(8) thereto.
(9) Eysell—strong vinegar, verjuice, or possibly catsup.
(10) Funges—mushrooms.
(11) thin.
(12) therefore—namely, for it.
(13) serue—serve.

208

of oone of p⁰ byrdes stucke at p⁰ oone ende
of p⁰ foyle, and a grete tayle at p⁰ op', &
dyuers of hys longe fedyrs sitteynne connynlye
alle aboute hym."

I had nearly forgotten to record some examples
of old-time pageants. The Salters do not possess
copies of many of their dramatic presentments,
and only one has been printed, as far as we are
aware. It is styled " Descensus Astreæ," which
consists mainly of a speech by one clad as a
Sea Nymph, who presented a pinnace on the
waters bravely rigged and manned to the Lord
Mayor at the time he took barge to go to Westminster, in 1591. There were great doings in
1684 when the Drapers organized a grand pageant
which consisted of twelve female characters
representing the twelve Companies. The Salters
were allegorically shown by Salina in a sky-
coloured robe and coronation mantle, both
fringed with gold ; bright hair, and chaplet of
white and yellow roses ; bearing in one hand a
buckler with the Company's arms depicted upon
it. No doubt the lady created a great impression
on the London crowds who flocked to see the
pageant pass, and looked very lovely. London
crowds always love a spectacle and a dream of
fair womcn as they passed would especially
please them. And with this account of this
interesting Company we must close our record
and pass on to its successor.

XIV. THE IRONMONGERS'
COMPANY

LONG before the City Gild which concerns itself with iron was founded, that useful metal had been discovered and worked. There was a late Celtic or early Iron Age which has left its products in this country and on the Continent of Europe, at Hallstadt and La Téne, ranging from the date 850–600 B.C. to about 150 B.C. There are the legends of the Scandinavian and Icelandic Sagas which tell of Weyland the Smith, the son of the Giant Wode, who worked wondrously in metals and was taught by the mountain dwarfs the art of moulding metals by fire, corresponding to Tubal Cain, the first artificer of metals, and the Roman Vulcan, and with the French giant who made the sword of Charlemagne. In this country iron bits have been found in connection with " Chariot-burials," as at Beverley and Kilhain, where the chariot of some ancient warrior was interred with his body. The Romans explored the iron-mines in this country. In Yorkshire, the Forest of Dean, the Weald of Sussex, and in other places there are immense beds of cinders, the remains of ancient iron-works in which Roman coins and pottery have been found. Maresfield, in Sussex, near Lewes, has the site of one of these many fields of iron scoriæ marking the existence of the extinct furnaces and forges of the Sussex Weald, in which have been discovered several coins of

IRONMONGERS' COMPANY

Nero, Vespasian, Tetricus and Diocletian. Similar discoveries have been made at Sedlescombe and Westfield. The scoriæ still contain much metal, showing that the Romans were not very skilful in smelting.

In Saxon times the art continued and indeed lingered on for a long period until in not very remote times the forests of the shire were cut down and the fuel exhausted. In Sussex we often find fire-backs made in these works and in one church we have seen a grave-slab made of iron. Domesday Book records that iron-working was carried on in Somerset, Hereford, Gloucestershire, Cheshire and Lincoln.

The first notice of the Ferones or dealers in iron in London is recorded in the *Liber Horn*[1] which informs us of a serious complaint made against the iron-workers of the Sussex Weald to the Mayor and Court of Aldermen of the City of London in the year 1300. They complained that these iron-founders brought in irons for the wheels of carts to London which were much shorter than anciently was accustomed, to the great loss and scandal of the whole trade of ironmongers. Whereupon an inquisition was taken of lawful and honest men, who presented three iron rods of the just and anciently used

---

[1] The *Liber Horn* is an ancient MS., one of the most important preserved in the archives of the City of London, and was compiled about the year 1311. It is very neatly written on thick vellum, and illuminated. The author was Andrew Horn, Chamberlain of the City in the time of Edward II.

THE CITY COMPANIES

lengths of the strytes (*strytorum*), and also of the length and breadth of the gropes (*groporum*), belonging to the wheels of carts, which rods were sealed with the seal of the Chamber of Guildhall, London ; whereof one remains in the said chamber, and another rod was delivered on the Monday before the Purification of the Blessed Virgin Mary, in the 29th Edw. I to John Dode and Robert de Paddington, ironmongers of the market, and the third was delivered the same Monday to John de Wymondham, ironmonger of the bridge : which John, Robert and John were sworn upon the Holy Evangelists that from day to day they should warn and give notice to all merchants bringing such iron to the City of London, as of the Wealds or elsewhere, that they hereafter should not bring such iron unless it was of the length and breadth aforesaid, upon pain of the forfeiture of such iron, and that such iron as they should find against the aforesaid assize after the feast of Easter next should be wholly forfeited.

The earliest mention of the Fraternity occurs in 1351, when the Mayor summoned two men of the various mysteries, the " bones gentz " of their crafts, to meet him and the Aldermen and Sheriffs, in order to consult upon " some heavy business touching the state of the City." The following Gilds are mentioned, the Drapers, Grocers, Mercers, Fishmongers, Goldsmiths, Woolners, Vintners, Weavers, Tailers, Cordwainers, Ironmongers and Butchers. The precept of the Mayor was sent to John Deyner and Richard de Eure, Ironmongers, and the Wardens selected for the important conference were Henry de Ware and William Fromond, Ironmonger, 1390 ; Thomas Mitchell, Ironmonger, 1527 ; Richard Chamberlain, Ironmonger and Sheriff, 1562, and also Alderman and " a Merchant Adventurer and free of Russia " ; Alderman Campbell, Ironmonger and Lord Mayor in 1613, etc. Strype mentions the subsequent removal of the Ironmongers of Ironmongers' Lane to Upper Thames Street, which (according to the History of the Company by Mr. John Nicholl) still continues to be the principal market in London for bar-iron and castings, and where in former days resided many worthies of the trade.

The Ironmongers by this time had become an important and flourishing community. Several of their brethren became Mayors, such as Sir Richard Marlow, citizen and ironmonger, who served the office in 1410 and 1417, when Henry V reigned. John Stow informs us that during his " mairalty there was a play at Skinners Hall which lasted 8 days, to heare which most of the greatest estates of England were present. The subject of the play was the Sacred Scriptures from the creation of the world." It certainly rivalled in length, if not in treatment and subject, Mr. Bernard Shaw's " Back to Methuselah."

213

THE CITY COMPANIES

" They call this Corpus Christi play," observed
Mr. Weever, " which I have seen acted at
Preston and Lancaster, and last of all at Kendall
in the beginning of the reign of King James,
for which the townesmen were sore troubled,
and upon good reasons, the play finally supprest,
not onely there, but in all other townes of the
kingdome." Sir Richard Marlow, who was
sheriff in 1402, was a charitable person and gave
£20 to the poor of Queenhithe ward and 10 marks
to the Church of St. Michael Queenhithe, in
which church lie his remains and those of his
wife Agnes.

Another worthy was Sir John Hatherley, *alias*
Adderley, citizen and ironmonger, a native of
Bristol, who became Lord Mayor in 1442.
Several public works of importance were inaugurated during his mayoralty. The supply of water
was always a trouble to London citizens until
Sir Hugh Middleton inaugurated the New
River Scheme. During Sir John's mayoralty the
citizens set up several conduits of fresh water
with standards and other devices and leaden
pipes that ran above three miles, both above and
under the earth, and a common granary, and to
repair the great Cross in Cheap, erected in 1290
by Edward I, in memory of his Queen Alianora
(Eleanor) ; the King having granted a licence
to the Mayor and citizens, in order to set forth
these works to buy 200 fodder of lead anywhere
in the realm, and to hire with their money work-

men, masons and plumbers, as many as they would from time to time.

The Company possesses some interesting old books relating to their history and amongst others the *Ancient Book of Orders*, a volume written on vellum, containing much interesting matter relating to their ancient annals. Its opening sentence runs as follows :

> " In the xxxiij yere of the regne of King henry the vith Richard Flemmyng & Nich'as Marchale stode wardeyns of the ffelaship of Ironmongers, having than nor long before no maister but ij wardeyns."

From this it is evident that the Company had no Master but was governed by two wardens as was the case with some of the other Gilds ; but in this case shortly afterwards a Master ruled the Company. There are other items recorded in this priceless little MS. We learn how the brethren kept the obit of John Guyva, and how there was an important dispute between them and the rector of "Alhalows Stayning," and how they managed to settle the affair by a "compremyse." We are also told about the position of the "yeomanry." These were the freemen of the Company ranking below the Livery Court which regulated the affairs of the Gild. In 1497 they considered that they ought to have higher privileges; so they sent a petition to the Master, Wardens and Court of the Livery, praying their "grete wysdomye" that they might have licence to choose two new "rulars" for themselves annually, and also have a supper twice a year in the Hall. This was, of course, granted, and later on we find that the supper was changed into a dinner in the hall wherein no doubt there were gay doings, much feasting and doubtless many songs and speeches galore.

Another proof of the increasing honour and position of the Gild is that it received a grant of arms from Lancaster, King of Arms, Marshal to Clarencieux, King of Arms, A.D. 1455, and it was then styled "The Honorable Craft and Mystery of Ironmongers." This grant was ratified by William Harvey, in the time of Henry VIII, and again in 1560 during the reign of Queen Elizabeth, and again in 1634. They are thus described : *Argent, on a chevron gules, between 3 gads of steel azure, as many pair of shackles, or ; crest on a helmet and torso, 2 lizards combatant proper chained and collared, or.: motto,* "God is our strength." It is a question whether these creatures called lizards should not be described as salamanders, a creature supposed, like iron, to live unhurt in fire. But the Ironmongers preferred to call these animals lizards, and so named their Irish estate "the Manor of Lizard." At first their Arms had no supporters, but later on the two ferocious-looking "lizards" were added, but it seems a little doubtful whether according to Heraldic laws the Company is entitled to these supporters. The ancient motto

216

A WATER PAGEANT

was "*Assher Dur*," which is rather cryptic but may be interpreted in modern orthography " *acier dur* " (hard steel) in allusion to the three gads of steel which form the principal charges of the Arms.

A few years later, in 1483, the Gild emerged from a licensed fraternity into a fully incorporated Company by the granting of a Charter by Edward IV, in which they are styled " our well beloved and faithful liegemen, all the freemen of the mystery and art of Ironmongers of our City of London and suburbs thereof." The usual privileges were granted to them and need not be here enumerated. Edward IV, who granted this and other Charters to other City Companies, was a far-seeing monarch, and has been well styled the Merchant King. He amassed riches as a trader himself. His ships were annually freighted with tin, wool and cloth, to the ports of Italy and Greece, and he strove to make London the principal mart of Europe. The English merchants in this reign easily accumulated riches. At the great fairs of Brabant, which were the resort of traders from all parts of the world they were the chief buyers and sellers, while their ships sailed in every sea and brought them abundant wealth. They made good use of this, devoting much of their riches to charity, building churches in their native villages and almshouses for the poor, and in promoting the welfare and prosperity of their Companies. The importance of the use of this

THE CITY COMPANIES

metal was clearly recognized about this time, as the Act of 28 Edward III prohibited all iron made in England, and all iron imported, from being carried out of the realm on pain of forfeiting double the value exported. In the same reign thirty-two Companies were in 1363 invited to send an offering to the King for carrying on the war with France when the victories of Crecy and Poictiers showed the valour of the English arms. The Ironmongers joyfully complied with the Royal command and sent £6 18s. 4d. towards a total of £452 16s. raised by the Companies and appear the eleventh on the list.

In the time of Edward III an important question arose concerning the governance of the City. Hitherto the members of the common council and also the Mayor and Sheriffs had been elected by the Wards of the City ; but the Companies having increased in numbers and importance, now claimed the right of electing the chief officers and of making ordinances for the government of the City. Doubtless there was much contention. However, the Mayor, acting on the advice of several Aldermen in order to produce peace, summoned a meeting at the Guildhall, which decided that the Gilds and Companies should elect the members of the common council and the Mayors and Sheriffs. This was somewhat of a revolution ; but the arrangement continued in force until 1384, when the mode of election reverted to the ancient custom and

IRONMONGERS' COMPANY

the Wards and not mysteries discharged the election business.

We have seen that in Old London each set of traders had their accustomed locality as the street nomenclature at the present day still bears witness to this arrangement. Thus, the bakers had their shops in Bread Street, the sellers of fowls in the Poultry, the leather-sellers in Leather Lane, the soapmakers in Sopers' Lane, the sellers of milk in Milk Street. So the Ironmongers lived in Ironmongers' Lane nigh Mercers' Hall, and in Old Jewry, " where they had large warehouses and yards, and exported and sold bar-iron and iron rods ; they also had shops wherein they displayed abundance of manufactured articles which they purchased of the workmen in town and country, and of which they afterwards became the general retailers." [1] Many of the worthies of the Company were buried in the churches of the adjacent parishes of St. Olave, Jewry, and St. Martin's, Ironmongers' Lane ; such as William Dikman, Ferroner or Iron-monger, one of the Sheriffs of London, 1367 ; at his funeral, which was somewhat sumptuous, Rober Havelocke paid for 2 deacons, clerk for ringing bells, " prest and clark for dyrge and masse, 2 gallons of Gascon wine, 3 lbs. of ' chumffits,' 3 gallons of sweet wine, a Suffolk cheese, a Banbury cheese, roses and lavender, sweet ' hally water '," etc., etc., etc.

[1] *Lond. Redivivum i .*

219

THE CITY COMPANIES

When the Queen (Anne Boleyn) came from
Greenwich the Ironmongers spent £11 18s. 1od.
Some of the items were as follows :

	s.	d.
Payd for oure barge from Grenewych	xxvi	viii.
,, for a kyllderkyn of alle and		
beryng to ye watter syde	ii	—
,, ,, grete ells		xv
,, ,, viii banner staves ..		xvi
,, ,, Painting the same ..		xvi

The refreshments required on board the barge
were many and various and besides the ale and
great ells mentioned above there were claret
wine, ling, gurnets, fresh salmon, bread and
cheese and other dainties.

Mistress Anne Boleyn seems often to have come
from Greenwich to Westminster and to have
been met by the Company in their barge. After
the funeral of a member there was always " a
dener at ye beryall " in the Hall.

The setting of the Midsummer Watch on
the Eve of St. John the Baptist Festival was
always a splendid function which delighted the
citizens. These have already been mentioned
in our accounts of the preceding Companies.
Processions of about 2,000 persons clad in divers
costumes marched along the streets, and hundreds
bore cresset lights, and there were pageants and
morris dancers and minstrels, and constables
who wore bright armour and chains of gold.
The Ironmongers include in their accounts sums

paid for the cressets and the cresset-bearers, and to those who kept the lights burning during the two nights of the Festival. The Watch was kept until 1548 and was then discontinued, as the authorities saw political danger in the assembly of so many armed men and the possibility of riot and disturbances.

Henry VIII showed his usual rapacity in 1523 when he demanded a large sum of money from the City, and ordered that an inventory of all · the money and plate belonging to every Hall and craft in London be drawn up, so that the money he demanded might be lent the more easily. So the Ironmongers lament: " he had all our money belonging to our Hall, xxv *li* xiiijd, and had to sell our plate." A goodly list follows of gilt and silver-gilt vessels, standing cups and covers, the residue being " layd to pleg," while many of the individual members of the Company lent to the King large sums. It is a mournful tale, especially as there was small hope of receiving back the money.[1]

The records of the Company reveal intimately the lives of the members, and the items of expenditure are curious and interesting. Payments were made in 1540 for the State barge on the river, for 20 sacks of " coll " (coal),

---

[1] The total result of the business is thus summed up, " the King hadde owtt off oure Hawle ciijxj *li* xiiijs ijd (£340 14s. 2d.). The individual members lent £219. The master, Sir William Denham, lent £30, and other sums were £20, £15, £5, down to 40s. and 33s.

THE CITY COMPANIES

for rushes (presumably for their Hall), for bread, ale, wine, fish and other victuals for a dinner at the Hall at the burying of Mr. Denham ; for a dirge and mass for Mr. Thomas Dorcheseter at Saynt Marchill for ij years. They loved their garden and , paid a gardener for cutting the vines and dressing the roses and for cutting the knotts of ye rosemarie. The payments for our " sollem mas " include xijd for the " cewrat of the church."

The Ironmongers suffered with their kindred Gilds from the spoliating acts of Henry VIII and Edward VI for " the dissolution of colleges, chantries and free chapels at the King's Majesty's pleasure " and the appointment of Commissioners to examine into all payments made by Corporations and Mysteries for the maintenance of priests, obits, and other superstitious observances." They could do nothing but submit to the Royal decree, and, as Strype observes, " purchase and buy off their rent charges and get as good a pennyworth as they could of the king, and this they did by selling other of their lands to enable them to make their purchases."

Many precepts were issued by the Mayor and Aldermen or by the Sovereign, requiring the Ironmongers to subscribe sums of money or provide men and arms for the service of the realm. It was a praiseworthy custom of the City to buy and lay up large stocks of corn in time of plenty, to store them in the granaries of the City, and then retail the corn to the poor at less prices in time of scarcity. In 1545 the Ironmongers subscribed £40 for this useful service. Ireland was then a troublesome and distressful island, as it is now. Rebellion was in progress, and the Company had to provide several men at various times for the Queen's service, and when the Armada threatened, frequent was the demand for men and arms. There is a mysterious order for an intended voyage to Rochelle, presumably for the relief of its siege. Sedition and plots were in the air, such as the plot to set Mary Queen of Scots on the English throne, Stubb's book against the Queen's marriage with the Duke of Anjou, the preaching of wandering Jesuits, the threatenings of Spain; so the Queen ordered the Companies to aid her in the suppression of seditious books and libellous publications. The Wardens were ordered to try to discover if any such things were current amongst the members. The Ironmongers devised a curious plan for discovering these without disclosing the person of the possessor. They appointed " a secret place " in the court room to which every man present was compelled to ascend, put in his hand and then return ; " which was to the end that such persons of the Company as had any of the same seditious book, should there let them fall ; and being only one man at a time, there was none to accuse him that had any book." It does not seem to have

THE CITY COMPANIES

occurred to the deviser of this scheme that the safest plan for the possessor of any obnoxious book was to leave it at home.

Again, we are overpowered by the abundance of information concerning the doings of this important Company. They were very careful to regulate and rule their own trade with wise observances and laws, which are too long to be quoted here. They had their pageants such as a famous one in 1629 when they exhibited a representation of " Lemnion's Forge, with Vulcan, the smith of Lemnos at work, surrounded by his servants, in black hair waistcoats and leather aprons. A fire blazed in the furnace, lightnings flashed and thunders rolled ; and at intervals harsh music and songs sounded praises to iron, the anvil and the hammer."

The Ironmongers showed a curious impartiality during the Civil War and refused to lend vast sums to the Royal or Parliamentary cause, though subsequently under compulsion they were forced to yield, and were obliged in the end to sell all their plate to satisfy the rapacity of Parliament. The money these unfortunate corporations were compelled to raise for divers objects was enormous ; and when " the king enjoyed his own again " and the Restoration came, they resolved to give a present to the King of £12,000, and the Lord Mayor informed the Ironmongers that their share was £480. They hastened to remove the arms of the Common-

IRONMONGERS' COMPANY

wealth from the Company's streamers and to set up again His Majesty's arms.

The subsequent history of the Company is not very eventful. The control and management of their Irish estate, styled the " Manor of the Lizard," caused them a large amount of trouble. Their Hall escaped the Great Fire. They seem to have always delighted to honour gallant sailors. Lord Hood was made an honorary freeman and a little later Admiral Lord Exmouth for his great victories at Algiers, his freeing of British subjects and those of other nations from slavery in Algiers, Tunis and Tripoli, and also Rear-Admiral Sir David Milne, K.C.B., the second-in-command of that victorious fleet.

THE HALL

The Ironmongers' Company was the most unfortunate of all the City Gilds in having their Hall destroyed by German aircraft in the Great War. Extensive precautions were taken by all the Companies for the preservation of their treasures, their plate and other movable valuables being all removed to places of safety, but no Hall was struck by a bomb save that of this Company. This fell upon the doomed building in 1917, and reduced the whole structure to a heap of shattered ruins. Desolation reigned and also in the hearts of the members who witnessed the complete destruction of their ancient home. Their new home has been built on a different

225   P

THE CITY COMPANIES

site, in Shaftesbury Place, Aldersgate, which I will describe presently, after recording the story of the old which I visited some years before its destruction.

It was situate in Fenchurch Street, off Mark (a corruption of *Mart*) Lane, on the site of which several previous buildings, representing the homes of the Ironmongers' fraternity have stood. This site is first mentioned in a deed dated 1344, and is described as near to the church of All Saints Stayning, to which church the Company has always been attached, and in 1457 the house built upon the site was sold to certain Ironmongers, and this became the earliest Hall of the Company. There is an entry in the Churchwardens' Accounts of the above-mentioned church in 1494 :

> " Payd for a Kyl cherkym of good ale, wich
> was drunkyn in the Yronmongers Hall, all
> charges born 12s. 2d."

The Hall was repaired in 1540 and rebuilt in 1587 because it was then " ruinous and in great decay." The accounts of the rebuilding are still preserved, but they are too long to be quoted here. I gather that Elias Jerman was the architect, and much money was spent in beautifying the hall, making the garden, adding new sun-dials, cutting off the arm of the middle mulberry tree, securing its privacy, and buying tapestry and furniture.

Although the Hall was not burnt during the

IRONMONGERS' COMPANY

Great Fire, it was in considerable danger, and the Clerk had to employ men to keep watch for several nights and to remove the treasures and documents to a place of safety. The authorities of the City naturally were inclined to provide remedies for any future conflagration. Amongst other methods they ordered all householders to have hand squirts, which do not seem likely to have been very efficacious in extinguishing fires. This primitive " fire-engine " consisted of a tube about nine inches in circumference and $27\frac{1}{2}$ inches long, including the nozzle. There were two side handles. The tube contained an ordinary bucketful of water which was propelled by a wooden piston or rod like an ordinary garden syringe.

Several menus of the Company have been preserved which reveal the good appetites of our forefathers and invite attention, but owing to lack of space, their attractions must be firmly resisted. The Hall was let for divers purposes, for funerals, for a lottery devised by Mr. Thomas Hatfield, for the meetings of the gentlemen merchants and traders of the " Bahamic Islands," for a ball and to Mr. Topham, a dancing master. In 1745, when Bonny Prince Charlie was creating excitement in the North of England, the Company decided to pull down their Hall and build a new one. Mr. Holken was appointed architect, and five years later it was completed and re-opened with a ball. Amongst the items of expense on this occasion was a hogshead of port wine, ten

227

THE CITY COMPANIES

dozen of Lisbon, half a chest of oranges, and half a hundred lemons.

Unfortunately the builders did not execute their work very well. The foundations were not very firm. So in 1817, in 1827, and 1829, and again in 1845 considerable alterations had to be made. The centre of the front had four Ionic pilasters. Over the door was a Venetian window. The spaces between the outer pilasters had windows with pediments, and the whole front was described by the architects of the day as " neat and elegant." On entering we found a large vestibule divided by six Tuscan columns into avenues, with chambers on the left, an entrance to the Court Room on the right, and the stairs to the Dining Hall on the first floor. This was a fine hall decorated in the Elizabethan style and was entered through folding doors set in a high portal supported by Roman Ionic columns adorned with arabesques and above was the effigy of St. Laurence, the patron saint of the Company. The Arms of Masters and benefactors were emblazoned on the walls. The buffet or frame at the back of the dais was supported by four colossal caryatid figures while in the pediment appeared the arms of the Company and the Royal Arms of England. At the end was the Minstrels' Gallery. The ceiling was a magnificent work of art.

It was pleasant to wander through the other chambers, now all vanished, and see the numerous portraits of Masters and benefactors which

adorned the walls, and have happily survived.
Amongst these I notice a former Clerk and
Master, Sir John Nicholl, F.S.A., a very learned
antiquary who compiled in 1851 from the records
in his custody an excellent "History of the
Worshipful Company of Ironmongers," a copy
of which I am glad to possess, and to which I am
indebted for much information. His biographical
notes on the members are most valuable.

After the fatal bomb had fallen and the Hall
was reduced to a heap of ruins, the Ironmongers
determined that it should be rebuilt when Peace
at last had been declared. They were uncertain
at first whether to erect it on the old site or seek
"fresh fields and pastures new." The Mark
Lane site was very valuable and could be sold
with advantage, and another good situation for
a hall presented itself in Aldersgate, where it
was resolved to build, and some interesting London
history is associated with the spot. Aldersgate
was situated immediately south of St. Botolph's
Church, and beyond the old London Wall to
the north was a lake which was a continual source
of trouble to the Corporation. The great ditch
which was almost a waterway between the
Wallbrook and the Fleet, was cut in 1211-13,
the effect of which was to reduce the lake to a
marsh. The task of filling up this marsh was
entrusted to Nicholas Leat in 1606, and after
the purchase of the site the Company was pleased
to discover that he was their Master in 1616,

THE CITY COMPANIES

1626, and 1637. Thus this former Master actually laid the first foundation for their new Hall. Shaftesbury Place formerly formed part of the site of Thanet House, built for John Tufton Earl of Thanet by Inigo Jones in 1644. After his death Anthony Astley Cooper, 1st Earl of Shaftesbury, entered into possession, and from that date it was known as Shaftesbury House. During Shaftesbury's ministry the Duke of Monmouth is said to have been concealed here. Between 1720 and 1850 Shaftesbury House saw many changes; it was an inn, a hostelry and dispensary (the first in London). The garden was converted into a court, containing a large number of tenement houses wherein lived a very rough population, a sort of Alsatia, into which it was not safe for single policemen to enter. These were pulled down in 1910. Thanet House was demolished in 1882. On the site of the tenements the Ironmongers have reared their new Hall, and a very fine palace it is, conferring great credit on the architect, a member of the Company.

The entrance porch faces Shaftesbury Place, and on it the arms of the Company are displayed. You enter a lofty hall which contains some old treasures, including a large mediæval chest which was much knocked about by the German bomb, and a remarkable clock, fashioned by Messrs. Hill & Harper, which was presented to the Company by one of their Masters in 1650. All the walls of the passages and chambers are

230

beautifully panelled in oak, and the ceilings are finely plastered in the Elizabethan style. The Clerk of the Company, Mr. J. F. Adams Beck, whose family has held the Clerkship for three generations, kindly welcomed me in his office, and escorted me through the building. We visited the Court Room where the chairs used by the Master and Wardens date back to 1730, the Drawing Room, the Great Hall, and many other chambers. The windows contain excellent stained glass showing numerous coats of arms, fashioned by Messrs. Clayton & Bell, and along the corridor are small windows showing arms and figures of persons connected with the Company, such as the Patron Saint St. Laurence, St. Dunstan, the Duke of Monmouth, Inigo Jones, and many others. The large wooden statue of St. Laurence stands in a corner of the main staircase, carved in 1740 for use on the Company's State Barge, and opposite to it is a large wooden ostrich which was carved for the Pageant on the election of Sir James Cambell as Lord Mayor in 1629. He was Master of the Company in 1615, 1623, and 1641, and his portrait is in the Hall. Many of the portraits of distinguished members were happily saved, and have been transferred to the new. Amongst these are Viscount Exmouth by Beechey, Viscount Hood by Gainsborough, Isaak Walton, Sir William Denham (1534), Sir Charles Price (Master, 1723), Thomas Michell (1527), Roland Haylin

231

THE CITY COMPANIES

(1614), John Child (1786), and several other paintings of Masters and benefactors.

Many charitable bequests have been made to the Company to be administered for the benefit of the poor and other worthy objects. They expend large sums out of their corporate income to support their trust funds ; they seek for objects that are worthy of their help, and few Gilds have done more than the Iron-mongers in supporting the City and Gilds of London Institute which does so much for the training in handicrafts of the youth of London.

XV.   THE VINTNERS' ❧
❧   ❧   COMPANY

WE will now journey to the Vintry, the home of the Vintners, where many strange and curious old customs survive, recalling features of the ancient life of the City. It fell to the lot of the present writer to act as Chaplain and preach the sermon on the occasion of the installation of the Master of the Company. Having robed and joined the marshalling of the chief officers, the Master, wardens, assistants, clerk, etc., he was presented with a fine bouquet of flowers. This was, of course, to protect him from the plague which used occasionally to ravage the City, and before the Great Fire was always prevalent, and lurking in the crowded alleys and streets, seeking whom it could devour. Though it was a summer day and Thames Street was as smooth and clean as a pavement of tar could make it, the porters armed themselves with brooms and swept the road as the procession marched along to the church of St. Michael Paternoster. The porters had done this for centuries, reminding us of the time when Thames Street was a sea of mud and well-nigh impassable without the aid of the porters' brooms. Then we wended our way to the interesting old church of St. Michael Paternoster Royal, created by the genius of Sir Christopher Wren in place of one destroyed by the Great Fire which was a collegiate church built from funds bequeathed by Sir Richard Whittington and in which he was *three times* buried. Stow tells us that he was buried by his executors under a fair monument, that a scandalous parson, thinking that some great riches had been buried with him, rifled the tomb in the time of Edward VI, stole the lead in which the body was encased, and buried him the second time ; but in the reign of Queen Mary, the parishioners were compelled to take him up again, encase the body in lead, bury him the third time, and to place his monument, or the like, over him again, and " so he rested." And yet the memorial of this great and good man was not allowed to rest, and his monument was destroyed in the Great Fire, and " no man knoweth of his sepulchre unto this day." And as one preached to this congregation of Vintners, one's thoughts flew back over the vanished centuries and recalled the countless generations of men who had worshipped on this spot, besought the blessing of God on their fellows, their families, and their trade, and deemed it no sin to supply the people of England with good wine, and had never heard the name "teetotaller." As we shall see presently, they did their utmost to check intemperance to control the tavern-keepers by strict regulations, and to close wine-shops which seemed to them to be redundant with all the severity of a modern bench of licensing magistrates. Another old custom I accounted strange, but the revelation of this must be postponed and related in its proper place.

The annals of some of the Companies are not always easy to explore. Some have large and elaborate histories written by some enthusiastic member, and printed privately. Little is known of others either because their documents were all destroyed in the disastrous Great Fire, or because no member has been keen enough to search and examine them, and no stranger has been allowed to pry into the mysterious secrets locked up in the strong-room. The Vintners have an excellent history compiled by Mr. Thomas Milbourn, a copy of which by the courtesy of a former Master and the Clerk, I have been allowed to possess.

The trade in wine has a long history and the vine was cultivated in Britain in very early times. The Romans had vineyards in this country, and the *win-wringa* or wine-press was in existence in Anglo-Saxon times. In many monasteries grapes were grown and wine made, though perhaps its quality would not suit the educated palate of a modern judge of good wine, being somewhat sour and weak owing to the lack of sun and bad weather of our English climate. Sometimes as at Abingdon in Berkshire, a street or lane is still called the Vineyard. There was a vineyard in the Tower of London. The exact birthday of the Vintners is not known, but their trade must have been in existence for a very long period,

THE CITY COMPANIES

far longer than the actual date of their charter. Stow informs us that they were anciently known as the Merchant-Vintners or Wine-Tunners of Gascoyne, and are so named in the records of Edward II and Edward III. Indeed, the connection between England and Gascony is earlier still, and dates back to the marriage of Henry II with Eleanor of Acquitaine, which laid the foundation of our traffic for wines with Bordeaux. The Vintners were divided into two classes, the Vinetarii and the Tabernarii. The former were importers of wine, great merchants who lived in stately stone houses in the Vintry adjoining the wine wharves. There Sir John Giser, Vintner and Lord Mayor and Constable of the Tower, dwelt, and Henry Picard's mansion was in Three Cranes Lane, and Stodie's in Broad Street, one of the roads leading to the wharf, and so called because it was wider than the others. The Tabernarii were a lower class of men, and were keepers of taverns, inns and cook-shops, over whom the Vinetarii exercised a severe and constant control.

Long before the first Charter was granted, the ships of the Vintners and the merchants of Bordeaux could be seen sailing up the Thames and anchoring off Botolph Wharf, near Billingsgate, which Edward I granted to the Vintners for the landing of their tuns of wine, the Company paying a silver penny as an acknowledgment. The King profited by the coming of the vessels,

THE VINTNERS' COMPANY

as he was entitled to two tuns for his own use
out of every cargo. The wines that came to
London port were sack, beloved of Falstaff,
styled so subtly " Sir John Sack-and-Sugar,"
and who exclaimed " If sack and sugar be a
fault, God help the wicked "; and Canary, or
sweet sack, the grape of which was brought from
the Canaries, " that marvellous searching wine,"
and Malmsey, in a butt of which the Duke of
Clarence was foully drowned. The prices were
limited. Gascoyne wines were sold not above
4d. a gallon, nor Rhenish wines above 6d.,
when the Third Edward reigned. Other wines
which came to Botolph Wharf were Muscatell,
a very rich wine ; Date wine, which was a sort
of Rhenish ; Stum, a strong new wine ; Alicant,
a Spanish wine and made of mulberries ; Sherry,
the original sack, but not sweet ; and Rumney,
a sort of Spanish wine. Sack was a term loosely
applied at first to all white wine. It was probably
those species of wines that Fitzstephens, the monk
of St. Bartholomew's, Smithfield, in the reign of
Henry II, mentions to have been sold in the
ships, and in the wine-cellars near the public
place of cookery on the Thames bank.

The exact date of the Charter granted to the
Vintners has been much in dispute among our
earlier antiquaries. Stow and Anthony Munday
contended that their first Charter was given by
Edward III in 1365, but this it was asserted was
not a regular Charter, but one authorizing them

237

to carry on an exclusive trade to Gascony for the importation of wines. However, I think it may be concluded that Edward III's Charter was a real incorporation which was confirmed by Henry VI, entitled "incorporation of the Vintners of London," that being a re-incorporation with the granting of several new privileges. The following is the text of the

Charter, 15th King Henry 6th, dated 23rd August, 1437.

"Henry, by the Grace of God, King of England and France, and Lord of Ireland, to all to whom these presents shall come, greeting : Know ye that we, of our special grace, have granted to the freemen of the mistery of Vintners of the City of London, that the mistery aforesaid and all the men of the same from henceforth may and shall be in dux, and in name, one body and one perpetual Company, and that the same Company every year shall and may chuse, and make out of themselves, four Masters or Wardens, to oversee, rule, and govern the mistery and commonalty aforesaid, and all men and business of the same for ever, and that the same masters, or wardens, and commonalty shall and may have perpetual succession, and that they and their successors have a common seal, to serve for the business of the said commonalty and that they and their successors for ever shall and may be persons able and capable in law to purchase and possess in

THE VINTNERS' COMPANY

fee perpetuity, lands, tenements, rents, and other possessions whatsoever ; and that they the wardens, by the name of the master or wardens of the commonalty and mistery of Vintners aforesaid, shall be able to implead or be impleaded before any judge whatsoever in any action whatsoever. And further, of our abundant grace we have granted that the master, or wardens, and commonalty of the said mistery shall be able to purchase lands, tenements, and rents within the City of London, and suburbs of the same, which are held of us, to the value of twenty pounds a year, to be had and holden to them and their successors for ever, towards the better support, as well to the poor men of the said commonalty as of one chapel, to celebrate divine service for ever daily, for our state whilst we live, and for our soul when we are departed, and for the souls of all our ancestors, as also for the state and souls of the men of the said mistery and commonalty, and the souls of all the faithful deceased, according to the ordinances of the said masters or wardens and commonalty in this behalf to be made, the statute of lands and tenements not to be purchased in mortmain, made, or to be ordained notwithstanding. In witness whereof we have caused these our letters to be made patent. Witness ourself at our Castle of Kenilworth, the twenty-third day of August, in the fifteenth year of our reign."

Such is the document. It may seem to us very

239

trifling and insignificant and somewhat verbose. But it was very precious to the Vintners and the forerunner of several other similar Royal decrees. The above was the second Charter granted by Henry VI, a former one granted in the sixth year of that monarch being an inspeximus Charter headed "ample confirmation for the Merchant Vintners of London of their liberties." Edward VI caused the Company some trouble as his Parliament passed an Act limiting the number of taverns and inns and greatly injuring their trade. The tavern-keepers were limited to 40, in York to eight, and in other cities in like proportion. So when his brief reign was over they besieged the ear of Queen Mary, who listened to their grievances and tried to remedy them by issuing letters patent. They were, however, still harassed by actions and proceedings inimical to their business, so another Charter was sought and granted by Philip and Mary which allowed them to conduct their trade according to the ancient liberties, franchises, and customs of the City of London, notwithstanding the same statute. This Charter was renewed by Queen Elizabeth and by James I, who added to their privileges and gave them additional rights. It is curious to note that after the severe restrictions on the sale of drink ordered by Parliament in the reign of Edward VI, the pendulum swung the other way, and the Vintners made great complaints to Queen Elizabeth, because "large multitudes did

THE VINTNERS' COMPANY

daily set up taverns, not only such as neither were
nor ought to be allowed by the said licence, but
also foreigners and strangers, and in excessive
numbers to the great hurt of the common weal
and the manifest peril of bringing the whole
licence into question." So the Queen granted her
Charter and the monopoly of the Vintners was
again safeguarded.

Reverting to the course of the fraternity's
history, we must refer to the Grant of Arms.
According to Maitland these were given by
Clarencieux, King at Arms in the year 1442,
but according to a Visitation Book of the Heralds,
the date is stated to have been September 17th,
1447, and subsequently confirmed by Thomas
Benolt, Clarencieux, in the 22nd year of Henry
VIII. They consist of " Sable, a chevron cetu,
three tuns argent, with a Bacchus for a crest."
As early as the time of the Third Edward, the
Company became wealthy and important. They
contributed a much larger sum of money to
the King for the French wars than did many of
the other Gilds, and sent six members to the
Common Council of the City, quite as many as
the most important Companies.

The Vintners exercised severe control, as I
have said, over the tavern-keepers, and made
strong regulations against fraud. They were very
strict about the early closing of inns and taverns,
and as soon as the curfew sounded all had to be
closed under a penalty of half a mark. They

241   Q

THE CITY COMPANIES

appointed four officers who were required to
inspect all taverns. Customers were to be allowed
to see their wine drawn from the cask, lest they
should be defrauded by having bad liquor served
to them, as some rascally taverners did not scruple
to sell droppings from the taps of the casks and
lees and putrid liquor, or good wine mixed with
dregs instead of sound wine. Such persons were
severely punished. No taverner was allowed to
have a cloth or curtain hung before the door of
his cellar in order that his customers might see
the wine drawn direct from the cask. There was
a case in 1364 when a certain John Penrose was
found guilty of selling unsound and unwholesome wine in the tavern of William Doget in
Estchepe, " to the deceit of the common people,
the contempt of the King, to the shameful disgrace of the officers of the City, and to the
grievous damage of the community " ; this
punishment was severe and ingeniously " fitted
the crime." He was imprisoned a year and a day
and had to drink a draught of the bad wine, and
to have the rest poured over his head, and to
forswear the calling of a Vintner in the City of
London for ever. Another pleasant method was
to place the casks of condemned wine in the
streets, break their heads, and cause the liquor
to run through the City like a stream of rain-
water, in the sight of the people " whence there
often issued a most loathsome savour." This
was inflicted on the Lombards, who were found

242

THE VINTNERS' COMPANY

guilty of corrupting their sweet wine. The Vintners also provided a means of punishment in their Hall, where they kept a movable pair of stocks for refractory taverners and 'prentices.

Another duty devolving upon the Vintners was the overseeing and regulation of measures used in their trade. Foreigners were not allowed to sell their wines in retail—that was the Company's monopoly, but only in gross, and the measures used were the tun, pipe, and hogshead, which is a corruption of oxhide. Sometimes by fraud these measures were found to be defective, and also the drinking vessels used by the taverners. Hence the officials of the Company were called upon to examine these and to protect the public from wrong measure. They had also to grant a licence to a tavern-keeper before he was allowed to set up his shop, and used to be very careful in considering whether the site was convenient and suitable, and in granting new licences. Thus, on one occasion, in 1629, Nicholas Banaster wished to start a tavern in his house. The warden and others went to view the same, but they did not approve. They found that the position was not in any way suitable, as it was near certain alleys, in a back place which lent itself to secret wickednesses, debauchery and drunkenness. Also it had a bowling alley and a pair of butts where poor people will spend their thrift and cause brawls. Bowling and archery one would imagine were harmless sports ; but

243

THE CITY COMPANIES

the City authorities also seem to have set their faces against them, and if an apprentice was in the habit of frequenting such places, he was duly censured and punished.

The Vintners had many things to contend against. Sometimes royalty interfered with their monopoly by appointing some Court favourite to issue and grant licences, as did Queen Elizabeth to Sir Walter Raleigh. Their trade was heavily taxed. Monarchs demanded loans. Charles II seized their Charters under the *Quo warranto* proceedings, but these were restored to them by James II when he found his sceptre slipping from his feeble grasp, and confirmed by William and Mary, who thought it wise to conciliate the City and the Companies. Since that exciting period their history has been smooth. They have diligently carried out their trusts, supported all good causes, kept their feasts and their pageants and tried to do their duty.

I must describe one of their pageants which was held at the beginning of the reign of Queen Anne, when Sir Samuel Dashwood, a distinguished member of the fraternity, became Lord Mayor, who afterwards entertained the Queen to a banquet in the Hall. It must be premised that St. Martin is the patron saint of the Vintners, who so charitably divided his cloak with a beggar. The Lord Mayor was first saluted by the Artillery Company, at whose head rode St. Martin on a stately white steed richly plumed and caparisoned ;

THE VINTNERS' COMPANY

himself armed *cap à pie*, having a large mantle or scarf of scarlet. He was followed by several cripples and beggars supplicating his charity, attended by twenty satyrs dancing before him with tambors, two persons in rich livery walking beside his horse, ten halberdiers with rural music before them, and ten old Roman lictors in silver head-pieces with axes and fasces, all marching before the Company to St. Paul's Churchyard, and there making a stand. The beggars cry, and to silence them the saint severs his scarf with his sword, and delivers to them a part. A vineyard, the Triumph of Bacchus, and other scenes, complete the pageant.

THE HALL

Stow, and his continuator Strype, inform us that the Vintners dwelt in that part of London which is called the Vintry, and that " Sir John Stodie in 1357, a Vintner, gave it with all the quadrant wherein Vintners' Hall now stands, with the tenements round about, unto the Vintners ; the Vintners built for themselves a fair Hall, and also thirteen almshouses for thirteen poor people which are kept of charity rent free."

As I have to relate, somewhat monotonously, the Great Fire swept this away, and the Company had to resort to inns for their meetings, the " Bell " in St. Nicholas Lane and the " Fleece " in Cornhill being their houses of refuge. The

245

THE CITY COMPANIES

ruins of the Hall had scarcely become cool when they began to rebuild it, and it was ready for use in 1671. It was a large edifice built of brick. The hall itself was paved with marble and richly wainscoted with fine carvings. There is a grand screen at the east end and figures of Bacchus with fauns and St. Martin and the cripple and the coats of arms of the Masters of the Company. There is an interesting list of the distinguished members who have had the honour to be Lord Mayor ; which list carries us back to very early times as we find the name of John Adrian who was Mayor in 1270. The Master's chair has been used for centuries, as fortunately it escaped the Great Fire. I have wandered through the Court and other rooms of this princely palace of the Vintners and observed their pictures and portraits, and the charming carvings of Grinling Gibbons, Rubens' splendid painting of St. Martin dividing his coat with the beggar, the royal portraits of Charles II, James II, William III and Queen Mary, and many other treasures. The Vintners have often been honoured by royal personages accepting their Livery, and I believe the last was H.R.H. the late Duke of Albany.

When I began this record of the Vintners I said their Company is a home of old customs. Two have been mentioned and a third remains. When one dines with the Vintners and when the toast of the Company is proposed, it is greeted with " five times five " cheers. This custom dates

246

THE VINTNERS' COMPANY

back to the time of Edward III, when Sir Henry Picard, Lord Mayor in 1356 and Master in 1363, had the honour of entertaining five kings, namely: Edward of England, David of Scotland, John of France, the King of Denmark and the King of Cyprus. It is curious that this event should have been held in remembrance five and a half centuries. The conduct of Picard and the unsportsmanlike character of His Majesty of Cyprus after this famous dinner are worthy of notice. The host and King played at dice and hazard together and the King of Cyprus lost fifty marks and was much annoyed, or as the chronicler states "took it in ill part." But Picard said, "My Lord, be not aggrieved; I covet not your gold, but your play ; for I have not bidde you hither that I might grieve you, but that amongst other things I might try your play," and then gave him his money again.

The Vintners are one of the six Companies who have retained their funeral state palls. It is made of cloth of gold with purple pile. Figures of St. Martin as a soldier and as Bishop of Tours, in each case with the familiar beggar-man and a Pieta and Death adorn the sides, and a rich tracery pattern occupies the centre of the pall.

A very remarkable piece of tapestry is preserved in the Hall. It is not known how it came into the possession of the Vintners. It is probably of English manufacture and of the date 1466, or not later. We see St. Martin performing his

247

THE CITY COMPANIES

charitable act, St. Dunstan saying Mass, and listening to an angel choir singing the Kyrie with additional notes and to an air before unknown. A scroll held by two angels reveals the notation of the music which is still to be found in the Sarum Missal as St. Dunstan's Kyrie. A monk, holding the Archbishop's cross, stands before the saint, and the people are waiting in surprise at the long pause in the service, for the angels' song is by them unheard. The black-letter inscription below desires the prayers of the faithful for the souls of John Bate and Johanna, his wife, and states that it was given in 1466 by their son, Walter Hertford, who was a monk at Canterbury. It seems to have been intended for a reredos for an altar, and is said to have been worked by nuns. It is one of the greatest curiosities of its kind in this country.

The Vintners with the Dyers and the Crown, own the swans on the Thames from time immemorial. The earliest record of this is a charge recorded in their books for " upping of swans " in 1509. One of their Company is appointed yearly as Swan Master, and he, with the herdsman and those of the Crown and the Dyers, make an expedition once a year to mark the cygnets with the swan-mark of the Company. The possession of a swan-mark has always been regarded as a token of high rank and dignity. In recent years the form of the mark has been changed. The Society for the Prevention of

A VIEW of CHEAPSIDE, as it appears on LORD MAYORS DAY [left]

THE VINTNERS' COMPANY

Cruelty to Animals interfered some years ago, and asserted that the old mark inflicted suffering on the birds. This the swan-herdsmen of the Companies and the Crown denied. However to satisfy the Society's officials a slight modification was made.

In accordance with the duties performed by other fraternities, the care of the poor members of the Gild has always been a matter of concern to the Vintners. In former days they had a set of almshouses nigh their Hall which Guy Shuldam devised to the Company in 1446. These were destroyed in the Great Fire, and instead of rebuilding them on the same site, they erected others in the Mile End Road. These were pulled down at the beginning of the last century and rebuilt by Benjamin Kenton, who rose from the position of a poor boy to a man of great wealth and was a most generous benefactor of the Company. Other generous members have also bestowed much wealth for the comforts of the almsfolk. An account of the Vintners' treasures will be found in the last chapter of this work.

XVI.   THE CLOTHWORKERS'
✿   ✿   COMPANY

THE Clothworkers' Company is the last of the famous Twelve, and has a distinguished record of good work faithfully performed, and a notable history which it is not easy to trace, as the clothworkers were concerned with all the trades connected with the making of cloth, its fabrication, finishing and vending of the same. The cloth trade was the most important industry in the country, and wool was declared to be " the flower and strength and revenue and blood of England." It rendered the country prosperous and the farmers used to say :

> " I thank my God and ever shal,
> It was the sheep which paid for al."

The English fleeces brought wealth to England, and no wonder that in the grand pageant of the Company the Clothworkers chose Jason for their hero, who slew the dragon and won the golden fleece, and as Elkanah Settle, who was an adept at cunningly devised phrases, said in his own quaint and elaborate style :

> " The grandeur of England is to be attributed to its golden fleece, the wealth of the loom making England a second Peru, and the back of the sheep, and not the entrails of the earth, being its chief mine of riches.   The silkworm is no spinster of ours, and our wheel and web are wholly the

CLOTHWORKERS' COMPANY

clothworkers. Thus as trade is the soul of the kingdom, so the greatest brand of it lies in the clothworkers' hands ; and, though our naval commerce brings us in both the *or* and the *argent*, and, indeed, the whole wealth of the world, yet, when thoroughly examined, it will be found 'tis your cloth sends out to fetch them. And whilst the Imperial Britannia is so formidable to her foes, and so potent to her friends, her strength and her power, when duly considered, to the clothworkers' honour it may be said, 'tis your shuttle nerves her arm and your woof that enrobes her glory."

Thus does Master Settle ennoble and glorify this ancient Company. How ancient the trade is it is difficult to determine. Weaving cloth was known in prehistoric times. The Romans taught us the art of weaving, and had woollen factories here. Cloth woven in this country had a high reputation abroad, especially the product of the Winchester looms. The wool of Britain is often said to have been spun so fine that it is in a manner comparable to the spider's thread. Thomas Deloney in his fanciful romance entitled *The Pleasant History of Thomas of Reading or the Sixe Worthie Yeomen of the West*, tells a story which, if we might take it as evidence of the state of the industry in the time of Henry I (an assumption which is scarcely warrantable) might prove that in that reign the trade was very flourishing. The hero of the tale is Thomas Cole, clothmaker of Reading, whose numerous wains laden with cloth arrested the progress of

251

the King and divers of his nobility as they rode
from London towards Wales. He demanded of
the drivers whose wains they were. They
answered " Cole's of Reading." The King was
much interested in his " worthy yeoman," and
when he died he desired to be buried near his
good clothiers " who, living, were his heart's
delight." He was buried in Reading Abbey.

Deloney was a greater authority on the condition of the trade in his own time than in previous centuries. He lived in reigns of the later
Tudors, and his description of the clothing
industry may be taken as fairly accurate. " The
art," he says, " was held in high reputation both
in respect of the great riches that thereby were
gotten, as of the benefit it brought to the commonwealth. Among all crafts this was the only chief,
for that it was the greatest merchandise, by the
which our country became famous throughout
all nations. And it was wisely thought that the
one-half of the people in the land lived in those
days thereby, and in such good sort, that in the
commonwealth there were few or no beggars
at all ; poor people whom God had blessed with
most children did by means of this occupation
so order them that when they were come to five
or seven years of age they were able to get their
own bread. Therefore it was not without cause
that clothiers were then both honoured and
loved."

In early times the cloth woven in England was

very coarse, very different from the produce of the Flemish looms, and English wool was exported in large quantities to Flanders where it was in great demand, and to the London merchants was granted the sole privilege of exporting woollen cloth. Edward III conferred a great benefit on the English trade by importing from Flanders weavers and dyers and fullers, and prohibited the exportation of English wool abroad, in order to foster the home industry. In the 14th and 15th centuries our clothiers and clothworkers were very prosperous. Men like " Jack of Newbury " or John Winchcomb, were very wealthy, and often spent their wealth in good works, building churches and almshouses and schools in their native towns and villages, whence as poor boys they had been sent as apprentices to London, and there made their fortunes. In the Cotswolds and East Anglia there are many evidences of their bounty. Newbury Church was built by the famous " Jack." Fairford, remarkable for its wondrous stained-glass windows erected by Sir John Tame, Lechlade and many others might be mentioned. The wool staple was fixed at certain places. Staple Inn in London at the entrance to the City from the West Country was originally the Staple for London, and Calais owned by England, was the great staple for exported goods. It is noticeable that the highest dignity of the legal profession is the woolsack.

Cloth Fair, in Smithfield, was the chief place

THE CITY COMPANIES

where cloth was sold. It was first established by
Henry II. The several processes of the manufacture of cloth necessitated the existence of
various trades, and each trade had its own Gild
or Company. There were fullers and sheermen,
and burrellers, and testers, and dyers, all connected with the making of cloth, and all of them
seem to have sprung from the ancient Gild of the
Tellarii, or woollen weavers. The Gild of the
latter is very old, and still exists as a separate
Company. It possesses a Charter under the seal
of Henry II granted " to their gild to be had in
London with all the liberties and customs which
they had in the time of Henry my grandfather."
Hence it must have been in existence in the time
of Henry I (1100-1135) and probably, like the
Saddlers, had a pre-Conquest origin. They
resided in Spitalfields and plied their looms and
sang songs as they wove. Shakespeare makes
Falstaff say, " I would I were a weaver ; I could
sing all manner of songs."

The burrellers, mentioned above, were engaged
in the measuring and inspection of cloth. The
width of cloth was ordered to be two ells wide
from list to list, which were termed *burrells*.
The Clothworkers' Gild was formed by the union
of the two first-mentioned fraternities, the Fullers
and Sheermen, while the Burrellers and Testers
were absorbed by the Drapers' and Merchant
Taylors' Companies, the Dyers preserving their
own individuality. Sheermen's Hall stood in

CLOTHWORKERS' COMPANY

Mincing Lane on the same site as Clothworkers' Hall stands to-day, having been granted to the former by one John Badby in the names of John Hungerford and other Sheermen of London. This took place in the time of Henry VI and Henry VII granted to them a Charter of incorporation. Fullers' Hall was in Billiter Street, and the members plied their craft in Whitechapel, that district being known as " Villa Beata Maria de Matfellon." The derivation of " Matfellon " is rather puzzling, but I find that it takes its name from a herb called " matfellon," or fuller's teasle, which was much used by the fullers in their industry and grew extensively in a field nigh their tenter grounds. The Royal grant was bestowed upon his beloved lieges who were authorized " to found to the praise and honour of God and the most glorious Virgin Mary, His Mother, a certain fraternity, or perpetual gild of the men of the mystery of Fullers."

So the Sheermen and the Fullers preserved their separate existence until the reign of Henry VIII who gave them a Charter which grants that the said mysteries shall thenceforward become one entire art or mystery, and that in future they shall be one perpetual commonalty by the name of Clothworkers only and no other. Their complete title was henceforward to be " The Masters, Wardens, and Commonalty of the Gild or Fraternity of the Assumption of the Blessed Virgin of the Art or Mystery of the Clothworkers

255

THE CITY COMPANIES

of the City of London." The usual privileges
were assigned to the united Company of holding
land, electing the governing body, having a
livery which must be changed each year or on
alternate years, the right of search over denizens
or aliens, the punishment of offenders, and the
prevention of foreigners plying their trade unless
they became members of the Company.

This Charter was confirmed by subsequent
monarchs. Charles II was rather troublesome
to the Clothworkers, somewhat restraining their
privileges, claiming the right to elect the officers,
and as a safeguard of his throne, requiring the
officials to take the oaths of supremacy and
allegiance. The " Merry Monarch " was never
very considerate of the feelings of the Companies
as evinced by his *Quo· warranto* proceedings,
and proved himself most ungrateful for the large
sums extracted from them by his predecessors.
Perhaps he remembered that the City in the years
of the Civil War favoured for the most part the
Parliamentary Party, although the people welcomed cordially the Restoration, and General
Monk, the hero of the piece, they feasted royally
in their Halls, as did the Clothworkers. The
speech that was made to him on that occasion is
still in existence and was published in a broadside. Nor was James II more obliging until
certain events in his brief reign compelled him to
curry favour with these powerful bodies ; while
for the same reason the victorious Prince of

CLOTHWORKERS' COMPANY

Orange when he ascended the throne of England, restored their Charters and privileges.

Our study of the Charters has drawn us away from the general history of this fraternity. When it embarked upon its career as a joint Company of Sheermen and Fullers and received the Charter of Henry VIII, a new set of Ordinances was drawn up, and it is interesting to note that these were signed and approved by Sir Thomas More, Lord Chancellor and one of the martyrs of ruthless Henry's rule. Long extracts from these are given in Herbert's *History of the City Companies.* They have the usual features which we have already marked in the records of other fraternities, and we can attend in imagination the annual assemblies, the procession to church attired in new liveries, the election of the Master and Wardens, the presentation of the yearly accounts by the Clerk, the flocking of their poor folk to the Hall to receive their relief, the stately funerals of deceased members, the abundant feasts, the examining and punishment of refractory apprentices in a manner which we have already described, and correcting the manners of unworthy seniors who were guilty of rioting or insubordinate behaviour to the Master or Wardens or unbecoming conduct unworthy of a Clothworker. The civilizing influence of female society was recognized, and " sisters " were welcomed as members as in some of the other fraternities.

The pride of place amongst the Companies

257   R

we have seen evinced in other cases when these bodies struggled for precedence and fights and riots ensued. There was much feeling and severe contests between the Clothworkers or Shearmen and the Dyers as to their position in the " guyings (disguising) in all processions, as also other guyings, standyngs, and rydyngs." As we examine the lists and order of the Companies, we notice many divergences. The Dyers often rode, or processed, or had their standings before the Shearmen or Clothworkers, as did the Merchant Taylors before the Skinners, or the Grocers before the Mercers. However, at last peace was restored in the time of Henry VIII, when Sir William Boteler was Lord Mayor when the fellowship of the Dyers consented " lovingly and charitably to follow the Clothworkers without any further strife or debate," and while the Clothworkers became last of the great Companies, the Dyers consented to come after them and be the first of the minor fellowships. This certainly speaks well for the good spirit and friendly feeling of the Dyers. The Shearmen were very jealous of their rank and status, and this is further exemplified by their conduct with regard to the election of Alderman Bayley to the Mayoralty. It was and is the custom for a candidate for that high position, being a member of a minor Company, to join one of the major ones. So this worthy Alderman sought the membership of the Drapers. This enraged the

CLOTHWORKERS' COMPANY

Shearmen, who said that their Company was quite as good as any other, stated that Bayley had declared that he would live and die a true Shearman, and proceeded to insult him, charge him with perjury, and made a great disturbance. However, the instigators were brought before the Court of Aldermen, and punished by fine and imprisonment.

James I was interested in this Company and became a freeman, and they joined in his Ulster Plantation Scheme, their land then being named the " Clothworkers' Manor." It was for many years a great burden to them, but it is now sold.

THE HALL

As I have already stated, the Hall stood in Mincing Lane and was the home of the Shearmen while the Fullers had theirs in Billiter Street. After the amalgamation of the two Companies under the title of Clothworkers, the Mincing Lane Hall became the possession of the united fraternities. It was used for the usual meetings of the Masters, Wardens and Livery and assistants, wherein they transacted the affairs of the Company, and had their feasts. The ordinary freemen, called also yeomanry, and their wives, caused some trouble by objecting to the autocracy of the governing body, and there were often disputes. However, the use of the Hall was granted to the freemen for their sports, recreations, and assemblies on condition that they behaved

259

well and showed respect to the Masters, Wardens
and Fellowship. Hence it was the scene of many
bright social gatherings. In the map of Agas
(1560) a rude sketch appears showing its proxi-
mity to the Church of All Hallows Stayning.
Nothing else is known of it. It was partially
destroyed by the Great Fire. Far be it from us to
question the usual accuracy of Samuel Pepys,
but in the case of this building he was somewhat
misled. He wrote in his *Diary* : " But strange it
is to see Clothworkers' Hall on fire these three
days and nights in one body of flame, it having
the cellars full of oyle." However, it seems only
to have been much injured, as the *Gazette* of
September 8th, 1666, announces that the fire
stopped near Clothworkers' Hall in Mincing
Lane. Two years later it was in danger again
from another fire.

In 1708 the Hall was restored and we learn
from Hatton's *New View* what it was like. He
describes it as " a noble rich building. The Hall
is a lofty room, adorned with wainscot to the
ceiling, where is a curious fretwork. The screen
at the south end is of oak, adorned with four
pilasters, their entablature and compass pediment
of the Corinthian order, enriched with their
arms, palm-branches, etc. The west end is
adorned with the figures of King James and
King Charles I, richly carved as big as life in
their robes, with regalia all gilt and gold, where
is a spacious window of stained glass, and the

CLOTHWORKERS' COMPANY

Queen's arms. Also those of Sir John Robinson, Knight and baronet, His Majesty's lieutenant of the Tower of London, Lord Mayor of this honourable City, *anno* 1663, and president of the Artillery Company, who kept his mayoralty in this Hall, in which year their majesties (Charles II), Queen and Queen-Mother, and their Royal Highnesses the Duke and Duchess of York, and towards the re-edifying of this Hall a worthy benefactor. His coat of arms, 6th and 4th gules and or quarterly embattled, the 2nd and 3rd vert semi of trefoils, a buck trippant or ; and the like buck for a crest."

Samuel Pepys was an honoured member of the Company and Master and benefactor. His arms appeared in a window, and those of William Howard, Master and benefactor, 1687, Sir Joseph Williamson, Knight, Master, 1676, a privy councillor and Secretary of State, and also the arms of the Company, which are : " Sable a chevron ermin between habiceks in chief argent and a tassel (or thistle) in base or ; crest, a ram passant or; supporters 2 griffins or pelleted. Motto : ' My trust is in God alone.' " The outside of the Hall must have been curious and remarkable. It was adorned with curious brick fluted columns with Corinthian capitals of stone.

The present Hall was built in 1859, and is worthy of the greatness of the Company. The entrance is very fine ; a wide stone staircase leads to the Hall itself, and the roof is supported

261

THE CITY COMPANIES

by Corinthian columns. In the binding-room, where men and women are made free of the Company, there are copies of the documents conferring the freedom of the Company on Prince Albert, the late Duke of Devonshire, the Duke of Leeds, Baroness Burdett-Coutts, Lord Kelvin, the late Lord Dufferin, the late Rt. Hon. W. E. Forster, and other distinguished members. The Court Room contains portraits of William Hewett, Lord Mayor in 1559 ; Sir J. Musgrove, Lord Mayor in 1851 ; William Lamb, Master in 1569, the founder of the Grammar School at Sutton Valence and a great benefactor (Lambs-Conduit Street is named after him) ; Sir Edward Osborne, Lord Mayor in 1583 ; Thomas William Wing, a worthy benefactor who in 1889 left £70,000 for blind persons ; Sir Owen Roberts, F.S.A., the late esteemed Clerk of the Company, whose acquaintance I had the honour of making when I was exploring the annals of the Companies, and whose name is associated with so many schemes of public benevolence and educational enterprise. He lived to a great age and for very many years guided the affairs of the Clothworkers in the management of their great estates. Some of the glass with arms from the old Hall is placed in the windows, and also the arms of William Hewers, Master in 1686, who acted as clerk to Pepys. The Hall itself is a noble room lighted by five windows. The royal statues from the old Hall are placed here.

CLOTHWORKERS' COMPANY

Massive pillars support the arches of the roof, and the ceiling is adorned with paintings.

Happily, some of the old books have been preserved and it is intensely interesting to browse among the papers. Here are some of the items :

> " 1553-4 Towards suppression of Sir Thomas Wyatt's rebellion, £28 10s. 4d.
>
> 1555-7 Setting forth soldiers about the Queen's affairs and business.
>
> £47 for the protection of Queen Mary and her Spanish husband.
>
> £137 for a Show before Queen Elizabeth at Greenwich."

There is a melancholy Court Minute in 1643, which records the misfortunes attending the Civil War " and the sad state " of the Company when " on account of the many great pressing and urgent occasions which they have for money as well for the payment of their debts and the danger of the City by reason of the great distractions and civil wars of this kingdom," so that they were obliged to sell their plate. But they determined to preserve the names of the donors, to the end that the same plate " might be repaired and made good *in statu quo* when God shall enable this Company so to do." A subsequent Court Minute shows that 2,068 ounces of plate were sold, and 1,239 ounces retained by the Company. Happily in recent times the intentions of the Court in 1643 have been carried out, and a silver salver purchased and en-

263

graved with the names of the donors of the plate sold.

The rejoicings of the Restoration are set forth in the entry :

> 1660. Thanksgiving at S. Paul's 5 May 1660 : to put out and remove the arms of the Commonwealth, and to set in their stead the Arms of His Majesty.

> 1661. Proportion for Building the Pageants on the King's passing through the City from the Tower to Whitehall, £530.

We should refer to many other items, but time and space forbid. The Company is blessed with a large income which they expend with extraordinary wisdom. Scholarships at Oxford and Cambridge, and also at many colleges and schools for women and girls are only a few of their minor charges. Naturally they take much interest in the industry, with which their Company is associated. They built the Clothworkers' Wing of the Yorkshire College, Leeds, comprising the textile industries, dyeing and art departments, and equipped it at a cost of £70,000, with an endowment of £4,000 per annum. The City and Guilds of London Institute has received £100,000 and an annual subscription of £4,000. Far and wide does their generosity extend for technical schools. I may mention a few of them : Huddersfield, Halifax, Keighley, Dewsbury, Salt, Bingley, Wakefield, University College, Bristol,

CLOTHWORKERS' COMPANY

Trowbridge and Westbury (Wilts.), Stroud, Glasgow, and numerous Polytechnics in London. They are the governors of the Grammar School of Sutton Valence, in Kent, founded by William Lamb in 1576. The endowment is only £30 a year which they supplement by more than £1,000 a year, besides spending on the buildings £20,000. Philip Christian bequeathed £20 a year for a school at Peel, in the Isle of Man. Recently they have spent £10,000 on new school buildings.

The Company does not forget their poorer members. In old times they had a set of almshouses in Whitefriars on part of a garden belonging to Margaret, Countess of Kent, who held the ground under a demise from the Prior of the Friary. The Countess, who was a free sister of the Clothworkers, bequeathed some property to them for the support of her almshouses. In 1640, John Heath founded a set at Islington for the support of decayed members of the Company. In 1871 new almshouses were erected in Islington at a cost of over £8,000. The blind find in the Company a most generous friend, and as I have said Mr. T. W. Wing left £70,000 for their benefit, of which the Company are trustees.

It is impossible in this brief sketch to enumerate all the activities and charitable work of this munificent Company, which are so far-reaching and extensive. As I have written before in my former book on the subject of the Companies' charities, I may be allowed to repeat :

265

THE CITY COMPANIES

" For more than four centuries they have carried on their noble work : in every age they have done their utmost to promote the interests of the trade with which they are associated ; they have protected the clothworker, and have not forgotten the clothwearer ; and, while they have preserved their ancient inheritance and time-honoured institutions, they have not omitted to show themselves alive to the spirit of the age, and ready to adapt themselves to new schemes and new requirements. Bound by no iron fetters of custom and obsolete enactment, they have shown themselves to be free to reform themselves by a gradual process, and capable of active movement with the times in which they live, ever preparing new paths for continued progress, ever devising new schemes for the profit and benefit of mankind. This is the only kind of reform which all great institutions need."

XVII. THE MINOR
COMPANIES

I T would have been a pleasant task to revisit all the Halls of the so-called Minor Companies of London and to have recalled their histories, each one of which presents features of special interest. Indeed the term " Minor Companies " is almost a misnomer, as several of them are in wealth, dignity, antiquity and importance, in no way inferior to the leading Twelve. The annals of several date back to very early times, for example the Saddlers can boast of an Anglo-Saxon foundation. They possess Halls which can rival many which we have seen during our peregrinations through the City and possess plate and other treasures which rival the possessions of their greater brethren. Others are small, and have no Hall. The trades represented by several of the Minor Companies are entirely obsolete, such as the Bowyers, Framework Knitters, Horners, Stringers, Fletchers, etc.; whereas those of others are extraordinarily active. Of course the connexion of the trade with the Company is slight, and only a few members, if any, belong professionally to the craft which the guild nominally represents : although the Companies endeavour to promote the welfare of the trade with which nominally their gild is associated. It is not from any lack of regard and appreciation that we are compelled to give only a brief description of the work and history of the " Minor

267

THE CITY COMPANIES

Companies." There are still some sixty-four of these fraternities; a record of the annals of each would require a much larger work than is here intended, and I must content myself with furnishing only a resumé of the story of these lesser gilds, although many of them are fully entitled to a much longer description. Their names and titles are arranged in alphabetical order, and the question of precedence does not arise. And so with many apologies to these Minor Companies and especially to the greater of these lesser fraternities, we begin our records.

The Apothecaries have a charming little Hall in Blackfriars, and have for centuries waged war against unsound medicines and ignorant quacks. They would not allow anyone to " use or exercise any drug, simples, or compounds, or any kynde or sorte of poticarie wares, but such as shall be pure and perfyt good." Their good work continues. The Armourers and Braziers' Company performed useful duties in the days when the lives of knights and warriors depended on the good and true work of the makers of armour. They have an interesting modern Hall containing a good collection of their wares. The Bakers' Company is an ancient corporation, and received its Charter in 1307. The Barbers, or Barber Surgeons, were incorporated in 1461, but they existed at least a century earlier. They combined the skill of " healing wounds, blows and other infirmities, as in letting of blood and drawing

THE MINOR COMPANIES

teeth," with that of shaving, and no one was allowed to perform these duties unless he was a member of the Company. In their Hall they have the well-known picture of King Henry VIII granting a Charter to Barber Surgeons in 1540. The Blacksmiths have a long history, dating back to their incorporation by Edward III in 1325. They combined the trade of makers of ironwork with that of Dentists and Clockmakers, and were by Queen Elizabeth united with the Spurriers, or makers of spurs. The motto of the Bowyers' Company, " Crecy, Poictiers, Agincourt," tells of the prowess of our English archers when archery was the national pastime of Englishmen, as well as their support in war. Other allied crafts were connected with the bowyers' art, including the Stringers, or long bow string makers, and the Fletchers, who made the arrows. The Gild of the latter still exists, and forms one of our minor Companies. The Brewers were in existence in 1418, and were incorporated by Henry VI. The Broiderers, or makers of embroidery, flourished in the fourteenth century, and with them were united the Tapissers, or tapestry makers ; their artistic skill was remarkable, and the funeral palls still in the possession of the Merchant Taylors, the Vintners, and Fishmongers, are evidences of their excellent workmanship.

The Carpenters' Company ranks high among its fellows, and has a very interesting history.

269

THE CITY COMPANIES

Its first Charter was granted by Edward IV in 1477, but it existed years before, as Chaucer witnesses :

"An Haverdasher and a Carpenter,
A Webbe, a Deyer and a Tapiser,
Were alle yclothed in a livere
Of a solempne and grete fraternitie."

In the days of half-timbered houses their skill was in great request, and they had a large and flourishing Gild, which failed not to take part in all the pageants, processions, and " ridings in the Chepe," and in all the State functions of the city. They have a noble modern Hall, but one rather regrets the disappearance in 1876 of the old mansion house of the Carpenters, which survived the Great Fire and recalled many memories of the past. In order to " seek for and destroy faulty and deceitful work of clock and watchmakers or mathematical instrument-makers," the Clock-makers' Company was formed in 1631. Some of the members wanted a Hall, and objected to meet " in alehouses and taverns to the great disparagement of them all " ; but this dream has not been realized, and the Company use the Halls of other Gilds. The Coach and Coach-Harness Makers have a Hall in Noble Street, note-worthy as being the place where the Gordon Riots were organized. The Company was formed in 1677, and performed useful functions in exam-ining defective wheels and axle-trees and in the

THE MINOR COMPANIES

construction of coaches. The Cooks, formerly known as pastelers or piebakers, are a very ancient fraternity, but most of their documents were destroyed in the Great Fire.

An *inspeximus* Charter of George III, however, informs us that it was incorporated by Edward IV, but their history has been uneventful. The Coopers can date back their existence to the reign of Edward II, but were not incorporated until 1501, one of their duties being to pray for the health of King Henry VII and his royal consort Elizabeth while they lived, and for their souls when they shall have " migrated from this light." The wardens had power to gauge all casks in the City of London and to mark such barrels when gauged. Brewers were not allowed to use vessels which did not bear the Coopers' marks. They have a Hall, and a very interesting history, upon which we should like to dwell if space permitted.

The Cordwainers, or Allutarii, regulated the trades connected with the leather industry, and included the flaying, tanning and currying of hides, and the making and sale of shoes, boots, goloshes, and other articles of leather. The Curriers have a Hall, and at one time were associated with the Cordwainers. Their documents were burnt in the Great Fire, but their records are complete since that date. Their ranks were greatly thinned at the close of the sixteenth century, as we gather from the record, " the

271

journeymen free of the Company are altogether dead of the late plague." The Cutlers date back to the time of Edward III, and their trade embraced all manner of swords, daggers, rapiers, hangers, woodknives, penknives, razors, surgeons' instruments, skeynes, hilts, pommels, battle-axes, halberds, and many other weapons. They have a modern Hall in Warwick Lane, their former home having been destroyed by the erection of the Cannon Street railway station.

The Distillers' Company was founded by Sir Theodore de Mayerne, Court Physician to Charles I, for the regulation of the trade of distillers and vinegar makers, and of those engaged in the preparation of artificial and strong waters, and of making beeregar and alegar. The Dyers have an ancient and honourable Company, which once ranked among the first twelve. Theirs was a very flourishing industry in mediæval and later times, when the coloured liveries of the Gilds and the brilliant hues of the garments of both male and female city-folk testified to the extent of the Dyers' industry. A Charter was granted to them by Edward IV, and they have taken their share in the great events of civic and national history. They, with the Vintners, have the right to keep a " game of swans " on the Thames. The Dyers' mark was formerly four bars and one nick denoting the ownership of the swan by the Company.

The Fanmakers obtained a Charter from good

THE MINOR COMPANIES

Queen Anne, their Company being the youngest of all the Gilds. They encourage the production of a female weapon, which was often used with much effect in the warfare of courtly fashion and intrigue. The Farriers were incorporated by the Merry Monarch, in order to prevent unexpert and unskilful persons destroying horses by bad shoeing, and have extended their good work to the present day by devising an admirable system of examination and national registration of shoeing smiths. The trade is naturally an ancient one, and a Gild existed as early at 1356, and we read of one Walter de Brun, farrier, in the Strand, in the time of Edward I, who had a forge in the parish of St. Clement on the peculiar tenure of paying to the King six horseshoes.

The Feltmakers, incorporated by James I, regulated the manufacture of felt hats. Of the Fletchers, or arrow-makers, whose motto is "True and Sure," we have already written. The Founders extended their jurisdiction over the manufacture of candlesticks, buckles, spurs, stirrups, straps, lavers, pots, ewers, and basins made of brass, latten or pewter, and have an interesting history. They had a Gild in 1472, when they began their career with "twenty-four poor, honest men." Their ancient ordinances contain directions about masses, burials and almsgiving, the carrying of wares to fairs, hawking them, and the governing of apprentices. Their young men caused much difficulty. They

273   S

THE CITY COMPANIES

loved riots and sport, and one of the ordinances of 1608 prohibited the playing of bowls, betting at cards, dice, table and shovel-board. One of the principal duties of the Company was the approving and signing of all brass weights within the City, which were ordered to be brought to Founders' Hall and there " sized and made lawful according to our standard of England," and then marked with the common mark of the mystery, " being the form of a ewer," the Company taking an ancient allowance for sizing. This was a very important public trust, which the Founders continue to discharge.

The Framework Knitters' Company owes its existence to an ingenious curate, one William Lee, of Calverton, who invented the stocking-loom in 1589. We should like, if space permitted, to dwell on his romantic story, but in this brief sketch it is impossible. The Company of Framework Knitters sprang into being in the time of Charles II, and was then extremely prosperous, indulging in expensive pomp and pageantries. A gilded barge, a large band of musicians, a Master's carriage, attendants resplendent in gold lace liveries, and banners emblazoned with their arms, were some of the luxuries in which they indulged. But their glory waned and their trade passed from London to the Midlands, and little of their ancient state remains.

The Fruiterers have an active little Company incorporated by James I, and still do useful work

THE MINOR COMPANIES

in promoting the cultivation of home-grown fruit by cottagers and small holders of land. The Girdlers' Company is an ancient fraternity, once styled the "Zonars," and formerly had the regulation of the manufacture of girdles of silk or wool, or linen and garters. Though the use of girdles has died out more than two centuries, the Company remains, and has a charming Hall and some valuable property. It owed its origin to a lay brotherhood of the Order of St. Laurence, the members of which maintained themselves by the making of girdles, and the Gild was in existence in the days of Edward III, who addressed them as "*Les ceinturiers de notre Citée de Loundres.*"

The Glass-sellers have a Charter granted by Charles II, "to his well-beloved subjects the glass-sellers and looking-glass makers," which authorized them to search in all places where glasses, looking-glasses, hour-glasses and stone pots, or bottles, shall be made, showed, or put to sale." The ordinances are very severe on apprentices, who, if guilty of haunting taverns, alehouses, bowling alleys, or other misdemeanours, were brought to the Hall and stripped and whipped by persons appointed for that purpose. Another Company connected with the same substance, the Glaziers, has little history, and we pass on to the Glovers, who existed in 1349, and have had an honourable career. Gloves have played such a notable part in our national life that it

275

THE CITY COMPANIES

would be a pleasant task to record their history, but we must confine ourselves to their makers. These had many allies and were united with the Pursers, and later on with the Leather-sellers. In 1638 they recovered their independence, and their Charter states that 400 families were engaged in the trade, and were impoverished by the confluence of persons of the same art, a disordered multitude, working in chambers and corners, and making naughty and deceitful gloves. Queen Victoria confirmed the Charter of the Glovers, whose corporation was the only Gild so honoured during her late Majesty's long reign.

The Gold and Silver Wyre Drawers have an ancient Gild incorporated by James I though existing in 1461. They were concerned in fashioning the gold and silver embroidered finery of our forefathers, who loved to make themselves, their pages and their horse-gear resplendent with gold and silver. The Gunmakers perform the useful work of protecting our countrymen from the dangers of defective guns, and their Company was incorporated by Charles I on the ground that divers blacksmiths and others inexpert in the art of gun-making had taken upon them to make, try and prove guns after their unskilful way, whereby the trade was not only damnified, but much harm and danger through such unskilfulness had happened to His Majesty's subjects. They had the power of

THE MINOR COMPANIES

destroying all false hand-guns, and pistols—
to stamp all sound goods with the letters G P
crowned. This good work is still carried on
by the Company. The Horners, in the days of
horn cups and winding horns, were a prosperous
community, and their Company existed in the
days of Edward III, exercising the right of
search at the fairs of " Stirbridge and Elie," their
fortunes declining when glass vessels were used
instead of the old horn cups. The Innholders
remind us of the old-time inns of London,
which Mr. Philip Norman, F.S.A., has so
well described. At one time they were styled
hostelers or herbergeours, and objected to the
former title inasmuch as their servants were
really called hostillers, the hostlers or ostlers of
modern time. St. Julian was their patron saint,
for he made a hospital or inn by a river where
men passed oft in great peril. Very curious
regulations were ordained for their government,
and no one was allowed to remain at an inn more
than one day and a night unless the innholder
was willing to answer for him. They have a
Hall, which has been newly erected, and some
good portraits.

In no work was the amazing subdivision of
labour so marked as in that which related to
wood. Carpenters, joiners, sawyers, and planers
had each their own separate work and organization. The joiners' work was concerned with
cupboards, bedsteads, tables and chairs, and

277

"rayles, sealinge boards, vainscott, chappboards, and bedd timber" were their raw materials. Their Company was in existence in 1309, and they have a Hall in the Vintry. The Leather-sellers have an active and flourishing Gild, which is first mentioned in 1372, when their *probi homines* or *bone gentz* petitioned for some regulations for the prevention of the sale of fraudulent leather. By the Charter of James I they have the full oversight of "skins and felts called buff leather, shamoy leather, Spanish leather, and that of stags, bucks, calves, sheep, lambs, kids frized or grained, dressed in oil, allum, shoemack, or bark or rawed." All proper leather was stamped with the arms of the Company. They have a fine modern Hall, and can show a good record of useful work.

The ancient Loriner made bits, spurs and all the smaller trinkets of a horse's harness, and the Gild dates back to the days of Henry III, but its history is uneventful. The Masons have few records. By their Charter of Elizabeth they had power to view stones intended for buildings—as to whether these were of proper length and measure, and well and sufficiently wrought. The Musicians some years ago celebrated their tercentenary, commemorating the granting of their Charter by James I in 1604. They might have claimed a longer period of existence, as their first Charter was granted by Edward IV. Their by-laws are particularly interesting, and give minute directions with regard to their profession. They tested the skill of music and dancing masters, forbade the singing of ribald, wanton or lascivious songs, or the playing of any instrument under any knight or gentleman's window without the Company's licence. The Needlemakers existed in the time of Henry VIII, but have little history. The Painters' or Painter-stainers' Company suggests many reflections on their art and skill, and its history would require many pages. Their Gild existed in the time of Edward III, and received its first Charter from Edward IV. Their by-laws order that if any member be found rebel and contrariwise to the Wardens he shall pay one pound of wax for certain altar-lights. No tin-foil might be used but only oil-colours. They derive their name Painter-stainers from the custom of calling a picture a " stained cloth." The principal artists in England were members of the Gild, and in their Hall are numerous examples of the work of its members. The Patten-makers' Company suggests a picture of the condition of the streets of London in mediæval times, when garbage and refuse were thrown into them, when drains and watercourses were things unknown, and pattens were invented as a useful footgear, and clogs and goloshes were sorely needed. The Company appears on the scene in the fifteenth century, and the name of the City church of St. Margaret Pattens, Rood

THE CITY COMPANIES

Lane, points out that locality as the seat of the industry. The Pewterers, a Company of " friendly and neighbouring men," existed in 1348, and did much to make English pewter famous and highly esteemed in other lands. They visited markets and fairs throughout England, and seized and condemned base pewter ware, brass goods, and false scales. They furnished men with arms for the defence of the City, and kept in their Hall, corselets, calyvers, bill pikes, and other weapons, and paid an armourer to keep them in good order. Their history, written by Mr. Charles Welch in two large volumes, abounds in interesting facts, and we can only here refer our readers to those records.

The Plaisterers, formerly known as Pargetters, were skilful in contriving curious, elaborate and beautiful ceilings, which form such an attractive feature in many old houses. They were incorporated by a Charter of Henry VII. The Playing-card Makers' Company was founded in 1628, with the object of counteracting the deceits and abuses practised by the inexpert in the art and trade of making playing-cards, and the importation of foreign cards into this country. It has no records and little history. The Plumbers' Company stands high in public estimation, and has been in existence several centuries, though not incorporated until 1611, when a Charter was granted " for the utility, advantage and relief of the good and honest, and

280

INTERIOR OF BARBERS' HALL

THE MINOR COMPANIES

for the terror and correction of the evil, deceitful and dishonest." Their modern efforts to initiate a national registration and training of plumbers are worthy of the highest praise.

Every citizen knows the Poultry in the City—the locality where the Poulterers anciently carried on their trade, selling " rabbits, fowls and other poultry." The trade was not without its dangers. Unsound poultry doomed the seller to the pillory, the articles being burnt under him—a peculiarly disagreeable penalty. The Company existed in 1345, but was not incorporated until 1504 and its history has been uneventful. The Saddlers' Company is a very honourable and wealthy corporation, and possesses records of unusual importance, dating back to Saxon times. The early colony of saddlers settled near the church of St. Martin-le-Grand, and they have never strayed far from there, their present Hall being in Fetter Lane. They can boast of having received many charters, the earliest having been granted by Edward I. In early days they were associated with a collegiate brotherhood, the house of which was situated where the General Post Office now stands. This religious fraternity offered masses for the souls of deceased saddlers, and shared with them a common graveyard. They disputed much with the joiners, painters, and loriners, who were always trying to trespass upon the rights of the saddlers. The introduction of coaches alarmed them as much as the invention

THE CITY COMPANIES

of railways frightened the coachmen, but with less cause. The saddle trade prospered. The Civil War caused many saddles to be made and many emptied. Their records tell of much old-time civic life and customs. They had a barge on the river ; they buried their deceased members with much ceremony, and their old hearse-cloth still remains ; they can boast of having a Royal Master, Frederick Prince of Wales, in 1751.

The Scriveners formerly discharged many of the duties now performed by solicitors, such as making wills, drawing up charters, deeds relating to lands, tenements and inheritance and other documents. They were known as the " Scriveners, or writers of the Court Letters of the City of London." Their earliest set of ordinances was granted to them in the time of Adam de Bury, Mayor in the 38th year of Edward III, a document couched in old Law French. They complained bitterly against certain chaplains and other men out of divers countries who called themselves scriveners, and took upon themselves to make testaments, charters and other things belonging to the mystery, to the great damage and slander of all honest and true scriveners. Their apprentices caused them trouble, because they had not their " perfect congruity of grammar, which is the thing most necessary and expedient to every person exercising the science and faculty of the mystery." Every apprentice found deficient was ordered to be sent to a grammar school until

THE MINOR COMPANIES

" he be erudite in the books of genders, declensions, preterites and supines, equivix, and sinonimes." Their first charter was granted in 1617. John Milton, the father of the poet, was a member of the Company.

The Shipwrights have had a corporate life of four centuries, originally known as the Bretheren and Sisters of the Fraternity of SS. Simon and Jude, and were established on the river side at Southwark or Bermondsey. The use of " good and seasonable timber " in the building of ships was enjoined by their ordinances. Their well-stored yards of timber were, however, considered dangerous to the City, and the constant noise of hammering offended the ears of the citizens ; hence the shipwrights migrated to Radcliffe, and they had much trouble with a colony of " foreigners " who dared to set up their yards at Rotherhithe, and actually obtained a Charter from King James. A long and bitter struggle for supremacy ensued, and was not settled until 1684. The art of shipbuilding has been revolutionized by the advent of steam and the use of iron ; the Thames side is no longer the great centre of the industry, and the importance of the Company has waned, though it still exercises some useful functions.

The Spectacle-makers' Company has no great history, though their first charter dates back to the time of Charles I. Its membership is large, including many illustrious names, and no less

283

than twenty Lord Mayors. It does much good in modern times by improving the skill of opticians. The Stationers have a noteworthy history, which has been graphically told by Mr. C. R. Rivington, and celebrated their five-hundredth birthday four years ago. For an account of their powers, privileges and the story of their copyright register, I must refer the curious reader to Mr. Rivington's book, or to my former history of *The City Companies of London and their Good Works.*

The Tallow Chandlers can boast of great antiquity, and possess several Charters and documents of much interest, and also the Tinplate Workers', alias Wire Workers' Company. The Tylers and Bricklayers formed a fraternity in 1356, and have received Charters from Queen Elizabeth and subsequent monarchs, which contain no remarkable provisions. The Turners or "Woodpotters" showed their skill in mediæval times in the manufacture of household furniture, and their fellowship was recognized in 1310. They received a Charter from James I and in modern times have shown much activity, and have enrolled many distinguished men in their rank of Freemen. The Upholder is really an upholster or upholsterer, who now supplies furniture, beds and such-like goods. His Company was founded in 1460, and received a grant of arms from Edward IV. Cornhill was the original home of the upholder, or fripperer, as he was sometimes

THE MINOR COMPANIES

called, and he used to deal in old clothes, old beds, old armour, old combs, and his shop must have been a combination of old curiosity shop and store-dealer's warehouse. Later on, he concentrated his attention on furniture, his status improved, and his Gild became an important association, though never very wealthy or remarkable.

The Wax Chandlers lived in palmy days, when they furnished the great halls of the nobles with the produce of their skill, and innumerable lights burned before every altar in our churches. Their Gild existed in 1371, and was qualified to make " torches, cierges, prikits, great candles or any other manner of wax chandlery." They still possess a Hall in Gresham Street and Gutter Lane. The weavers claim to possess the oldest Company of all the City Gilds. It certainly existed in the time of Henry I, and they have a Charter of Henry II which is signed by St. Thomas of Canterbury, and no less than eleven others. In the palmy days of the cloth industry they were prosperous, but unfortunately few records of their former greatness remain. The Wheelwrights' Company suggests the fascinating study of the introduction of coaches and cars, upon which we cannot now embark, nor listen to the wails of the Thames watermen, who complained against newfangled ways. This Gild received a Charter from Charles II, and did good service in protecting the lives of his Majesty's

285

subjects from " the falling of carts and coaches through the ignorance and ill-work " of foreign craftsmen. Last, but not least, on the list stands the Woolmen's Company, founded in 1300, when the trade in wool was at its zenith. It has borne several names, and was identical with the Gild of Woolpackers or Woolwinders. Woolcombers were also licensed by the Company. A noted member of this ancient fraternity was Sir John Crosby, the founder of Crosby Hall, " Grocer and Woolman," alderman of the City in the reign of Edward IV, whose noble house London has at length declined to spare, but happily it has been removed bodily and set up again in Chelsea. Efforts are now being made to utilize it as a hostel for young women engaged in business.

XVIII.   THE TREASURES
OF THE CITY COMPANIES

IN our accounts of the story of each Company
we have alluded to some of their treasures.
Much of their ancient plate has passed
away from their possession in the times when
misfortunes assailed them. As we have already
noticed at certain periods of their interesting
careers, when the Tudor and Stuart monarchs
regarded them as convenient institutions for
exacting forced loans which were never repaid,
they were compelled to sell a large quantity of
their plate, or during the Commonwealth period
when they were mulcted by both contending
parties, and worst of all when the Great Fire
laid their buildings low and often destroyed their
goodly store of silver cups, rare paintings, funeral
palls and other treasures. We can imagine the
feelings of the sorrowing freemen when amidst
the ruins of their former homes they set themselves to gather together the remains of their
hoards all melted by the raging fire. Some
treasures had extraordinary escapes: as in the case
of one Company they had been hidden in a
drain and so were saved. In this chapter we
propose to enumerate some of these valuables,
which will cause the envy of the collector who
might be inclined to wish that misfortunes might
again visit the fraternities so that their treasures
might again find their way into the auction room
and fall victims to the auctioneer's hammer.

287

THE CITY COMPANIES

We venture to utter a wish that no such troubles should ever assail the Companies and that no hostile hands should ever be raised against them.

The Mercers were fortunate. None of their plate was destroyed by the Great Fire, but on account of their losses, they decided to sell part of it in order to provide funds. The sale realized £702 16s. 8d. Four pieces only were preserved, and are still in their possession. One of them is a noted piece. It is a waggon and tun, the gift of William Burde in 1573, all gilt. It had a coachman once, but he is unfortunately lost. It was intended to move along the table, being impelled by clockwork, so that no one need exclaim, " Pass the wine." The gift of Sir Thomas Leigh is a standing gilt cup with the Mercers' maidenhead and unicorn enamelled on it. This is a remarkably handsome vessel and is called the " Leigh Cup." The date mark is 1499-1500 and it was presented in 1554. It bears the inscription :

" To elect the Master of the Mercerie hither I am sent
And by Sir Thomas Leigh for the same intent."

Three gilt beakers presented by John Bancks, and a gilt salt-cellar by Sir John Dethick. The first contribution to the post-Fire collection of plate was William Hurt's, whose cup is adorned with his arms and those of the Mercers, and was given, according to custom, for not accepting the office of Warden in 1673. The date mark,

however, denotes that it was fashioned before
the Great Fire, in 1650. The maidenhead crowned
with hair dishevelled appears on the staves of
office made in silver in 1679, which are very
handsome. Twelve silver tablespoons (1685),
two silver salts (1684) follow, and two large
loving-cups are especially interesting, as they
were the gift of the Bank of England in 1694.
The occasion of this gift was the lending of
Mercers' Hall to the newly formed Bank wherein
the first meetings were held. The collection
was further enriched by the gift of William
Sydenham, who borrowed the Hall for a lottery
in 1699. They are extremely handsome pieces
of plate with lion handles and scalloped edges
and fluted centres bearing the arms of the
Company and those of the Sydenham family.
We may conclude that this lottery was most
successful. In gratitude for the use of the Hall
the English East India Company gave the Mercers
two circular silver salvers in 1700, which Company was raising two millions of money for the
further extension of their business in the East.

I know not what " ye Corporation of ye Mines
Royall, ye Minerall and Baths Works " may
have been ; but this Company borrowed the
Hall for the taking of subscriptions for the
insurance of ships and merchandise, and in
gratitude gave to the Mercers two plain silver
flagons 18 inches high bearing two shields of
arms emblematical of the donors. These with

the monteiths are engraved in Sir John Watney's book on St. Thomas of Acon and the Mercers, from which I have derived much information. An inventory of the plate drawn up in 1756 gives the weight thereof to be 1,100 ounces. Subsequent gifts include a very handsome silver oblong plateau or table ornament with an epergne to hold lights or flowers, 26 inches high, presented by the Commissioners appointed by Act of Parliament for the issue of Exchequer Bills for the assistance of commercial credit as a testimony of the liberality and readiness with which the use of the Hall was granted in 1794.

The Gresham Committee which manages the Royal Exchange and other institutions founded by Sir Thomas Gresham in 1845, presented to their Clerk, Mr. James Barnes, a silver inkstand, who also received from the Mercers a silver copy of the Warwick Vase. These gifts were subsequently presented to the Mercers by a relative of their former Clerk. A curious history is attached to a massive loving-cup and two salts belonging to the Warden and poor men of the Trinity Hospital in Greenwich which the Mercers manage. It was founded by Henry Howard, Earl of Northampton, whose remarkable history is well known. His father and elder brother died on the scaffold in 1546 and 1572 respectively, and he only escaped the same fate by dying before his trial and execution could take place. He was a very learned man,

THE TREASURES

founded three hospitals, and was the builder of Northampton House, afterwards Northumberland House, at Charing Cross. The cup was given by Thomas, Earl of Arundel and Surrey, great-nephew and heir of the founder of the Hospital. The principal portraits of the Mercers have already been recorded.

I am not sure whether I have described the etiquette of drinking from loving-cups, these *pocula charitatis*, of which all the Companies possess some. Standing, you receive the cup from your neighbour on your right, who bows to you very politely, having wiped the brim with a napkin. You sip the beverage, and while you do this your left-hand neighbour stands, so that you are guarded on both sides, so as to prevent any miscreant from attacking you with a dagger or other weapon while you are in a defenceless position when drinking. Having finished your sip, you bow and repeat the process with your left-hand neighbour who is thus guarded by yourself and his other neighbour. It is a curious and interesting custom of great antiquity, and is observed at all City banquets whether held in the Mansion House, Guildhall, or the Halls of the Companies.

Owing to the demands of the Crown and the destruction caused by the Great Fire the Grocers have no old plate. The Drapers are more fortunate. They have a silver and gilt cup by Cellini which was presented in 1578 bearing the inscription :

291

THE CITY COMPANIES

" A proctor of the poor am I,
Remember them before I die."

A fine monteith bears the hall-mark of 1685, and amongst other examples of the silversmith's art I may mention a large voiding knife of the date 1678, as big as a sabre, for removing crumbs from the table. They possess many portraits of illustrious personages, life-sized paintings of Hanoverian Kings, a fine portrait of Nelson by Sir William Beechey in 1805, of Mary, Queen of Scots, and her son, by F. Zuccaro; the founder of the Green Coat School at Greenwich, Sir William Boreham. There are portraits by Gainsborough of John Smith, by Richardson of Sir Robert Clayton, a copy of Holbein's portrait of Henry VIII, an imaginary one of Henry Fitzalwyn, first Mayor, and of others. There are busts of Queen Victoria and Prince Albert and of other royal personages—a goodly list of treasures.

The Fishmongers are rich in plate,[1] though pre-Fire examples are very few, as their Hall was overwhelmed in the great conflagration. A frosted silver cup inscribed, " The Company of Fishmongers, London, anno dni. 1664," appears to have been made before the Fire, but that inscription is misleading. The date-mark is 1667, and it was given by the donor after the Fire, the former date denotes his year of office.

[1] I described the plate of the Fishmongers in the *Connoisseur* for April, 1916.

THE TREASURES

There is also a silver salt, 14 inches high, given by John Rushout, Prime Warden in 1654. He came from Flanders and was an ancestor of Lord Northwick. It is a curious piece formed of three escallop shells, supported by tails of dolphins ridden by boys holding coral and escallop shells, and in the centre is a naked boy. The earliest post-Fire piece is a silver tankard with cover and bow handle bequeathed by Daniel Pennington in 1666-67. It bears the hall-mark of 1666, and is 6 inches high and 5½ in circumference, weighing 30 ounces. A frosted cup on a baluster shaft bears the inscription, " The gift of John Owen, Esq., Prime Warden, anno dni. 1668, 1669, 1670, in which yeares this Hall was newly built after ye dreadful fire in 1666." The date-mark is 1671.

During the next decade several gifts were made. In 1671 Dame Anne Dawes gave for her late husband, Sir Jonathan Dawes, Sheriff and Master, a large loving-cup, silver-gilt with a large baluster stem and acanthus leaves, 15 inches high. A large silver basin and ewer were given by William Allington in 1676. They were made in 1670. This basin or rosewater dish is 24 inches in diameter and bears the arms of the Company and donor. A large silver-gilt loving-cup was given by Richard Norton in 1678 and a silver tankard by Sir Richard How in 1680, weighing nearly 90 ounces ; and another by Sir Simon Lewis. On the top of the handle are two dolphins,

293

THE CITY COMPANIES

and this was given in gratitude " for the extraordinary favour to him for the use of the Hall
and rooms in the tyme of his late Shrievalty."
An old Hungarian silver alms-dish, dated 1681,
was presented by Mr. Travers Smith in 1890.
The store was gradually increasing. James
Paule, Master 1690, gave a loving-cup, and
another was given by an unknown benefactor,
but the arms denote that he belonged to the
family of Peake. A huge monteith, called the
" John Bull Bowl," was presented by Sir Thomas
Abney in 1696, and is the earliest example of
that kind of vessel known. These punch-bowls
derived their name from a gentleman of fashion,
named Monteith, who was remarkable for wearing
a scalloped coat. In King's "Art and Cookery"
occur the lines :

"New things produce new words and so Monteith
Has by one vessel saved himself from Death."

Like this gentleman's coat the vessel had " a
moveable rim ornamented around the top with
escallops," in which glasses were placed with their
feet outwards, for the purpose of bringing them
into the room. The bowl was, of course, brought
in empty, each gentleman fancying that he had
an especial talent for concocting the beverage,
and a silver ladle and a lemon strainer were
brought in with it.[1]
There is another similar monteith (1698)

1 *Old English Plate*, by W. J. Cripps, C.B., F.S.A., p. 329.

THE TREASURES

made by John Ruslen " at ye golde cup in Swithin Lane," who also made the ladle, and a large silver salver. The Fishmongers became wealthy in the 18th century, and they kept Master Ruslen briskly employed. Another salver, a tankard with cover, silver candlesticks, one pair, were given by Sir John Buckworth, Sheriff, and were inscribed :

> " Amicitiae Tessera
> John Buckworth, Mil⁸ et Bar^tt
> Societatis Pisca Custo⁸ P^ml
> et Vic Com⁸ Londini
> Anno 1704."

The Tyrone Cup (silver-gilt) is very handsome and elaborately adorned with fruit and flowers, and on the base the four elements. On the cover are shown the four seasons and the four quarters of the globe enriched with fruit surmounted by an Indian pineapple. The handles consist of two satyrs' heads and a representation of Music. This wonderful cup was made by William Grundy and is inscribed, " The gift of the Right Honble. Marcus, Earl of Tyrone, 1747, on the granting to His Lordship a Lease of 3 lives the Company's Irish Estates known as the Manor of Walworth." This is indeed a wonderful cup and a triumph of the silversmith's art. The most striking of recent works of art is the Doncaster Race Shield of 1866 which formerly belonged to the Marquis of Hastings

295

THE CITY COMPANIES

and was purchased by the Company at the sale of his effects. There is one gift which they might like to throw into the Thames. It is a handsome gold snuff-box which was presented by the ex-Kaiser in memory of his visit to the City. Amongst other treasures there is a silver model of a Viking ship, and a snuff-box made from a fragment of a tree under which the Duke of Wellington stood for some hours while the Battle of Waterloo was being fought.

It may be gathered that the Fishmongers are rich in treasures. However, I happen to know more of these than of several other Companies, as through the kindness of the late Clerk, Mr. J. Wrench Towse, I have been able to make use of his admirable work on the subject.

The Fishmongers possess also a statue of St. Peter, the patron saint of fishers, a banner presented to Admiral Earl St. Vincent in 1797, many royal portraits and busts, a portrait of Lord Hatherley, by Wells, and two fine paintings by Romney of the Margrave and Margravine of Anspach. In the drawing-room are the portraits of the Dukes of Sussex and Kent and of Queen Victoria. The Walworth Pall is a remarkably fine specimen of needlework and is said to have been worked by nuns previous to 1381, and is in good preservation. It is more probably the work of the 16th century. The arms of the Company, and the presentation of the keys to St. Peter appear in the work. It was said to

APOLLO DISTRIBUTING REWARDS TO THE ARTS AND SCIENCES AND MISERY, CROWNING THE GENIUS OF ENGLAND.

Sir

You are desired to meet the rest of the Mystery of GOLDSMITHS, at the

at Ten of the Clock in the Morning precisely, there to hear a Sermon, and from thence to Accompany them to Goldsmiths-Hall in Foster-Lane to Dine with Your Friends and Servants,

Ambrose Stevenson   *William Chase*
William Owen   *Edward Chenne,*
Jeremiah Lammas,   *Charles Jones.*

STEWARDS.

Pray pay the Bearer 4 Shillings.

AN INVITATION CARD

have been used at Walworth's funeral, and another interesting relic is his dagger with which he slew Wat Tyler. It has been in the possession of the Company since the deed was wrought. It is preserved in a glass case which bears the inscription : " With this dagger Sir William Walworth, Lord Mayor of London, Citizen and Fishmonger, slew the rebel, Wat Tyler, in Smithfield, Anno Domini, 1381." The Company possesses some good paintings of fish by Arnold von Halken, 1767, and Scott's pictures of old London Bridge and Westminster Bridge, prior to 1757. They have a large representation of a pageant in former days.

The Goldsmiths naturally have a fine collection of plate. Amongst these there is the much prized Queen Elizabeth's cup which was used by Her Majesty at her coronation. There is also a fine collection of antique silver, Elizabethan chalices, a unique collection of apostles' spoons, salts, a helmet cup, candelabra from the Duke of Buckingham's palace at Stowe, a remarkable two-handled gilt cup and cover, and a splendid ewer of 1741 date. It is covered with figures of children and flowers, and the handle is ornamented with the demi-figure of a bearded naked man, possibly representing Father Thames or Neptune. Opposite the entrance is a bust of the figure of the founder, Edward III, and sculptures of the Lybian Sibyl and Cleopatra, by Storey. Amongst other treasures we find a painting of St. Dunstan,

THE CITY COMPANIES

portraits of Sir Hugh Myddelton (1644), Sir
Thomas Vyner, Sir Martyn Bowes, three times
Lord Mayor, and a bust of Walter Prideaux,
Esq., who held the honourable post of Clerk of
the Company for thirty years, and was succeeded
by his son, Sir Walter Sherburne Prideaux.
I also discovered many perfect specimens of
modern art, including a magnificent silver vase
and shield by Vechte, which were exhibited at
the Exhibition of 1851. The Goldsmiths have
many other priceless treasures, and when their
banquets are spread the tables are loaded with
their works of art.

The Skinners have some valuable and interesting plate, consisting of gifts from past and
present members of the Company, and including
loving-cups, salts, plates, etc., dating from the
16th century. It was the fashion of that period
to make cups and other plate in the shape of
beasts or birds, and the Skinners possess five
loving-cups in the form of cocks, of which the
heads must be removed for the purposes of
drinking. They were bequeathed by Mr. William
Cockayne in 1598, and doubtless intended to be
a kind of pun upon his name. The cock is
represented as a very perky bird with flowing
tail, treading upon a snake ; and the cups are
wonderful examples of the skill of the silversmith of the period. In accordance with a
covenant made with the executors of the donor
these peculiar cups are used annually at the

election of the Master and Wardens. The Skinners also have another curious loving-cup of the same sort of design. It is called the Peahen Cup, and is shaped in the figure of that creature. The hen has two chicks at her feet. The head must be removed for drinking, and it is inscribed: " The gift of Mary, ye daughter of Richard Robinson and wife, to Thomas Smith and James Peacock, Skinners, 1642." They have a snuff-box in the shape of a leopard.

The Merchant Taylors are very rich in plate, which on one occasion I had the pleasure of inspecting under the guidance of the late Mr. Nash, Clerk of the Company. As I have already stated, the Great Fire did sad havoc in the Hall, but was stayed on the premises, but the plate was almost all melted. The Master's Mace happily was saved, and the silver yard by which for some centuries the London cloth measures were corrected. A very fine silver basin of pre-Fire date (1590) is remarkable. It has a large beautiful boss in the centre enriched with a coat of arms, and three coats on the rim. It is used at banquets for holding rosewater which is passed round to the guests. A second rosewater dish was also saved. They have, also, a still more elaborately decorated silver salver of 17th century date, and two Irish tankards of the date 1680 which were presented by two Wardens, of whom John Hort was one. They possess two hearse cloths ; one of these was made about 1490-1512.

299

THE CITY COMPANIES

Of interesting pictures there is a great store. There is a picture of their patron saint, St. John the Baptist. A portrait of Henry VIII is reputed to have been painted by Paris Bordone ; and others represent the first Duke of Wellington, Lord Eldon, the Duke of York, the younger Pitt, by Hoppner, which was given to the Company by the Pitt Club. In the drawing-room I noticed two portraits by Kneller representing Charles II and James II, and two by Thomas Murray of King William III and Queen Mary. In the small dining-room over the fire-place is a portrait of Charles I by a pupil of Vandyck, and, on the sides, Charles II by an unknown artist, and a painting of three former Clerks of the Company, that of George Norten by Thomas Hudson, the master of Sir Joshua Reynolds.

The memory of Sir Thomas White, who was born at Reading in Berkshire, and who was the munificent founder of St. John's College, Oxford, and Master about 1535, is preserved by his portrait in the library. Another portrait of this worthy is in the court-room, together with that of Robert Dowe, Master in 1578, of Sir Thomas Rowe, Master about 1557, and others. Sir Godfrey Kneller painted three portraits of former Masters, namely, Alderman Sir P. Ward (1671), Alderman Sir William Pritchard (1673), and Alderman Sir William Turner (1685). In the ante-room to the court-room there is a curious picture representing Henry VII presenting the

300

THE TREASURES

Royal Charter to the Master and Wardens ; and here are also two Dutch landscapes attributed to Roland Severy and John Breughel. These are some of the treasures to be found in the Hall of the Merchant Taylors.

The Haberdashers have some valuable plate which survived the Fire. There is in their Hall a beautiful standing silver-salt of the date 1636. Carved on the sides of the cylindrical body appear some agricultural operations with cows and sheep and a man ploughing. The top and base bear scroll-work. There is another standing cup of 1637, and a loving-cup of 1649 ; inscribed round the rim are the words : " The guift of Thomas Stone, Esq." In spite of two fires several good portraits and paintings have escaped the conflagrations. I have already noticed the migration of two royal portraits of George I and Queen Caroline, which somehow wandered away into Devonshire, and were absent from their proper place in Haberdashers' Hall for a century. Happily they have been restored. Two other royal portraits, George III and Queen Charlotte, are the work of Sir Joshua Reynolds. Wren's fine ceilings adorn the court-room and drawing-room and there are many portraits of the Company's worthies. Amongst them I may mention George Whitmore, Lord Mayor in 1659 ; John Banks (1716); William Jones, merchant-adventurer and haberdasher, founder of a grammar school at Monmouth. It will be remembered

301

THE CITY COMPANIES

that he, after gaining much wealth, returned to his native village of Newland, Gloucestershire, where his welcome was not so cordial as he expected. Hence instead of bequeathing his money to Newland, he gave it to Monmouth, where he founded a grammar school and alms-houses and the Jones Charity has proved a gold-mine for the town. There are other portraits of benefactors, Thomas Alderney (1594), Thomas Skinner, Lord Mayor in 1775, D. Austin, 1832, Peter Pope, Robert Dike, William Adams, Sir Hugh Hammersly, Lord Mayor in 1776, First Colonel of the City, President of the Artillery Gentlemen, Governor of the Company of Russian Merchants, and the holder of many honourable distinctions. There is a portrait of Jerome Knapp, formerly Clerk of the Company, painted by Gainsborough. A fine painting of the Nativity by an unknown Master is in the drawing-room.

The Salters possess two royal portraits by Sir Joshua Reynolds—George III and Queen Charlotte. His Majesty is represented in his robes of State holding his sceptre. The portraits of Charles I, William Robson and Bernard Hyde, escaped the Great Fire.

In spite of the various pillagings of the Iron-mongers' treasures there are still some ancient specimens. One is a mounted coco-nut cup, similar to one with which I am familiar in my old Oxford College, Oriel. I used to be told that

THE TREASURES

this was a drift nut washed over to Europe from America by the sea, and that these nuts, strange to Europeans, led Columbus and other discoverers to start on their great adventurous voyages to discover the land whence they came. Sometimes they are called " hanaps " or " standing nuts." Another curious cup is a wooden bowl mounted with a silver-gilt rim on which is inscribed the words :

"Ave Maria gratia plena, Dominus tecum, benedicta tu in mulieris: et benedictus fructus ventris tui—In Annūciatioe Marie virg. Missale ad usum insignis ecclesiae Sarum 1527 fol. xvii, xxxii."

There is also a similar bowl with a plain rim. The Lion loving-cup is a wonderful work of the silversmith's art. Besides these there are two saucer-shaped bowls or Mazers,[1] and doubtless many new cups and treasures to replace those which hard fate and troublous times had deprived them of.

The pall and wonderful piece of ancient tapestry in Vintners' Hall have already been described, but the Company possesses some extremely interesting plate. They have a list only of their ancient plate, but much has been sold to satisfy the rapacious Tudor and Stuart monarchs, who " borrowed " so frequently from the coffers of this and other Companies, and like Sir John

---

[1] This word is supposed to be derived from the Flemish word *maeser*, signifying maple wood.

303

THE CITY COMPANIES

Falstaff "*did not like the paying back : 'tis a double labour.*" Amongst the archives of the Vintners a list of plate formerly owned by them was not long ago discovered, and this must have made the present generation sigh over the loss of former treasures. Amongst the pieces that remain we find an early one bearing the date 1518. Like that of the Ironmongers it is a coconut cup mounted in silver-gilt, and richly decorated. Another ancient piece is a Delft or stoneware tankard of the date 1563, finely mounted, bearing the motto: "Think and Thank," and also, "Thank David Gitting for this." Antony Pawle gave two pieces of plate in 1638 to His Majesty's wine porters. The milkmaid cup is a curious and interesting example of the quaint fashions which were sometimes adopted for drinking-vessels, and in this instance the "milkmaid" must have caused much merriment resounding through the banqueting hall from its use. It is in the shape of a female, whose petticoat forms the cup : she holds in her uplifted hands another smaller vessel which turns on a pivot. Both vessels are filled with wine, and some skill is required to empty one cup without spilling the contents of the other. There are also many other splendid specimens of plate of later work which gleam and sparkle on the tables when the banquets are spread. The list of portraits of worthies has been already recorded, and also the wonderful tapestry and carvings of

THE TREASURES

Grinling Gibbons and other beauties of the Hall.

The active and munificent Clothworkers were obliged to sell almost all of their ancient plate during the disastrous period of the Civil War in 1643, and I have already recorded the sad court minute passed when they found that this was inevitable. Wisely they decided to have an inventory drawn up of all that was sold, setting forth the names of the donors, so that the various cups and other pieces might be replaced when " God shall enable this Company so to do." A subsequent court minute shows that 2,068 ounces of silver were sold for £520 and 1,239 ounces were retained for the use of the Company. Not long ago they preserved the names of the former donors by purchasing a silver salver on which were engraved all these names. " Not forgotten " was evidently the motto of the Cloth-workers. Of the ancient plate that was retained is a handsome rosewater dish presented by John Burnall, Master in 1593, a Caudle cup of the date 1654, inscribed *ex dono* above the arms of the donor enclosed by a wreath with the initials P.C., and beneath Renter (Warden) 1654 ; and a salt of the date 1661. It is similar in shape to another which has already been described among the plate of the Haberdashers, and was the gift of " Samuel Waldo, Clothworker, Esqre." It bears his arms surrounded by scroll-work. Samuel Pepys, of Diary fame, was a member of the

305   U

formidable to the guests who are admitted to the banquets.

Of plate the Armourers have a goodly store. Some old plate they lost through the tyrannical conduct of Cardinal Wolsey, who was the first to discover that the City Companies were convenient bodies to be pillaged. He met with his deserts. In 1521 he ordered the Armourers to sell all their plate, which then consisted of six maser-bowls and a silver mace. This they were compelled to sacrifice and to sell, and to give the proceeds to the avaricious Cardinal who also demanded a fine. One of the maser-bowls was presented by a great benefactor of the Company, and first Master, Everard Freer. By some means it escaped the clutches of the Cardinal, as it is still in existence. Evidently it was hidden away when he seized the rest of the booty and much crushed, as it had to be repaired considerably when Wolsey was safely dead.

The Armourers possess more 16th century plate than many of the larger Companies, who were often, as we have already noticed, obliged to sell their stock. They were very fortunate. Charles I either on account of his love for their craft, or for some other reason, did not require them to sell, or make such demands upon them as to compel them to do so. Neither did the Cromwellian party succeed in seizing it, as the Master at that time was a prudent person and had been able to take it away and hide it in some place of safety. No

THE TREASURES

list, as far as I am aware, has been published, but I can testify that the Armourers' plate makes a fine display when it appears on the buffet and the tables when the banquet is spread.

In the reign of good Queen Anne the Brasiers' Company, founded in 1480, was invited with the Armourers into one loyal fellowship. The site of the Hall was owned by them as far back as 1346. Their first Hall was built in 1453. It happily escaped the Great Fire, but was rebuilt in 1795 and again in 1840.[1]

A visit to Barber-Surgeons' Hall is a special delight on account of the treasures it contains. Fortunately it escaped the Great Fire. Hence there are left many Charters granted by successive Kings of England, an ancient vellum book of ordinances, and other interesting and valuable adornments, several of which are important works of art, with portraits of the royal donors and splendid seals. Many of them are in excellent preservation with the exception of one which has been gnawed by rats. The Barbers are fortunate in having preserved a goodly store of plate of which any Corporation might be proud. They do not possess now all the store that once was theirs. Their records tell of many gifts of standing cups, bowls, silver double-gilt, and much else that has vanished. For reasons already given in our records of the Companies, they have been

[1] I am greatly obliged to Dr. A. Newton Pitt for much of the above information.

309

THE CITY COMPANIES

compelled to melt down their plate and to pawn or sell it. Thus, in 1643, they were assessed at £8 per week for three months towards the King's army, and disposed of 1,000 ounces of their plate. Happily they spared their greatest treasure, the royal grace cup and cover, which was the gift of King Henry VIII. Indeed the cup was sold during the Civil War, Alderman Arris protesting; but at the sale he bought it, and again presented it to the Company. It is of silver gilt and weighs 26 ounces, bearing the date-letter of 1523. It is very valuable and is believed to be one of the finest pieces of plate in existence. Mr. Francis Weston, Master, states that although the cup was made in 1523, it was not presented to the Company until 1540, and that it was refashioned for that purpose. He is of opinion that it was originally a standing mazer with a maple-wood bowl, held in position by strapwork mounts, which still show the original hinges used for that purpose. When the cup was altered the maple-wood bowl was removed and a silver-gilt bowl substituted, the cover being added. This was designed by Holbein, who was employed by Morett, goldsmith to Henry VIII, to make designs for him. " These additions," adds Mr. Weston, " caused the cup to be somewhat out of proportion, and a close examination shows that an extra member or rim was then added to the original base to complete the design. The cover and stem are richly decorated with

THE TREASURES

the Tudor Rose and portcullis and fleur-de-lis, surmounted by the Royal arms and crown. A Latin inscription on the outside of the cover runs thus : " Henrici R. munificentia ne Posteris Ignota maneat Johannis Knight, R.C.P., 1678."[1] In the bowl is an outline engraving of the old coat of arms of the Barbers, impaling the cognizance of the Surgeons. From the strapwork mounts hang down little bells. Samuel Pepys explains their use. He dined at Barbers' Hall in 1662, and observes : " Among other observables at Chyrurgeons' Hall we drank the King's health out of a gift cup given by King Henry VIII to the Company, with bells hanging to it, which every man is to ring by shaking after he hath drunk up the whole cup." This cup was stolen in 1615, but was happily discovered in a garret at Westminster. Four men who took part in this robbery were executed.

The Royal Oak Cup is another important treasure. It was presented by Charles II in 1676, and fashioned in remembrance of the King's escape at Boscobel by hiding in an oak tree. It is a wonderful example of early hammered silversmith's work. The stem represents the trunk of a tree, and the cup and cover are adorned with the leaves of the tree, branches, wreaths of flowers, escallop shells, and acorns. Lizards and snails appear at the foot, and it is surmounted

---

[1] R.C.P. stands for Regis Chir. Principal, or Chief Surgeon to the King.

311

by an imperial crown adorned with fleur-de-lis
and a cross. Pendent acorns hang below the bowl
as bells from shields. This splendid cup was
obtained for the Company by two distinguished
members, Dr. James Pearce and John Knight,
both surgeons to his Majesty. Dr. Pearce and his
wife are often mentioned by Pepys in his im-
mortal *Diary*. It is 16¾ inches in height. The
shields bear the arms and crest of the Company,
and an inscription, "Donum munificentissimi
Regis Caroli Secundi, Anno 1676," and another
recording the names of the king's surgeons just
mentioned.

Dr. Arris, who saved the Grace Cup, also
presented four beautiful silver wine-cups which
bear the date-mark 1646 and were given five
years later. Each is inscribed "The Guift of
Edward Arris, Chirurgeon, Master of the Company, Anno Domini 1651."

Another splendid piece of plate is the punch-
bowl, weighing 160 ounces, and made in 1704.
It was fashioned by Pierce Harache, a Huguenot
craftsman and court silversmith to Queen Anne.
The style and workmanship show the French
influence introduced by the Huguenot refugees,
which remained in vogue for many years. The
letters HA. appear as part of the hall-mark,
and are the two first letters of the artist's name.

During Cromwellian times other treasures
were added to the collection :

1654 Sir John Frederick presented a fine

STATIONERS' HALL

loving-cup with cover, which is surmounted by a Roman soldier holding a shield.

1654 A rosewater ewer by Thomas Collins, Master.

1652 A loving-cup by Martin Browne, Surgeon.

1654 A loving-cup by Thomas Bowden.

Of tankards there are several with covers :

1640 By George Gray (37 ounces).

1662 By Thomas Fothergill (24 ounces).

1663 By John Dorrington (39 ounces).

1663 Two hammered rosewater dishes by R. Andrews and Thomas Gill.

1663 Loving-cup, the gift of Thomas Bell, Chyrurgeon (63 ounces).

The Barbers also possess a large collection of punch-ladles, and when tea-drinking set in they received gifts of tea-urns and teaspoons. On the handle of one of these is the crest of the Company, an opimacus, a strange and fabled animal supposed to have been very fleet of foot and strong on the wing. I may notice also a silver-mounted Master's hammer, the gift of John Monforde, King's surgeon in 1540, which must have been in constant use when the repeated quarrels raged between the two branches of the Company, the Barbers and the Surgeons. They have also preserved the crowns or garlands used at the election of Masters and Wardens (1629), the Barge Master's silver badge, and the metal badges of the rowers, the beadle's silver maces, and a large store of 18th-century and modern plate, salts,

THE CITY COMPANIES

casters, punch-ladles with ivory handles, salvers, etc.

It will be gathered that the Barbers are fortunate enough to possess a collection of plate which exceeds many owned by most of the greater Companies. There are many other treasures which want of space prevents me from describing. The paintings include the very famous one by Holbein, showing Henry VIII presenting the Charter to the combined fraternities of Barbers and Surgeons,[1] portraits of deceased worthies, of kings and queens by eminent artists, and there is a goodly store of old furniture and china, and the Poor's box bought from Widow Lucas in 1636. One old screen of stamped and gilded leather is very remarkable. It was presented by one William Duell, who was hanged at Tyburn. His body was conveyed to the Hall for dissection, where he revived, and by the kindly surgeons was nursed, and then shipped off to the East, where he became a prosperous merchant, and presented this screen to the Company in token of his gratitude. With this memento of a gruesome episode in the history of the Company I must close this record, and conclude with the time-honoured toast " *Floreat Guilda Barbitonsoris.*"[2]

[1] It is suggested that this picture represents the union of the Barbers' Company with the Gild of Surgeons in 1540, and not the granting of the Charter in 1512.

[2] I wrote an article in the *Connoisseur* on the Plate of the Barbers' Company, and am obliged to the editor for permission

314

THE TREASURES

Many of the minor Companies, unlike the Barbers, have lost their Hall during the course of ages, and with their Hall their treasures. I am only able to allude to a few of those who amidst many vicissitudes have been able to retain them. The Brewers' Company possess a charming Hall in Addle Street, Cheapside, but I have not seen their treasures. The Broderers still have a small Hall in Gutter Lane, but it is not occupied by them, and on one occasion when I dined with them, the banquet took place in one of the large London restaurants, if I remember rightly. Their two valuable cups are always exhibited at their feasts. One is the gift of John Parr in 1606 ; he was embroiderer to Queen Elizabeth and James I. In Mr. Cripps' valuable book on Plate, the date is given 1611, which is probably correct. It is a handsome specimen of the silversmith's art, and with the cover is in the shape of a ball with a bulbous lower part, and a thin base and stem. An angel with outstretched wings appears on the central portion. The other cup is the gift in 1628 of Edmund Harrison, embroiderer to their Majesties, James I and Charles I. On State occasions on each side of the Master's chair, which survived the Great Fire, stand the

to republish portions thereof. I am also grateful to the officials of the Company, and especially to Mr. Francis Weston, Master, for the use of a valuable paper written by him and published under my editorship in the *Journal of the British Archæological Association*, and beg to acknowledge the assistance of the learned work of the late Mr. Sidney Young, " The Annals of the Barber-Surgeons."

315

staffs of the Porter and Beadle. The heads of both are silver and ancient, the former bearing the hall-mark of 1628. I must not omit the humorous Broiderers' Song, the refrain of which contains the quintessence of commercial morality and honour. It runs as follows :

> " Oh, give us your plain-dealing fellows,
> Who never from honesty shrink,
> Not thinking of all they should tell us,
> But telling us all that they think."

The Carpenters' is a very flourishing Company, to which the City owes much for its benevolent work. Its history has been ably written in a large volume by its Clerk, Mr. Edward Basil Jupp (2nd edition by W. W. Pocock). There is an inventory of its plate as early as the early part of the reign of Henry VIII, and as this and the other Gilds were of a religious character, their plate had an ecclesiastical impress, being ornamented with the figure of a saint or some other religious device. Thus we find in this inventory the following :

> ij great masers with I.H.S. in the bosses—23 oz.
> A maser of William Priest with image of St. Thomas-
> 6 oz.
> John Ruddokke gave a maser of silver gilt with a
> picture of Jesus.
> Silver spoon with Peter (apostle spoon)
>   ,,   ,,   Paul   ,,   ,,
>   ,,   ,,   Andrew ,,   ,,

and several others.

316

THE TREASURES

But all these and many others have long ago been sold at various crises in the Company's history, and need not be here recorded. The same events which agitated the other fraternities troubled this one. The worst period was that of the Commonwealth. They had a great fright when General Fairfax ordered soldiers to be billeted in the Hall, and they promptly sold much of their plate, and when they heard that, just before the advent of Charles II at the Restoration, General Monk had carried out the order of Parliament to demolish the gates and posts of the City, they were careful to secure their plate. However, they have retained some fine examples of the silversmith's art.

They have a silver-gilt cup of handsome design and elaborate workmanship, which is known as the Master's Cup. It is inscribed :

" John Reeve being Mr. ye second tyme made me for ye use of ye Mr. Wardens & Coi-altye of ye Mistery of Freemen of ye Carpentry of ye Cittye of London for ever without charging ye Coi-altye then being."

This was presented in 1611.

There are three Wardens' cups, the first given by John Ansell in 1611, the second by Thomas Edmones in 1612, and the third by Antony Jarman in 1628. The Carpenters have also preserved their garlands or crowns formerly used on election days. The Master's crown is

THE CITY COMPANIES

made of crimson silk and velvet embroidered with gold and silver lace. It bears the date 1561 and the initials " J.T." stand for John Tryll. The crowns of the Wardens are of the same date and very similar in design.

There is a remarkable series of mural paintings in the Hall which are worthy of close inspection. Their date is uncertain, but they were probably executed about 1561. The characters are represented in Tudor costumes, and are probably of the school of Holbein. The scenes depicted are Noah building the Ark ; King Josiah ordering the rebuilding of the Temple ; our Saviour in the carpenter's shop at Nazareth ; and His teaching in the synagogue, when the people said of Him, " Is not this the *carpenter's* son ? " For many years these paintings were hidden, and were accidentally discovered. There are some ancient portraits in the Hall, amongst these that of William Portington, Esq., Master Carpenter in the office of His Majesty's buildings for forty years, who died on March 28th, 1628, aged 84 years. He has a gigantic ruff, and is evidently engaged in some measuring work with a pair of compasses. There is also a portrait of John Scott, Carpenter and Maker to the Office of Ordnance in the reign of Charles II. He is a stern-looking personage with a Cromwellian collar and is holding a large pair of compasses in his hand together with a roll of parchment.

The Coopers' Company has an interesting

318

THE TREASURES

history and has a Hall in Basinghall Street which was granted to them in 1490, but the present Hall was built in 1868. During the Fire they saved their records and plate. Some was sold in order to realize money to meet the demands of the contending parties in the great Civil War, but much remains and many pieces have been added in modern times. They are specially proud of two silver salvers presented when Robert Williams was Lord Mayor in 1743. It has been mentioned when a member of a minor Company is exalted to that high office of dignity, he usually is transferred to some one of the illustrious " Twelve." But this Robert Williams refused to migrate and declared that he would prefer to remain a Cooper. The two silver waiters, the gift of his lordship, recall this pleasing example of the attachment of a Cooper to his own Company.

Owing to the Great Fire, the Cordwainers or Allutarii, a very ancient mystery which concerned itself with the leather industry, lost heavily and were forced to sell their Irish estates, and also their plate which consisted of forty-four pieces with engravings of arms and inscriptions of the donors on them, in order to pay off their debts. Their small eighteenth-century Hall is in Distaff Lane and faces Cannon Street, and subsequent benefactors have supplied the place of the old loving-cups and salts and other silver vessels which they were forced to sell. John Came,

Cordwainer, who died in 1796, left much wealth to the Company, and an urn and tablet by Nollekins record his memory. Of this Company the late Right Hon. Joseph Chamberlain was a freeman for fifty years and enriched the treasury by a handsome gift of plate, as his uncle and great-uncle did before him.

The Dyers rival the Great Companies in dignity, importance and usefulness. Amongst their treasures is a magnificent iron chest, a most beautiful work of art and several portraits of benefactors. All their old plate has disappeared.

The Fanmakers is the youngest of all the fraternities and obtained a Charter from Queen Anne. The store of treasures is mostly modern and has been much increased in recent years. These include the banners of the arms of Masters, a common seal, an ivory hammer, silver snuff-box, some silver-gilt loving-cups, a ram's head with silver snuff-box, a silver-gilt rosewater dish, and a gold chain for the Master.

The Feltmakers have no relics of any interest, except four banners, an iron chest, a poor-box, and a beadle's mace which is embellished with the representation of a hat. The Founders are more fortunate. They were not at one time a united body and we read of many quarrels caused by " false complainers, according to their perverse, proud and peevish minds," who as early as 1508 disputed about the custody of the plate, " napyre," and jewels belonging to the craft.

THE TREASURES

An inventory of 1497 discloses that they had a goodly treasure of valuable plate including eight masers, standing cups, a table for an altar with an image of St. Clement, and much " napyre." The demands of James I obliged them to sell some of their plate. In 1617 forty-eight spoons silver-gilt were sold and in 1620 twenty-five more. The Puritan Parliament ordered the destruction of their old hearse-cloth " embroydered with gould and Popish images, being contrary to a late ordinance of Parliament," and some tapestry described as " old Popish painted cloth." The Company is now rich in plate owing to the gifts of benefactors, amongst whom were John Relye (1638), Abraham Woodhall (1460), Mr. King (1802), and William Bond (1824), and many others. Some of their ancient plate has escaped from divers calamities, and includes a spoon, the gift of Humphrey Bowin in 1625, which is inscribed :

> " If you love me—keep me ever,
> That's my desire—and your endeavour."

They have two masers of ancient date. A curiosity is a loving-cup of Venetian painted glass of the fifteenth century, said to have been brought from Boulogne when that place was besieged and captured by the English in 1544. The stem is of silver-gilt, the original glass foot having been broken, it is supposed, during the siege. It is called the " Wioley's Cup," and was doubtless

321   x

part of the pillage of the town. Three handsome tankards were given by Thomas Fisher in 1708, and they have a curious copper treasure-chest given by Stephen Pilchard, Master in 1653, bearing the motto " Helpe the Poore." It was intended for money given every Christmas for distribution to the poor.

The plate of the Framework Knitters was sold in 1861 for the repair of their almshouses. The Innholders have some good plate, including two salts of the period of Queen Elizabeth, which, in accordance with the old custom in baronial halls, separate the guests of high degree from their lower companions, i.e., the Court and the Livery. They have also a fine standing cup, the gift of Grace G. Walter in 1599, and a valuable collection of apostle spoons. There are also some interesting portraits and pictures, including one of Sir Polydor de Keyser, Lord Mayor ; Dick Whittington listening to the sound of Bow bells, and Charles II driving away rebellion. The Joiners possess an old Master's chair and some plate which I have never had an opportunity of inspecting. The Leathersellers' Company is a prosperous corporation and has much plate. Their Charter granted by James I in 1604, has a very fine seal attached to it.

The Painter-Stainers' Company formerly included in their number the principal artists of England who have not failed to present to their fraternity good examples of their skill. Amongst their freemen have been Sir James Thornhill, Charles Carton, Master in 1761, Sir Peter Lely; and amongst the paintings we see Charles I by Vandyck, Charles II by Gaspari, Catherine of Braganza by Houssman, William III by Sir Godfrey Kneller, George Richmond by himself, William Camden by an unknown artist, a picture entitled " Choosing the Deity," by Edwin Long, R.A., and a view of the Great Fire of London. Other artists represented are Francis Barlow, Peter Monamy, S. Ricci, Sir John Modina, and R. Smirke, R.A. They have a few remains of their silver plate, chief amongst which is the Camden Cup, a standing bowl and cover of silver-gilt presented by William Camden, Clarencieux King-at-Arms.

The Pewterers have a curious painting of William Smalwood, who gave to the Company " for ever their common Hall with a garden and six tenements, the 15th day of August 1487." This painting is subsequent to the donation. The Saddlers, who date back to Saxon times, have a large income and some plate. Chief of this is the Rich Cup, presented by Peter Rich, Esq., 1681. They have an interesting ancient view of Cheapside showing the time when there were "ridings in the Cheap"; a royal or civic procession is passing along, and the Companies are arranged in their " standings," and the Cheapside Eleanor Cross had not been then thrown down. The Scriveners' Company

323

THE CITY COMPANIES

prospered greatly under the princely rule of
Sir Robert Clayton, who had a fine house in Old
Jewry and gave gorgeous entertainments and
feasts which Evelyn describes "might well
have become a King." His portrait is in Drapers'
Hall, as he forsook his old Company and joined
the Drapers when he became Lord Mayor ; of
their ancient plate all that remains is a loving-cup
and the Master's badge.

The Stationers' Company in ancient times
had a rich store of plate, each Master being
expected to present to the fraternity some piece
not weighing less than 14 oz. But owing to the
expense of rebuilding their Hall, they were
compelled to sell most of their gathered store
in 1693. Since that time they have received some
beautiful seventeenth century and eighteenth
century vessels, including cups, bowls and
flagons, a silver salver, the gift of the widow of
Samuel Mean, bookbinder to Charles II, who
was Master in 1679, two gilt monteiths, collars
made in 1729 out of old plate, and many other
interesting pieces. The principal vessels are
stored in a cabinet at Stationers' Hall and are a
very valuable collection. The Tallowchandlers
have a fine painting of Sir Joseph Sheldon, Lord.
Mayor (1676-7) attired in State robes and
mayor's collar and a very heavy wig, out of
which his face looks somewhat like an owl in
an ivy-bush. The Wheelwrights have no Hall,
but they still possess the silver badges worn by

THE TREASURES

the Masters and Wardens on all official occasions, and several loving-cups, banners and snuff-boxes.

Such is a brief description of some of the treasures of the Companies. I have not been able to explore all the strong-rooms and treasure-chests of all the fraternities, nor to see their beautiful things spread out on their banqueting tables; but enough has been written to reveal the richness of some of the stores which patriotic benefactors have bequeathed to their Companies, the affection of the freemen for their own fraternity which prompted the gifts, the trials and vicissitudes through which they have passed, obliging them with many heart-burnings to sell their plate, and the good fortune which has befallen them in many cases to fill again their treasure-chests with the rich and beautiful objects I have tried to describe.

INDEX

INDEX

INDEX

INDEX

330

INDEX

INDEX

INDEX

INDEX

BRISTOL : BURLEIGH LTD., AT THE BURLEIGH PRESS

www.ingramcontent.com/pod-product-compliance
Lightning Source LLC
Chambersburg PA
CBHW072133090426
42739CB00013B/3181